The Dragon's Debt

An Investor's Timeline to profits During china's financial Crisis 2019-2020

Marie Schoeppel

The Dragon's Debt: An Investor's Guide to Profits During China's Financial Crisis, 2019–2020

by Marie Schoeppel

www.globaltrendscycles.com

Published by Global Trends and Cycles

September 13, 2018

Book Cover & Interior Design: BookSavvyStudio.com

ISBN: 978-1-7323413-0-2 (Paperback edition)

ISBN: 978-1-7323413-1-9 (eBook edition)

First Edition

Printed in the United States of America

DEDICATION

For Dean Clairmont, my close friend, trading buddy, and enthusiastic supporter of this book project, who left us for paradise on May 26, 2018. May he have Spirit's infinite love and eternal happiness.

ACKNOWLEDGEMENTS

This book began as an article on the similarities between the 1997 Southeast Asian currency crisis and China's situation today. Ambrose Evans-Pritchard, the international business editor for *The Daily Telegrap*h, made a case for this similarity in his posts in 2015, so I decided to research the astrological conditions surrounding the 1997 currency crisis and found that they will repeat for China in 2019-2020.

The enthusiastic reception that I received from the participants at the Merriman Market Analyst Investment Retreat in 2017 when I presented my material on Southeast Asia led me to research other currency-related events and create a book of my findings. I thank Ray Merriman for giving me that opportunity; it was a big boost to my career as an astrologer.

I thank Mike Jenkins of *Stock Cycles Forecast* for his mentorship over the years, showing me the trading techniques and methods of W.D. Gann. Christeen Skinner has been an enthusiastic supporter of my work and has helped me avoid some pitfalls along the way. Ted Lee Fisher has also been very supportive as a friend and mentor. Thanks also to Chris Brennan and the astrologer behind *Regulus Astrology* for their advice.

My cover designer Chris Molé is a fantastic artist; she intuitively knew what I wanted for my cover and her design captures the spirit of my book's message. She has also given me valuable advice in other areas of my self-publishing journey. Deborah Mokma has been a very patient and thorough editor and she improved the tone of my book. Tiffany Huang has created a stunning website for me and has saved me much stress as my website guru.

I send heartfelt thanks to my mother, Rita, for her example of how patience can conquer difficult people. Following her advice saved this project from being derailed.

CONTENTS

How to Use This Book

I wrote this book for two primary audiences: Those who trade speculative markets; and astrologers, economic historians, and those interested in astro-economics.

In order to prove my case that China is headed for a financial crisis in 2019 and 2020, I have included my astrological research and many charts. I admit that the reader needs an advanced level of familiarity with astrology in order to understand some of the techniques shown here. I have made the effort to explain the terminology used.

This book is organized so that the reader who wishes to understand how I arrived at my conclusions can review my analysis of several cases of severe financial crises and currency devaluations, while those who simply want to make profitable trades can skip the analysis and get the dates for significant events that they want.

Chapters 1-5 provide astrological analyses of past cases, and Chapters 6 and 8 give forecasts for China based on astrological factors. Those who wish to understand how I arrived at my forecast will want to study these chapters.

But those (traders) who just want to know what to expect and hopefully profit from it can cut to the chase by reading Chapter 7, which contains a detailed timeline of events with no mention of astrology. However, I strongly advise these readers to carefully read the Introduction so that they are aware of the complexity of the situation that they are attempting to trade.

As always, each individual is responsible for his/her own investment decisions. This book is not meant as trading advice, but only as another source of indicators of what the trend may be.

INTRODUCTION

The purpose of this work is to prepare anyone who saves or invests their money, or actively trades in speculative markets, for the second phase of the global financial upheaval that began in 2007.

The main question for investors is, when will that second phase begin? But just as importantly, what are the events that trigger it?

This work identifies 2019 as the turning point, and China as the epicenter of another financial crisis.

By analyzing financial and political crises of the past in terms of astrological patterns, identifying a specific set of astrological conditions associated with such crises, and then using those conditions to develop a forecast of when and how similar crises will repeat, this analysis definitely points to turmoil emanating from China in 2019 to 2022.

The analysis will include significant financial crises of the 20th century revolving around severe currency devaluations to develop a specific set of astrological conditions that, when they repeat, can be expected to result in the same sort of crises. The debt problems and eventual defaults of emerging economies in Latin America in the 1980s, the collapse of the British pound in 1992, and the Asian currency crisis of 1997–1998 are the crises which are analyzed.

The common factor in all of these cases from the 20th century is currency devaluation. In the cases of emerging market economies—those of Latin America and Southeast Asia—another common factor is fast expansion of debt, whether public or corporate.

A large part of this work is devoted to analyzing the financial and political events of 1275 through 1350 for Europe in terms of the astrological patterns at the time. A major configuration that has occurred only twice since 1270 was a major influence in the 13th–14th centuries, especially for what was the international finance system at that time. This configuration occurs again in late 2019 and early 2020.

With respect to global finance, this analysis identifies when, and how, significant currency devaluations will occur in the near future. The most glaring instance of a country whose astrological chart will experience the set of conditions identified from past examples is China, during the period 2019 to 2022, and even beyond. Regarding the geopolitical landscape, the focus is also on China and the upcoming upheavals in its political and financial systems, as these upheavals are interrelated.

Why China's "Sustainable Debt" is a Mythical Creature

China's Debt to GDP Ratio

China's total debt to GDP ratio rose to 317% in 2017, as estimated by Goldman Sachs. This ratio has doubled since 2008, when it was 158%.[1] Its corporate debt to GDP ratio was 159% for 2017.[2]

The growth of China's aggregate debt rose by 13.5% (year over year in 2017), which was higher than its nominal GDP growth of 11.2% (year over year in 2017), also according to Goldman Sachs.[3] Many analysts say that credit growth was lower in 2017 than in 2016, but there are those who dispute this and claim that credit in 2017 was almost as high as in 2016. Despite which version is the accurate view, China has managed to do very little in the way of deleveraging.[4]

Countries which accrue too much debt, too fast, usually have a hard landing. The culprit is easy access to credit within the country, and much of China's debt is domestically funded. Easy access to credit has been used in a cyclic pattern by China's leadership to stimulate the economy, and then withdrawn to cool things down when speculation threatens to burst the bubble. This has been especially true in China's property market.

Debt and Corruption in China's Property Market

When the global financial crisis in 2008 slowed demand for China's exports, the government turned to the domestic property market as a way to keep the economy growing. By providing easy credit, many young urban Chinese were

1 https://ftalphaville.ft.com/2018/02/05/1517825168000000/Over-in-China--a-debt-boom-mapped/

2 https://www.bloomberg.com/news/videos/2018-02-02/china-s-corporate-debt-hits-159-of-gdp-in-2016-video

3 https://ftalphaville.ft.com/2018/02/05/1517825168000000/Over-in-China--a-debt-boom-mapped/

4 https://www.bloomberg.com/news/articles/2018-02-12/china-may-go-soft-on-financial-risk-curbs-to-shield-economy?in_source=video_page

able to buy homes, which led to a boom in property values. As home prices skyrocket, many Chinese are rushing to buy, under the assumption that if they don't buy now, they will be priced out of the market in the near future.

Qualifying conditions for a home loan have been lax in China, with banks allowing an applicant to spend up to 50% of their income on the loan payment while failing to confirm an applicant's stated income with their employer.[5] Does this sound familiar? Such reckless lending was a direct contributor to the United States' subprime crisis. Although the Chinese government began tightening access to credit to property buyers and setting down payment requirements in 2016, up until early 2018 this had continued to fuel even higher prices.

Household debt in China, which is mostly comprised of mortgage debt, reached 44% of GDP in 2016. As speculation has driven prices higher, disposable income has fallen. In 2017, the ratio of mortgage debt to household disposable income had risen to 90%, compared to 35% at the end of 2007. By 2020, that ratio could reach the same level as that of the United States just prior to the subprime crisis.[6]

China has relied on the property market to fuel economic growth since 2008. The property market is interwoven with state-owned enterprises (SOE's)—such as developers, utilities, energy, and construction firms—which are big corporations with large debts themselves. Property developers in China hold half of the corporate debt that will mature in the next two years. With corporate debt continuing to grow (especially for SOE's), and the current effort to rein in property values to prevent an even bigger speculative bubble, China will find it hard to use the property market as a way to prop up the economy in the future as growth slows.[7]

Property is a major source of revenue for cash-strapped local governments through the sale of land use rights. In June 1986, China began implementing incremental reform of the property market by passing the Land Administration Law, opening a new era in China's legal approach to property ownership. The main thrust of this law was to separate land ownership rights from land use rights, meaning that an entity other than the state could have the right to use

5 http://www.scmp.com/news/china/economy/article/2112873/chinas-household-debts-soars-it-being-stalked-subprime-spectre

6 Ibid.

7 https://worldview.stratfor.com/article/chinas-property-sector-groans-under-weight-its-debt

and develop the land, although the state retains ownership rights.[8] As Minxin Pei says in his book China's Crony Capitalism, "This paved the way for the Chinese government to permit the sale and transfer of land without having to change its legal ownership."[9] But the law did not thoroughly define ownership rights.

According to Pei, "Despite the absence of a formal legal basis for selling land use rights, the State Council indicated in April 1987 that land use rights could be transferred for a fee."[10] In December 1988, an amendment to the Land Administration Law allowed the transfer (effectively, the sale) of land use rights. Yet it was not until 1991 that the sale of land use rights increased dramatically.

In the period 2000 to 2010, local governments began aggressively selling land use rights, using the land as collateral for bank loans to fund infrastructure projects.[11] In turn, local government finance vehicles (LGTV) use the revenue from sales of land use rights to back the local governments' debts—with these loans used to fund infrastructure and property development. But as property prices decline, the solvency of local governments is threatened, as well as the ability of developers and construction firms to employ the local population.[12]

Thus, the fortunes of local governments are intricately interwoven with those of property developers and construction firms—one of the most indebted sectors of the Chinese economy.

Corporate Debt and China's State-Owned Enterprises

China's state-owned enterprises are notoriously inefficient. Although reforms were introduced during the late 1990's, which helped reduce SOE debt for several years, government spending to support SOE's has grown since the global economic slowdown began in 2008.[13] Loans to SOE's now[14] account for almost half of all corporate debt in China, and are the main reason for the increase in corporate debt.[15]

8 Minxin Pei, *China's Crony Capitalism* (Harvard University Press, 2016) pg. 61

9 Ibid., pg. 51

10 Ibid.

11 Ibid., pgs. 55–57

12 https://worldview.stratfor.com/article/china-no-easy-cure-local-governments-addiction-real-estate-revenue

13 http://www.eastasiaforum.org/2017/10/04/chinas-twenty-year-dream-of-soe-reform-still-unfulfilled/

14 As of February 2018.

15 "Reinstatement," *The Economist*, July 22, 2017, pg. 55

In 2015, another round of reforms was initiated. One of these reforms is restructuring through mixed ownership in which private companies can purchase equity in SOE's, or fund SOE projects.[16] This reform targeted parent SOE's, as 92% of SOE subsidiaries have already restructured their ownership, but as of 2016, 69 out of 101 parent companies had yet to be restructured.[17] In June 2017, the government ordered all SOE's to be restructured as corporations by the end of 2017.

As important as this reform could be in addressing the problems with SOE's, the underlying issue has not been fully addressed: Liquidating poorly performing assets. This is especially sensitive for SOE's in industries with excess capacity, such as steel.[18] The Chinese government, and the Chinese Communist Party, are loath to eliminate any operations that would impact a large number of laborers, as its power rests on the social contract to provide stable employment in return for the populace's acceptance of dictatorship.

SOE debt will remain on the books somewhere unless poorly performing operations are eliminated, although the accepted alternative has been to encourage mergers and insist that banks write off bad loans and assets.

China has avoided putting definite limits on SOE budgets, without which SOE debt and inefficiency—with their toxic effects on the economy—will continue to grow.[19] Furthermore, SOE debt is interwoven with other forms of debt in China, some of it in complex and hidden ways. It was this kind of interweaving in the United States' financial system and beyond that led to the 2008 global financial crisis.

In September 1999 a resolution was passed to speed up the privatization of small and medium sized SOE's, and to give economic preference to large SOE's. This effectively led to local governments selling off smaller SOE's to local private businessmen at very low prices. Local officials were happy to be rid of the costs of maintaining these SOE's, and they also now had a new avenue for establishing collusive networks with private businessmen, increasing their influence and ability to extract bribes.[20] Also, the taxes and debts of these SOE's

16 http://www.eastasiaforum.org/2017/10/04/chinas-twenty-year-dream-of-soe-reform-still-unfulfilled/

17 https://thediplomat.com/2017/11/chinas-soe-reform-challenge/

18 http://www.eastasiaforum.org/2017/10/04/chinas-twenty-year-dream-of-soe-reform-still-unfulfilled/

19 Ibid.

20 Minxin Pei, *China's Crony Capitalism* (Harvard University Press, 2016) pg. 67

were left unpaid in the process.

Pei's research in this area points to the interweaving of changes in China's property market, restructuring or sale of SOE's, and increased corruption within the Chinese Communist Party (CCP). Pei's premise is that all of these "reforms" have actually accelerated corruption within the CCP and are contributing to the downfall of the Chinese regime. His analysis sees China in the final stages of regime decay.

Corporate debt, as well as cronyism, played a big role in the financial collapse of Indonesia in the Asian currency crisis of 1997. The signs were ignored for years, but once Thailand was forced to devalue the baht, a speedy chain reaction of devaluations ensued across the region.

Local Government Debt in China

Related to SOE debt, there is also the problem of local government debt. Prior to 2014, local governments could not issue bonds to raise revenue; they were dependent upon a share of taxes collected at the central level, which was distributed to them. But they rarely received enough to fund their operations, and local governments got around these restrictions by using unregulated local government financing vehicles (LGFV) to raise needed funds. Some LGFV's were established as SOE's, although they were not banks or departments of the local governments, so they were unregulated. By the end of 2015, debt held by LGFV's amounted to 15 trillion yuan—and this was only the portion that had been reported, as much of it does not have to be reported in local budgets.[21]

China's central government has established a program to convert the LGFV debt into bonds, but Xi Jinping himself declared at a financial conference in July 2017 that the program was not working well enough, and that the two biggest threats to China's financial system are the LGTV debt and SOE debt.[22]

Shadow Bank Loans Disguised as Wealth Management Products

Wealth management products (WMP's) are sold by banks and act a transfer of investors' money to speculative assets. They are often part of the shadow banking system in China, although official banks do sell them. Banks also disguise their

21 "The Walking Debt," *The Economist*, November 18, 2017, pg.37

22 Ibid.

investment in loans of the shadow banking system as WMP's, for which neither the principal nor the interest are guaranteed, and these WMP's are reported as "receivables" rather than as loans.[23] Thus the official banks and the shadow banks of China are closely intertwined.

The whole idea of such WMP's is that they are devised as a way to circumvent banks' minimum capital requirements and their deposits-to-loans ratio. They are also exposed to corporate debt.[24] A troubling trend detected in 2015 was of these WMP's investing in each other, making their true risks difficult to decipher—much like the collateralized debt obligations of the subprime mess of 2008.[25] The government had begun a crackdown on shadow banking, and the growth of WMP's did begin to decline, but it increased in the last half of 2017, perhaps signaling that regulators might once again allow this form of financing.[26]

In March 2018, China's banking and insurance regulatory bodies were merged to provide more comprehensive oversight of the financial system.[27] In late April 2018, new asset-management regulations were passed to stem the growth of bad loans through WMP's. But Chinese banks have lobbied to have the compliance deadline pushed into late 2020, as economic activity has slowed.[28] Bank reserve ratio requirements have already been eased as companies have found it difficult to get funding.

With the threat of additional US tariffs triggering a stock market sell-off in China as this is being written in June 2018,[29] China's economy could slow even further, prompting an easing of regulations and reverting to reliance on shadow banking through wealth management products to provide funding. Because they help to fund corporate debt, especially that of the property market, the government may be willing to rely on them in order to keep the economy going.

---

23 http://www.bloomberg.com/gadfly/articles/2016-05-30/china-s-veiled-loans-present-a-lethal-hidden-danger

24 Ibid.

25 http://www.bloomberg.com/news/articles/2016-05-29/china-default-chain-reaction-threatens-products-worth-35-of-gdp

26 https://www.bloomberg.com/news/articles/2018-02-12/china-may-go-soft-on-financial-risk-curbs-to-shield-economy?in_source=video_page

27 https://www.forbes.com/sites/sarahsu/2018/03/19/chinas-new-financial-regulatory-system-may-overlook-some-risks/#6ebd2387b975

28 "Light on the shadows," *The Economist*, June 16, 2018, pgs. 59–60

29 https://www.bloomberg.com/news/articles/2018-06-18/china-s-struggling-stock-market-faces-hit-from-tariff-tensions

CONCLUSIONS

Debt as stimulus has become a persistent addiction of China's economic growth. This is especially true in the property market, as China's leadership has alternately restricted and then eased access to credit for home buyers over the years. This approach appears to have maintained economic growth and managed to rein in, if not fully prevent, a bubble in property values. But the bubble is there, and the temptation to reach for the bottle of easing credit to provide stimulus will lead to overestimation of their ability to calibrate the delicate balance. Property developers and construction firms need prices to go higher in order to service the debts they incurred with foreign banks under foreign interest rates, but to prevent most people from being priced out of the housing market, prices must fall, or at least stabilize.[30]

The most indebted sectors are dependent upon one another, and they play major roles in society. And one of those players is the shadow banking system, which is unregulated for the most part, although its finances are interwoven with the official banking system.

When a Party Becomes a Problem

China's economic growth has been phenomenal since 1978, when Deng Xiao Ping initiated reforms to move the country toward a market-based economy. This growth has lifted millions of Chinese citizens out of poverty, and has provided new areas of expansion for other countries' economies.

China supposedly espouses a system of "state capitalism" in which the government controls commercial activity and growth of all sectors of the economy, usually through state owned enterprises. Growth is directed more by governmental policy, and far less by free market forces. Maybe a better term would be "surface capitalism"—the limited use of capitalist methods for interacting with outside entities in order to draw in trade, investment, intellectual property, and expertise, while not allowing true supply and demand to measure which industries are the fittest to survive, or how capital will be allocated.

30 Most Chinese own their home. Only very recently has the government started a rental housing program, in hopes of moving people to accept renting as a good alternative to home ownership. But rents follow housing prices—or at least they do in a truly capitalist economy.

The true guiding principle of China's leadership is retaining the Chinese Communist Party's grip on power. China is still a dictatorship, something that many outsiders have ignored in their rush for profits in what appears to be an immense semi-open market, but a transition to full democracy and fully open markets is not consistent with the CCP's goal of maintaining its position of power. One glance at the astrological chart for the Chinese Communist Party (analyzed in Chapter 5) will convince anyone of the folly of those who thought such a transition to be in the works. When pushed against the wall, the CCP will choose to preserve its power over providing economic benefits to the Chinese people, or sustaining the illusion of economic growth.

The Dragon's Debt

CHAPTER 1

Financial and Political Crises of the 13th and 14th Centuries

The 14th century was a time of turmoil and decline for Europe, with developments in the last few decades of the 13th century paving the way for this decline. This period saw a major political shift of the strong influence of the Catholic Church being challenged, and dealt a mortal blow, leading to the subordination of religious authority in the West which has lasted up to the present day.

The finances of the Church played an important role in the financial system of the time. The conflict between England and France (and their monarchs' need to finance their militaries) intersected with the challenge to the Church's authority. This affected the condition of papal reserves—and ultimately led to severe financial crises.

The following astrological cycles and configurations were involved in these financial and economic crises of 1270 to 1350.

Capricorn Stellium of 1284

The "global" economy of the late 13th century—that is, the linked economies of countries across the Eurasia land mass—reached a peak at that time, and a series of financial crises began that involved the collapse of important banking concerns in Europe.

The dynamic that was developing was heavily influenced by a large cluster of planets in Capricorn in 1284 called a *stellium*. In late 1284 it consisted of the Sun, Mercury, Venus, Mars, Jupiter, Saturn, and Pluto. This stellium was the beginning of the cycles of each planetary pair with their conjunctions[1] in Capricorn, with the exception of Sun-Mars and Jupiter-Saturn, which began

1 Two planets are conjunct when they are at the same degree in the zodiac.

their cycles in Aquarius. It was also the culmination (or half-cycle point) for the Jupiter-Uranus, Saturn-Uranus, and Uranus-Pluto cycles.

December 8, 1284 has been chosen as the defining date for this stellium for two reasons: There was a solar eclipse at 24°51' Sagittarius on that day, and Venus went retrograde[2] in Capricorn on the following day, December 9, 1284.[3]

Capricorn Stellium
December 8, 1284
Venice, Italy

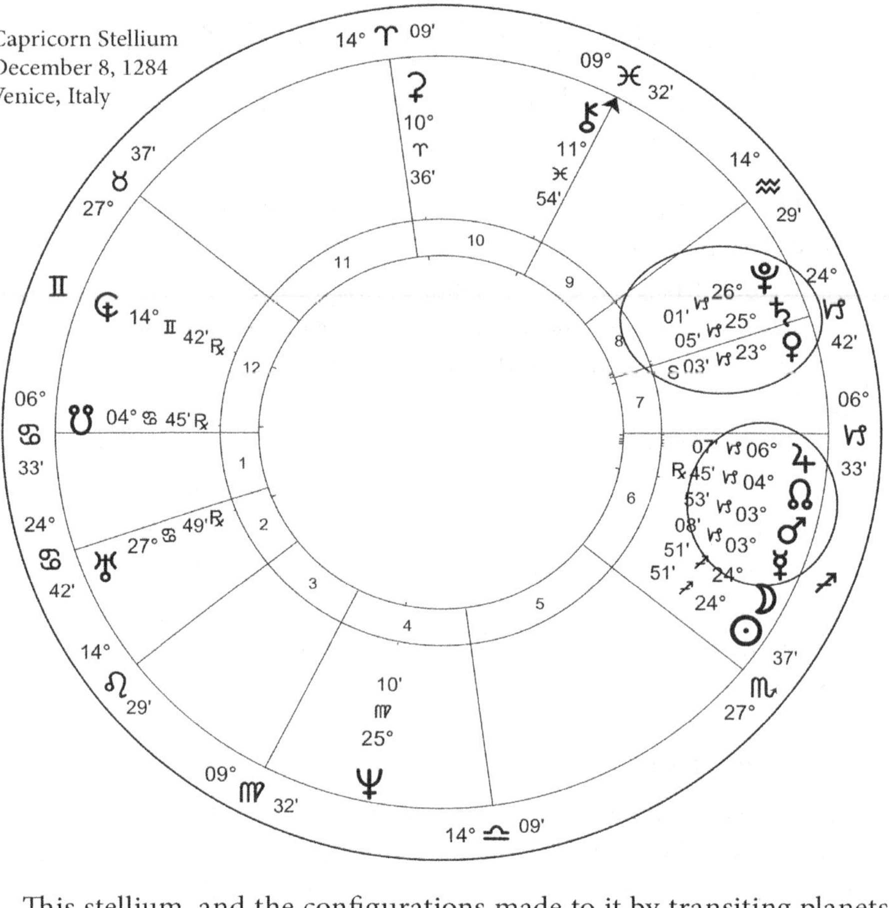

This stellium, and the configurations made to it by transiting planets, indicated two important developments in Europe in the late 13th and early 14th centuries that would shape Europe for decades to come.

2 A planet is said to be retrograde when it appears to be moving backward through the zodiac, which is due to the angular relationship between the perspective on Earth and the planet's orbit around the Sun.

3 Eclipse dates or stationary retrograde/direct dates that are within the time period of another major configuration are often the most accurate for forecasting the future effects of that configuration.

The most important of these developments was the beginning of the reign of Philip IV of France, who became king in October 1285 not long after the stellium occurred. The other development was that Europe's financial system would suffer a lack of liquidity, which alone could bring on a financial crisis. Astrological configurations in the 1290's to the position of this stellium and its central Saturn-Pluto conjunction indicated just such a crisis.

Strikingly, aspects made by transiting planets to the position of the 1284 Saturn-Pluto conjunction at 26°20' Capricorn over the following years seem to have been the most important triggers for major events.

Chart for Reign of Philip IV of France

Philip IV was a major player in events of the late 13th and early 14th centuries. His reign began on October 5, 1285, so it was not long after the December 1284 stellium that he came to power.

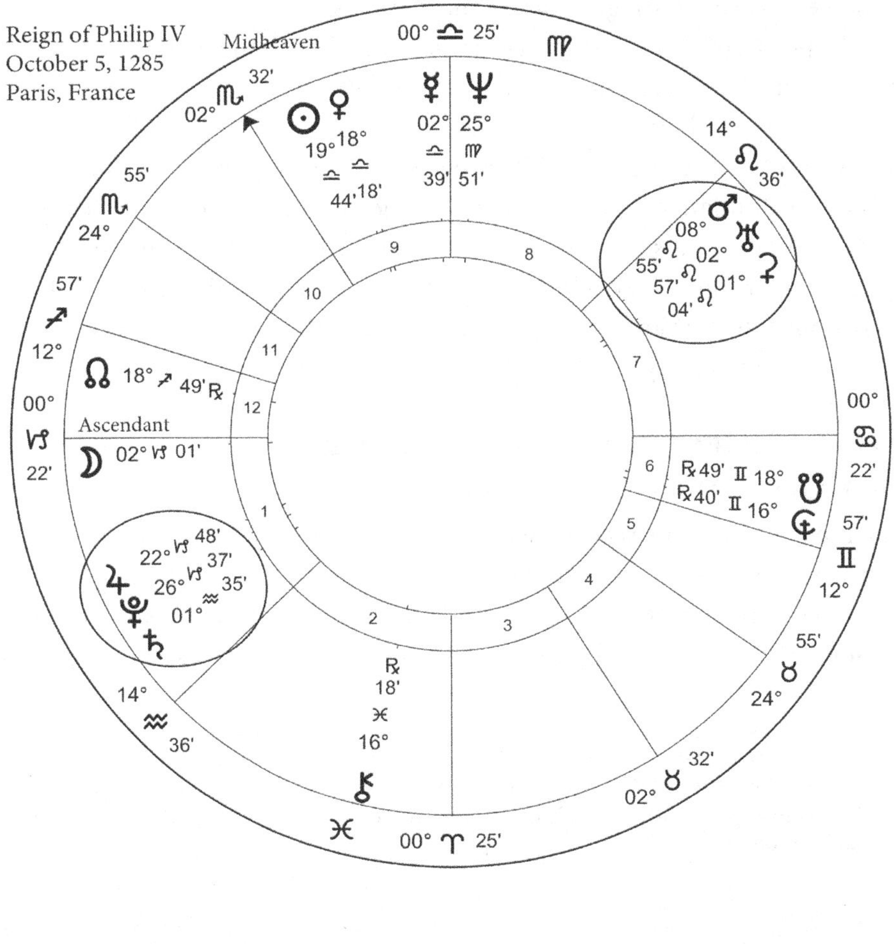

Using the time of 12:35 pm for this chart produces planetary rulerships within the chart[4] that accurately indicate the potential of Philip IV's reign. His autocratic style—which caused him to be an intensely disliked ruler—is indicated by the Midheaven 2°32' Scorpio[5] (the ruler of the country) squaring (90° angle) Uranus 2°57' Leo.

With Mars, the ruler of Scorpio, conjoining Uranus in the seventh house of war, Philip was often involved in conflicts. The many disputes of his reign are also shown by the Moon 2°1' Capricorn squaring (90° angle) Mercury 2°39' Libra (sign of war), and Cancer/Moon ruling the seventh house of war. With Aquarius/Uranus ruling the second house of finances, along with Uranus opposing (180° aspect) Saturn 1°35' Aquarius, the constant belligerence of his reign resulted in depletion of the country's coffers.

One of Philip's most contentious conflicts was an attempt to fill those coffers. He demanded that the clergy pay taxes, which caused him to face off with Pope Boniface VIII who strongly resisted these efforts.

The position of the 1284 Capricorn stellium falls in the first house, the area of the chart that reveals the character of the entity, indicating a heavy-handed and stern approach, intent on domination, which characterizes Philip's reign. That Venus went retrograde while she was part of the stellium indicated that the country's finances and diplomatic relations (areas associated with Venus in any chart) would suffer as a result of Philip's approach to other influential leaders and groups. As will be shown, Philip's track record was definitely one of economic decline and constant belligerence with others, especially those to whom he owed money.

Late 13th Century: The Credit Crunch of 1294 and Taxes on the Clergy

Papal revenue (i.e., taxes collected on behalf of the Church) was an important source of investment capital in the late 13th century. Italian merchant societies, particularly the Ricciardi, Gran Tavola, and Bardi, acted as bankers to the papacy and held papal revenue. They in turn would use this money to fund

4 An astrological chart is divided into twelve segments, called houses, each of which represents an area of life experience. A planet is said to rule a house when that planet is the one associated with the sign on the cusp (line of demarcation) of that house.

5 The Midheaven, or MC, is the point in the zodiac that was directly overhead at the time and location of "birth."

"loans" to governments or private parties, or to invest in commodity trading. They would also allow other merchant societies to use their funds for their financing activities.

By the first decade of the 14th century, Venice was the main exchange market of the Black Guelph group of northern Italian noble families such as the Bardi, Peruzzi, and Acciaiuoli who had established international banks. The Black Guelph ruled all of northern Italy except Milan, which was aligned with the Holy Roman Empire—and which the Black Guelph opposed.

The Black Guelph banking families, especially those in Florence, provided funds to the monarchs of Europe. In exchange for these "loans" (which couldn't truly be structured as loans, with usury considered a crime, as dictated by the Church), the monarchs were expected to pledge their tax revenue to the bankers. At this time commodities such as grain, wool, iron, and cloth were produced only under royal license, and were subject to taxation by the monarchies, so pledges of tax revenue gave the Black Guelph bankers control of commodities—and also of some functions of the monarchies.[6] These pledging arrangements reached a critical point in the 1290's when monarchs needed money to fund their wars, especially Edward I of England and Philip IV of France.

In 1291, Pope Nicholas IV agreed that a portion of papal revenue would be dispersed to Edward I as funding for his participation in a Crusade, with one payment made to him in June 1291. This money was held for him by the Ricciardi, an Italian merchant society.[7]

But in 1294, the outbreak of war between France and England over Philip's seizure of Gascony from England caused Edward I to try to draw upon the papal reserves which had been transferred to him. But the Ricciardi—which had made loans and investments with part of this money—could not easily call in the funds because of a liquidity crunch in the credit market.[8]

Ironically, this lack of liquidity was caused by the Pope drawing upon his own reserves in an attempt to dry up funding for this war, as well as Philip IV demanding new taxes from the Italian merchants.[9] And at the same time, the Ricciardi could not turn to other Italian merchants for short term loans,

6 Frederic C. Lane and Reinhold C. Mueller, *Money and Banking in Medieval and Renaissance Venice, Volume 1: Coins and Moneys of Account* (The John Hopkins University Press, 1985), p. 73

7 http://www.ehs.org.uk/dotAsset/2198856a-47ce-475b-8e49-0917b3b1f0d7.pdf

8 Ibid.

9 Ibid.

for they, too, were short on cash due to the depletion of papal reserves, a main source of capital and liquidity.

The Ricciardi thus were unable to meet Edward's demands. Understandably unhappy, Edward ended the agreement in which they collected customs on wool for him, and he also confiscated some of the Ricciardi's assets. This caused a blow that eventually led to their bankruptcy in 1301.[10]

In June 1291, when the pope released one payment to Edward I for his participation in leading another crusade, transiting Saturn 22° Aries was squaring (90° angle) transiting Jupiter 28° Cancer. This square linked into the 1284 stellium because Jupiter opposed (180° angle) the 26°20' Capricorn position while Saturn squared it. This particular payment held for Edward I by the Riccardi was the money that he wanted to draw upon in 1294 to fund his army in the war against France, but which the Riccardi couldn't deliver because of the lack of liquidity in the financial system at the time.

Capricorn Stellium
December 8, 1284
Rome, Italy

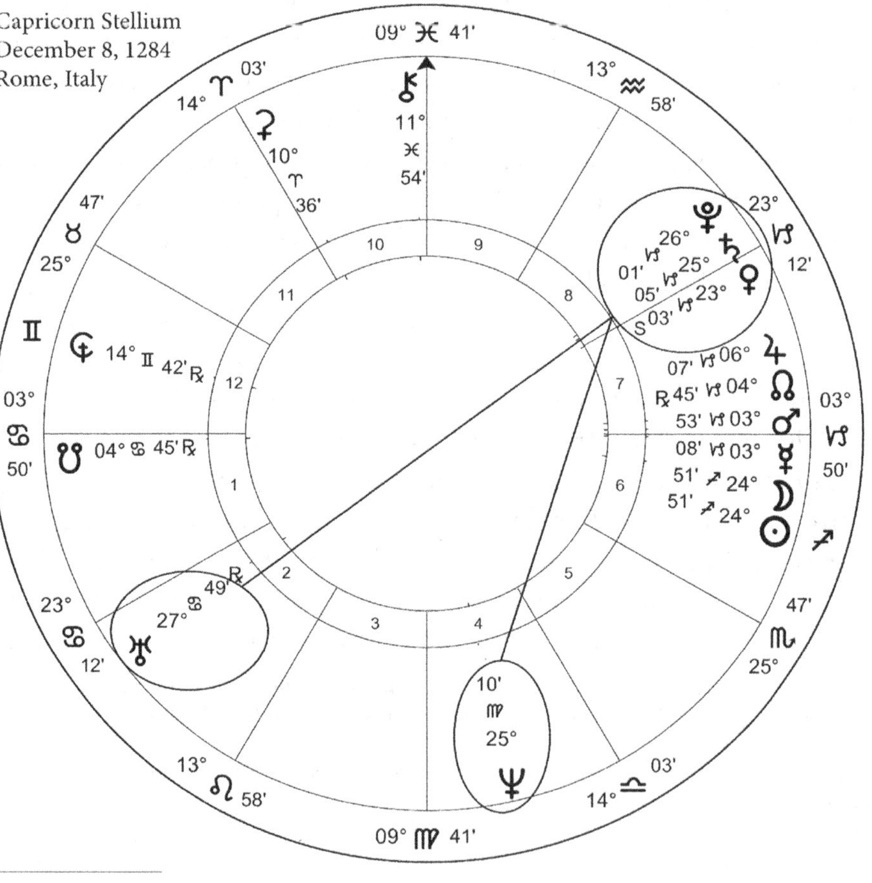

10 Ibid.

That the Church had been amassing considerable reserves is shown by the pattern of the outer planets in the 1284 Capricorn stellium chart. Aspects made by transiting planets in subsequent years indicated that the Pope would draw upon these substantial reserves in a large enough way to affect the flow of credit throughout the whole system.

This time period marked the culmination of several long-term planetary cycles: Saturn-Pluto, Jupiter-Saturn, and Jupiter-Pluto, all in Capricorn. At the same time, it was the half-cycle point (i.e., the opposition, or 180° angle) for Jupiter-Uranus, Saturn-Uranus, and Uranus-Pluto, with Uranus in Cancer. And the planets in Capricorn were all configured in a trine (120° angle) with Neptune in Virgo.

The configuration of Jupiter, Saturn, and Pluto conjoined in Capricorn, making a trine to Neptune, indicated that an established spiritual center (the Church, designated by Neptune[11]) was sitting on a large cache of funds (Jupiter-Saturn-Pluto). But with Venus, Saturn, and Pluto conjoined in the eighth house of foreign revenue and taxes, an extreme drain was forming, as indicated by their opposition to Uranus.

This conjunction of Venus with Saturn and Pluto is even more noteworthy in that Saturn and Pluto made only one conjunction marking the end of one cycle/start of a new cycle—they did not form three conjunctions due to retrograde motion. Thus, there was only one Saturn-Pluto conjunction, and it included Venus, the planet of finance.

The Capricorn stellium in 2020 repeats this pattern: Only one Saturn-Pluto conjunction, and Venus conjoins them (in December 2019). The same pattern occurred with a stellium in Libra in 1982, which indicated financial crises in Latin America in the early 1980's.[12]

As these planets continued their sojourns through the zodiac, the next major configuration to form among them occurred in mid-1290, with Saturn in Aries opposing Neptune in Libra, forming a T-square (first with Ceres, then with Jupiter) in Cancer. The excess of funds (Jupiter exalted in Cancer,[13] square Neptune) was

11 Neptune is associated with spirituality and religion.

12 See Chapter 2.

13 According to the system of essential dignities in astrology, Jupiter is said to be exalted in the sign of Cancer, meaning that Jupiter functions with great power in that sign.

about to encounter a restricting situation (Saturn in its fall in Aries[14]), thus the Saturn-Neptune opposition signaled the peak in the buildup of papal revenue.

A shift in the situation was indicated in October 1293, due to a Mars-Neptune-Jupiter conjunction in Libra. Now Mars and Jupiter were conjoining Neptune and interacting with the longer-term cycle of Saturn and Neptune, which reached its opposition (180° angle) in 1290. Considering that it was in 1294 that Philip IV and Edward I went to war over Philip's seizure of Gascony, the seeds of that conflict and its side effects were beginning to germinate in 1293 under this triple conjunction. With both parties in need of funds for their armies, their responses to acquire those funds were quite similar: Both demanded that the clergy pay new taxes to their respective states, which the papacy resisted—and this triple conjunction indicated the developing depletion of papal revenue as investment capital.

Philip IV was most demanding on the issue. Looking at progressions and transits for October 23, 1293 (the day that the Mars-Neptune conjunction was exact) to the chart for his reign, shows transiting Mars, Neptune, and Jupiter 14°–16° Libra, conjunct progressed Mercury 15°05' Libra, in the ninth house of the clergy. Mercury is a co-ruler of the eighth house of taxes in this chart, for Virgo is intercepted[15] in that house. Both Jupiter and Neptune are planets associated with religion and spirituality, and this interpretation of them is emphasized by their location in the ninth house of the clergy, with Mars in the mix adding an element of urgency and conflict. It is important to note that the progressed Moon 11° Aries was moving to oppose the position of this Mars-Neptune-Jupiter conjunction with progressed Mercury over the next few months, which echoes the natal Moon-Mercury square of Philip's chart. With both the square and opposition being harsh aspects, the level of hostility and belligerence increased. And, as this aspect also shows, Philip IV was firmly convinced that his position that the Church should do its part to support the state was correct.

14 According to the system of essential dignities in astrology, Saturn is said to be in its fall in Aries, meaning that Saturn is weak, and possibly more malefic, in that sign.

15 A sign is said to be "intercepted" in a house when the entire 30° of the sign is engulfed in that house; i.e., if Virgo is the sign that is intercepted, the boundaries of the house start in Leo (the sign preceding Virgo) and end in Libra (the sign following Virgo).

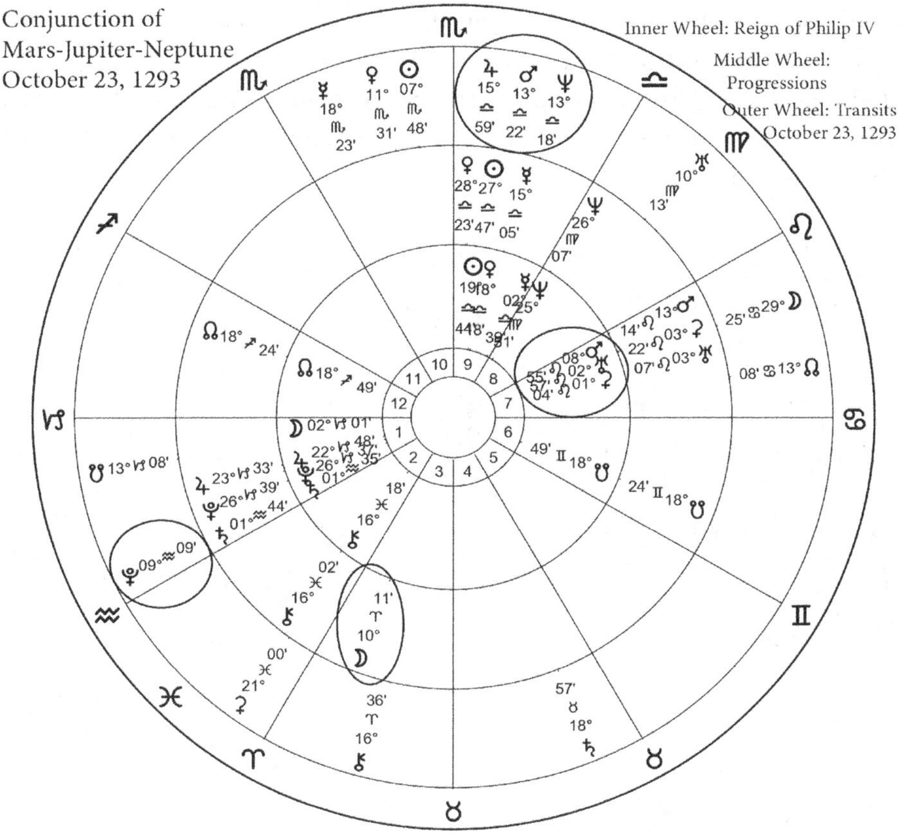

Furthermore, transiting Pluto 9°09' Aquarius opposes natal Mars 8°55' Leo, indicating the hardening of Philip's position and his willingness to destroy the position of his opponent. This he certainly did in the early 1300's as he faced off with Pope Boniface VIII who retreated, so emotionally shaken by the experience that he died.

The Mars-Neptune-Jupiter conjunction of 1293 indicated that the Church would be adversely affected by a brewing conflict. Pope Boniface VIII was concerned about the war between England and France because he felt that as long as both were involved in this secular conflict, neither would be willing to provide resources for another crusade. He tried to end their dispute somewhat indirectly by withdrawing some of the papal revenue that was financing the conflict. Furthermore, Boniface was concerned about Edward I taxing the clergy for half of their revenue in 1294, and Edward's demand in 1295 that the clergy vote to send him revenue regularly from their own reserves. The Pope viewed this development as an ominous sign that such taxation would continue indefinitely, so on February 5, 1296 he issued the *Clericis Laicos:* A papal bull forbidding all clergy from paying any revenue to laymen, and which threatened excommunication from the Church upon any layman who tried to collect such revenue from the clergy.[16]

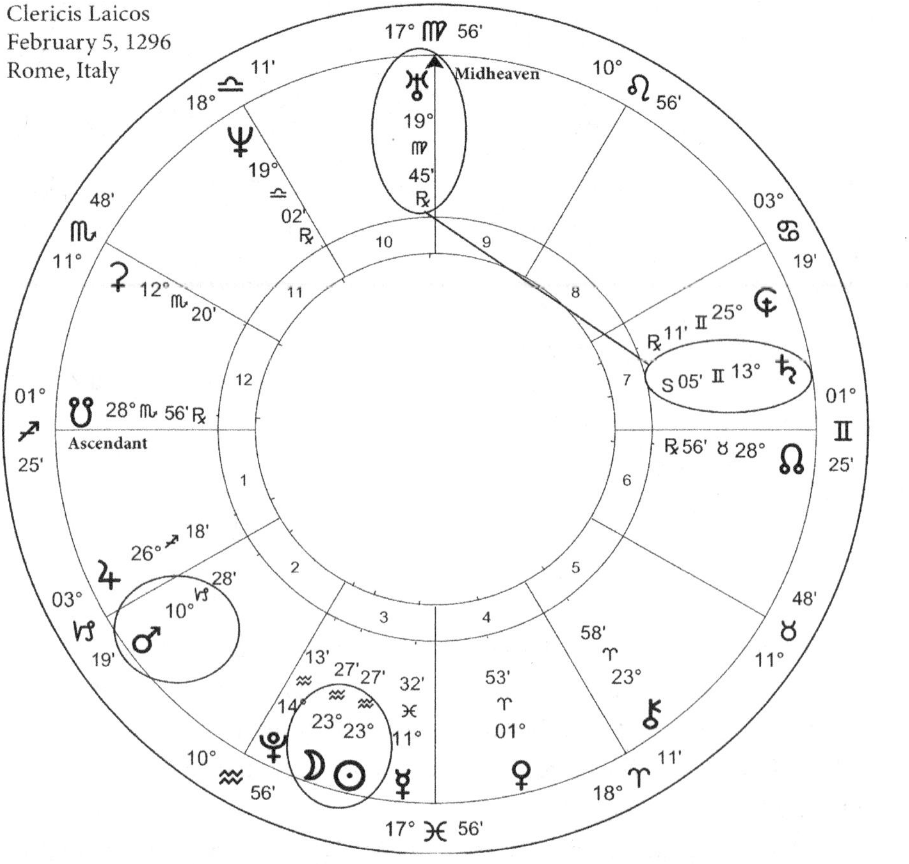

February 5, 1296 was the day of a New Moon, so this chart is cast for the moment of the New Moon at 23°27' Aquarius. Saturn, which went into direct motion the same day, is a co-ruler of Aquarius, so Saturn is thus doubly important in this chart because it rules the sign of the New Moon.

Uranus is the other co-ruler of Aquarius, so with Uranus conjunct the Midheaven a direct challenge to the status quo is indicated. And with Uranus square Saturn, the tension is increased between the ruling monarchs (represented

16 https://en.wikipedia.org/wiki/Clericis_laicos

by Saturn) and the Pope (the party making the declaration, who is represented by Uranus).

Mars in Capricorn is inconjunct (150° angle) Saturn, which rules Mars through its position in Capricorn. This definitely indicates very poor timing and an aggressive position that was bound to be rejected by those to whom the papal bull was directed.

Edward I, who was incensed by the papal bull, responded by declaring that any clergy who refused to pay levies to him would be charged with *outlawry*, which meant that they would no longer have protection under the law. He also confiscated some property held by bishops.[17]

Then, in August 1296, Philip IV countered the Pope by issuing an embargo on weapons, gold, precious stones, and currencies being exported from France. This had the side effect of keeping papal revenue in the country, for gold and silver

Philip IV's Embargo
August 2, 1296
Paris, France

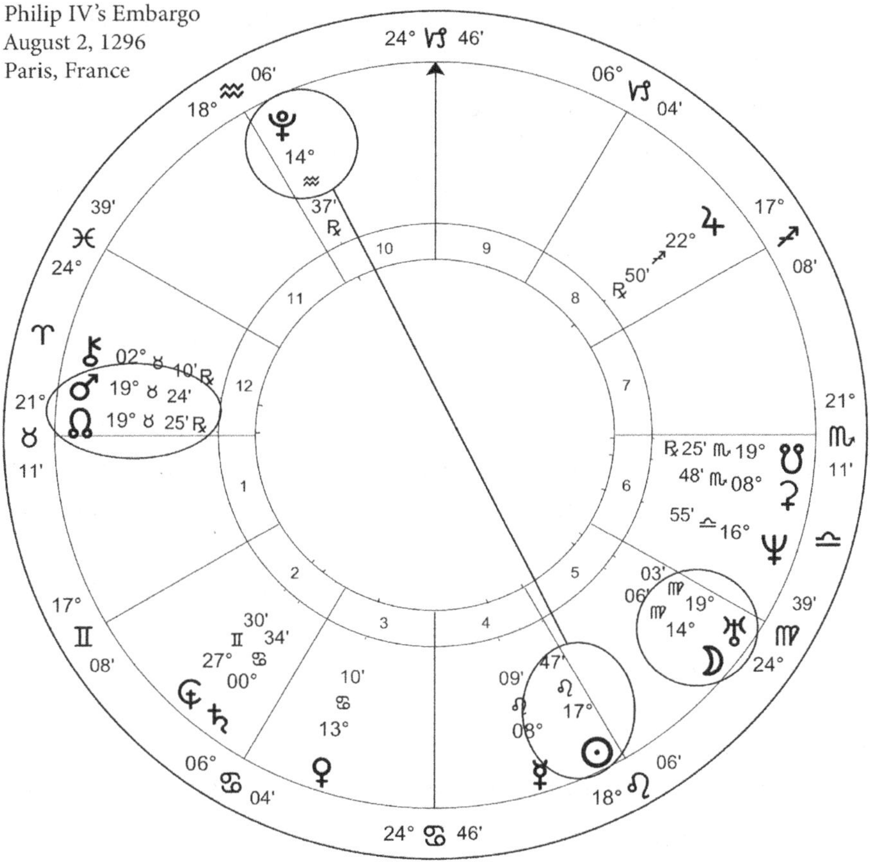

17 https://en.wikipedia.org/wiki/Edward_I_of_England

could not be sent out of the country, so papal revenue couldn't be transferred to Rome. Because of Philip's action, the Pope had to draw further on the Church's reserves to compensate for the shortfall, affecting the entire financial system that was administered by the Italian merchant societies. Philip also deported all papal agents who were raising money to fund a new crusade.[18]

The transits for August 2, 1296 clearly indicate this rebuttal to the Pope. Mars 19°25' Taurus was conjunct the North Node that day, forming a T-square with the Sun in Leo opposing Pluto in Aquarius. Such a combination of the Sun, Mars, and Pluto indicates an aggressive slap in the face to an opponent, as well as an association with war, as Philip could easily justify such an embargo during a war with England. With Mars trine Uranus, the strategy would be effective. Mars and Uranus forming angles to the North Node indicate a shift in the overall dynamic due to new tactics.

Progressed Saturn-Pluto Conjunction for the 1284 Capricorn Stellium Chart

That the summer of 1296 would be a critical time period was indicated by progressions for the 1284 Capricorn stellium chart. Progressed Pluto 26°21' Capricorn and progressed Saturn 26°23' Capricorn are almost exactly conjunct, another indication of a major shift in the financial system and the exchange of currencies, as these planets begin their new cycle by progression.

Transiting Mars and the North Node at 19°25' Taurus form a Grand Trine with transiting Uranus 19° Virgo, and progressed Venus 19°59' Capricorn.

The financial system was under pressure, and the greatest effect was on credit and currency transfers due to the eighth house influence of these two configurations. The eighth house of a chart is the area associated with "other people's money," such as debt, foreign currency, interest rates, taxes, and foreign investment. The two key planets, progressed Saturn and progressed Pluto, are in the eighth house. The ruler of the chart's eighth house is Aquarius/Uranus, and transiting Uranus forms a Grand Trine[19] with progressed Venus in the eighth house and transiting Mars, the planet naturally associated with the eighth house. In this case, taxes and the flow of currencies were the issues, and the Grand Trine, while being a configuration of ease, indicates that Philip's embargo would indeed easily put a crimp in the papacy's operations and achieve his goal.

18 https://en.wikipedia.org/wiki/Unam_sanctam

19 A Grand Trine is three planets or positions in the zodiac forming an equilateral triangle in the sky.

Capricorn Stellium
Progressed Saturn-Pluto
August 2, 1296

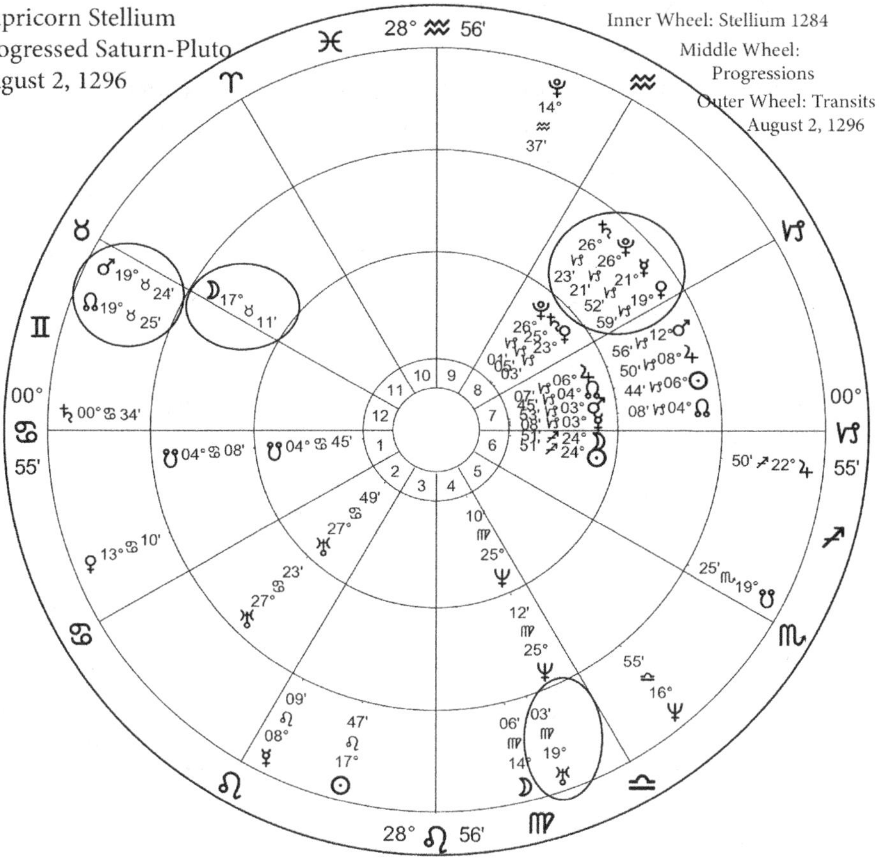

Transiting Mars and the North Node conjoining the progressed Moon 17°11' Taurus acted as a trigger to these eighth house configurations. The exact progressed Saturn-Pluto conjunction was in effect for several months, and with a range 3° of exactness, they were in effect for several years. Mars triggering the progressed Moon pinpointed the time when this conjunction would manifest a sharp effect.

Major Political Shift: 1295 Saturn-Neptune-Pluto Grand Trine

That both Philip IV and Edward I were able to extract new taxes from the Catholic Church could only have happened with a change in society's attitude toward the Church. Such a change was already apparent due to the reputation of Pope Boniface VIII as a corrupt and vicious leader as compared to the previous pope, Celestine V, who was pious and humble.[20]

This shift in attitude toward the Church, which for centuries had been regarded as not just the spiritual leadership of Europe but also the political leadership, is indicated astrologically by a Grand Trine of Neptune, Saturn, and Pluto in Air signs that formed in 1295.

Grand Trine of
Saturn-Neptune-Pluto
July 4, 1295

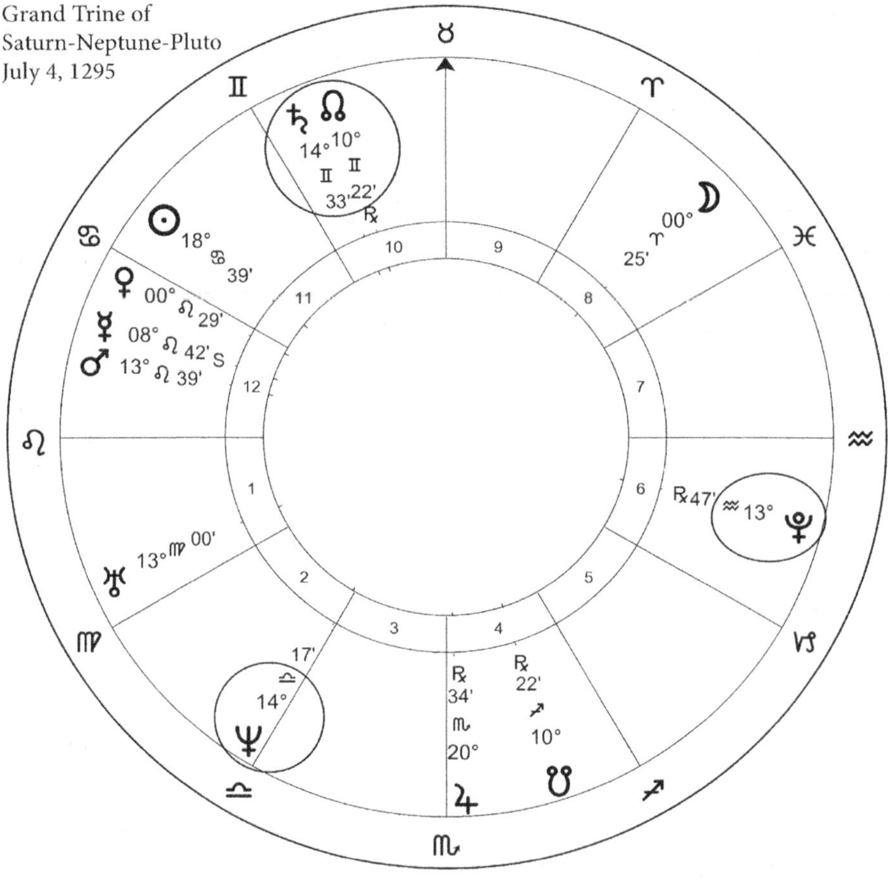

Neptune in Libra and Pluto in Aquarius had been moving in range of a trine aspect (120° angle) for years and would continue to do so. But in 1295, Saturn was in Gemini, trine to both of them. Saturn had also moved into the waning square portion of its cycle with Uranus, now in Virgo.

Neptune rules religion and spirituality, Saturn rules the established status quo and ruling governments, and Pluto rules the deep underpinnings of the financial system, which invariably involves the interweaving of the currencies

20 http://constructionlitmag.com/culture/philip-iv-takes-down-the-church/

and finances of individual entities, such as nations and city-states. With a trine considered to be an indication of beneficial cooperation and flow between the planets involved, this may have seemed so on the surface, but as this Grand Trine formed at 14° of Air signs, it was forming very ugly configurations with the stellium of 1284. If anything, this Grand Trine really indicated that a very delicate balance was about to be upset, due to Saturn's square to Uranus, as Saturn was involved in the Grand Trine. The Nodes were in sync with the Saturn-Uranus square in May and June of 1295, with Uranus first squaring the Nodes and then Saturn conjunct the North Node indicating a change in the established balance of religious, governmental, and financial system authorities.

When comparing the December 8, 1284 stellium chart to the July 4, 1295 chart, note that the Saturn-Uranus square in 1295 has its midpoint at 28°47' Cancer, which is conjunct the position of Uranus in 1284, at 27°49' Cancer. This means that the Saturn-Uranus square of 1295 formed a 135°–135°–90° triangle

Inner Wheel:
Capricorn Stellium
1284

Outer Wheel:
Saturn-Uranus Square
1295

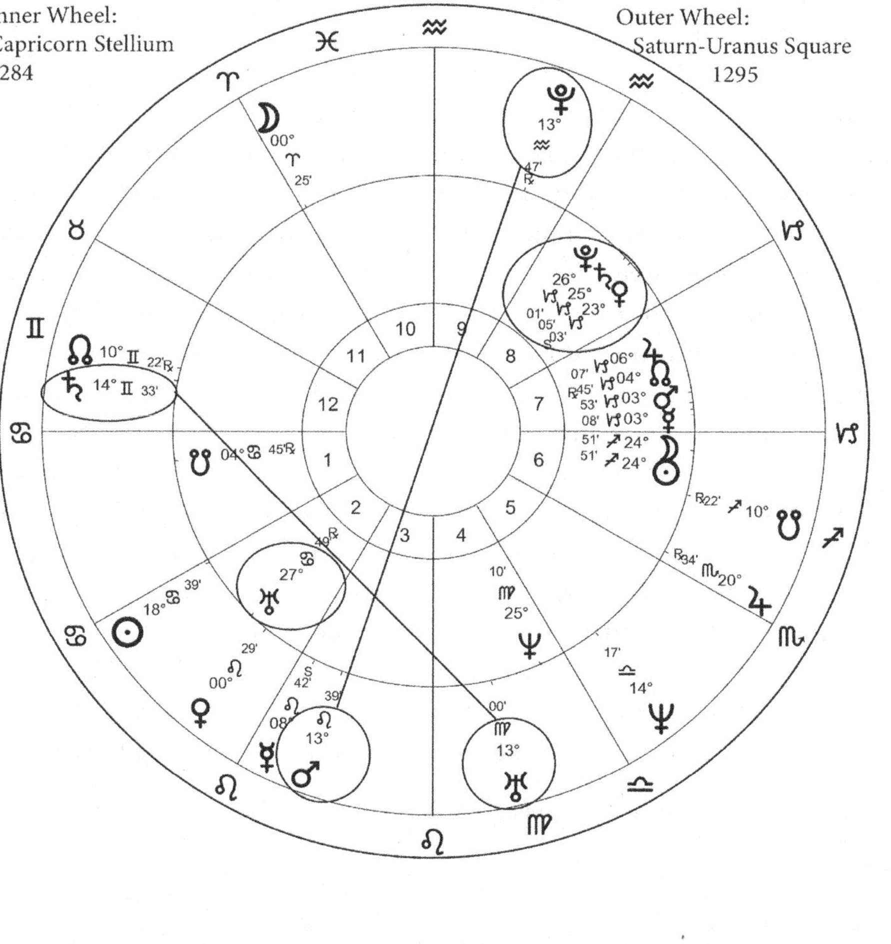

with the Saturn-Pluto conjunction of 1284. So, although the Saturn-Neptune-Pluto Grand Trine of 1295 indicated that things looked peachy on the surface, the situation was anything but. The Saturn-Pluto conjunction of 1284 is the apex of this triangular configuration, and with Uranus in 1284 opposing it, strong opposition had developed toward the existing system of church and state symbiosis. But it took this configuration of 1295 to bring this opposition to a head, and to open up a path of action to rupture that system (Mars opposing Pluto in the July 4, 1295 chart, with Uranus inconjunct Pluto).

Philip IV certainly did his utmost to unseat the Church as the final authority in France. His feud with Pope Boniface VIII intensified in 1301, when Philip had the papal legate Bernard Saisset arrested for inciting insurrection, and had him put on trial before the royal court. Pope Boniface responded with the papal bull *Ausculta Fili* ("Listen, Son") in December 1301, in which he implored Philip to submit humbly to him as the Vicar of Christ—but Philip upped the ante by having the *Ausculta Fili* burned before him and a crowd of supporters in Paris in February 1302.[21]

In November 1302, Pope Boniface issued the *Unam Sanctum*, a papal bull which stated that both spiritual and temporal power belonged to the Pope as the leader of the Church, and that kings were subordinate to the Pope. Later, in September 1303, French forces led by Philip's chief minister Guillaume de Nogaret attacked Pope Boniface at his palace in Anagni, and although after several face-offs between the two parties Pope Boniface was released, he was so badly shaken by the experience that he died in October 1303.[22]

The papacy was moved from Rome to Avignon, France in 1309, giving Philip IV an enhanced ability to bully the Church leaders. From 1309 to 1377, the seat of the Catholic Church was located in Avignon, with all of the popes during that time being French and essentially answering to the French king.

Politics was not the only area subjected to turmoil by Philip IV's aggressive rule. France became an economic backwater due to Philip's short-sighted blunders in attempting to grab funds to reduce his debts—which also affected the ability of other countries to assert their sovereign powers.

Some of the major financial institutions of the time collapsed in the first half of the 14th century, in part due to the mounting debts that France and other monarchies had accrued. A major astrological event in the early 14th century

21 https://en.wikipedia.org/wiki/Pope_Boniface_VIII

22 Ibid.

broadly indicated these financial crises and other events. But the financial crises in the last few years of the 13th century were influenced by two cycles which coincided.

Collapse of the Ricciardi and Gran Tavola: Saturn-Pluto and Chiron-Pluto Cycles 1294–1301

The Ricciardi suffered financial difficulties in 1294 and 1298 when Edward I wanted access to his money, which was being held by them (as explained above) essentially due to a credit crunch. The Gran Tavola began to collapse in 1298 due to a financial panic when Philip IV confiscated their assets in payment for what he claimed were debts owed to him by the Bonsignori (the family behind the Gran Tavola). This severely weakened the Gran Tavola's position and contributed to their loss of business from the Church for managing papal revenue. Although the Gran Tavola technically went bankrupt in 1298, they probably struggled on for a few more years.

When the Church took a loss due to the collapse of the Gran Tavola, which had further depleted the amount of papal reserves, it led to the rise of the Florentine merchant bankers who were now entrusted with managing papal revenue.[23]

These two periods in which Italian banks suffered great losses (1294 and 1298–1301) were times in which the Saturn-Pluto and Chiron-Pluto cycles coincided. In March 1294, Saturn 18° Taurus was semi-sextile (30° angle) Chiron 18° Aries, and Saturn squared Pluto 13° Aquarius. Although the Ricciardi's problems began at this time, they managed to survive until 1301.

It was the period of 1298 to 1301 that brought a shift in power in Italian banking circles. The Saturn-Pluto and Chiron-Pluto cycles coincided again in September–October 1299. On October 8, 1299, Chiron in Taurus opposed Mars in Scorpio, and they formed a Grand Cross with Saturn in Leo opposing Pluto in Aquarius—all around 15° of these fixed signs.

In terms of the 1284 stellium, and the outer planet cycles that either began or culminated at that time, in October 1297 Saturn was moving to conjoin the position of Uranus in 1284, and thus also oppose the position of the 1284 stellium. Saturn had moved 180°—halfway around the zodiac—since 1284, while at the same time Jupiter had completed an entire sojourn around the zodiac since 1284. Then, just as these planets reached these significant phases

23 https://en.wikipedia.org/wiki/Gran_Tavola

in their movements around the zodiac, Mars conjoined the South Node and formed a T-square with them.

Mars conjoining the South Node indicates that aggression and/or sudden change would be involved, with blatant disregard for diplomacy and rule of law, as Venus conjoins them, and the actions of Philip IV with respect to the Pope and the Gran Tavola certainly fit this description. Although this conjunction is in Libra, a sign ruled by Venus, she is retrograde.[24] And because the South Node is also a negative influence here, any existing conflict would take a turn for the worse under this configuration.

Saturn in Leo was within 11° orb of opposing Pluto in Aquarius from August 1299 through July 1301—a configuration that spelled doom for the Ricciardi and Gran Tavola, but which indicated restructuring and rejuvenation for the Peruzzi of Florence.

However, the Peruzzi eventually met their demise due to the next major coincidence of the Saturn-Pluto and Chiron-Pluto cycles in 1340, when Chiron was conjunct Pluto in Aries, as explained below.

Breakdown of Society: 1307 Triple Conjunction of Saturn, Uranus, and Neptune in Scorpio

The 14th century was a time of disaster and decline in Europe. The Medieval Warm Period ended around 1300 which contributed to lower crop yields and, eventually, floods and famine. War was prevalent, as monarchies competed for territory and financial advantage. Disease took a great toll as the Black Death spread across Europe.

In 1307, there was a conjunction of Uranus, Saturn, and Neptune at 11°–12° Scorpio. This is roughly a 700-year cycle. The next time these three outer planets were closely together at the same area of the zodiac was 1989–1993: First at 3°–12° Capricorn in 1989, involving all three planets, and in 1993, with Uranus conjunct Neptune 19°–20° Capricorn.

The 1307 instance of this triple conjunction signaled the peaking of overload of debt owed by European monarchies, the peak of deforestation and soil exhaustion across Europe, and the end of the Medieval Warm Period for the climate. It also marked the beginning of financial system collapse, decline of commodities' production and prices, famine, flooding, the spread of deadly

24 Furthermore, Venus was retrograde in the section of the zodiac referred to as the Via Combust (15° Libra to 15° Scorpio) which is considered to be a very malefic area of the zodiac.

diseases such as the Black Death, and the decimation of the European population over the following forty-five years.[25] This emphasis on the collapse of banks, natural disasters, and mass death is consistent with the areas ruled by Scorpio.

The 1989 instance of this triple conjunction also signaled a period of "overload" and impending decline, collapse, and reorganization. It triggered the collapse of the Soviet Union and the reorganization of governments across eastern Europe and central Asia. It was in 1989 that the Chinese Communist Party resisted a transformation to democracy and reasserted its rule with the brutal repression of the popular revolts of Tiananmen Square. And by the early 1990's, the Internet had become established as the new mode of doing business—with global reach available to even small companies—which led to a bubble in "dot-com" stocks and the resulting market crash of 2000. These themes of government control and reorganization, and changes in the way of conducting business on a global scale, are consistent with the areas ruled by Capricorn.

The similar factors of these two turbulent periods are social and economic disintegration, as well as serious financial decline for those entities that lose their competitive advantage due to a lack of resources required for adapting to new developments. And, it is important to note, during these kinds of turbulent periods there will also be entities that control the trend, ultimately profiting from it.

Uranus, Saturn, and Neptune were in their tightest configuration in September 1307. The chart on page 20 is cast for September 15, 1307, 11:22 pm when the Sun made its ingress into Libra, for location of Venice, Italy.

Pluto 29°03' Aquarius forms a sesquiquadrate aspect (135° angle) to the North Node 14°22' Libra. This is a dangerous indication overall, and depending upon how this configuration falls in the natal charts of the cities and states involved, they will be either at a severe disadvantage in the coming years, or able to profit from the adverse conditions that this aspect portends. As Pluto and Uranus are in mutual reception in 1307 (Pluto is in Aquarius, the sign ruled by Uranus; Uranus is in Scorpio, the sign ruled by Pluto), this configuration could also be interpreted as *both* Pluto and Uranus sesquiquadrate the North Node. It's as if Uranus and Pluto are conjunct in Aquarius, an indication of a severe upheaval in society—which is exactly what the 14th century was for Europe.

---

25 Evan D. G. Fraser, *Economic Crises, Land Use Vulnerabilities, Climate Variability, Food Security and Population Declines: Will History Repeat Itself or Will Our Society Adapt to Climate Change?* (University of Leeds, March 2009), https://www.see.leeds.ac.uk/fileadmin/Documents/research/sri/workingpapers/SRIPs-15_01.pdf

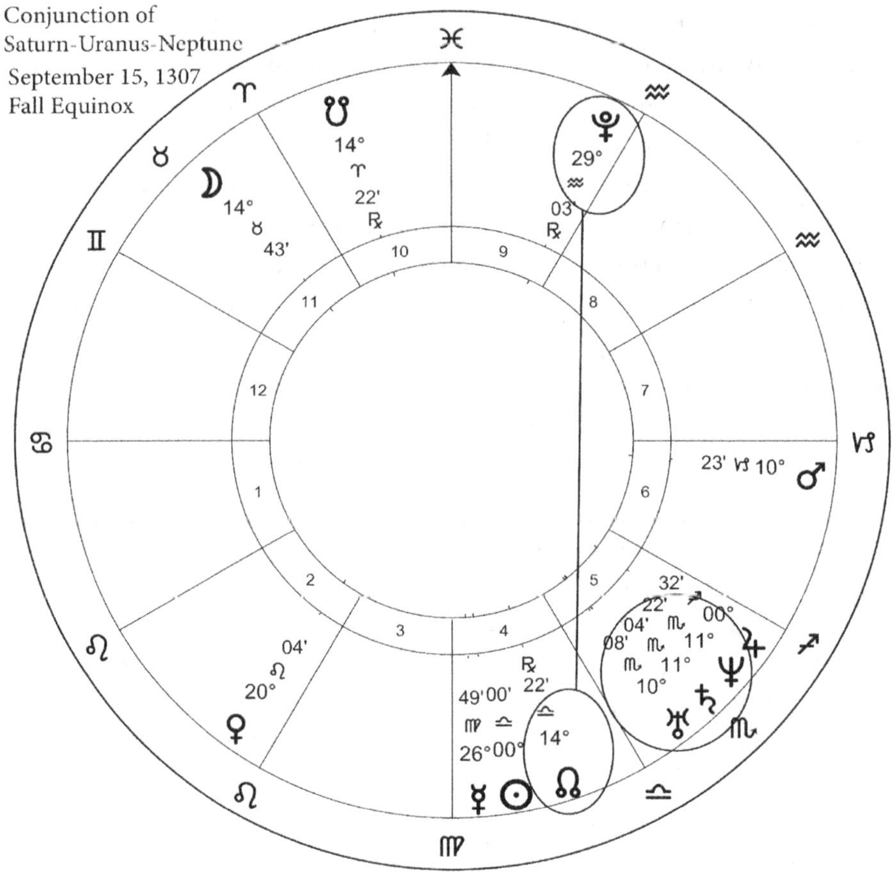

But the natal chart of one political entity at the time showed that it would benefit greatly from the triple conjunction. That entity was the city-state of Venice, Italy.

Chart for Founding of Venice

The Venetians have always claimed that their city was founded on Friday, March 25, 421, exactly at noon.[26] There isn't substantial evidence in the form of historical documentation to support this; even John Norwich, the author of the reference source, disputes this date as perhaps being too early. But by using the astrological chart for this date, and checking significant events in Venice's history against it, it is clear that the Venetians knew that this chart worked for them!

The Sun conjoins Uranus and the Midheaven at 5°–6° Aries. Both the

26 John Julius Norwich, *A History of Venice* (Vintage, 1989), p. 5

Founding of Venice
March 25, 421

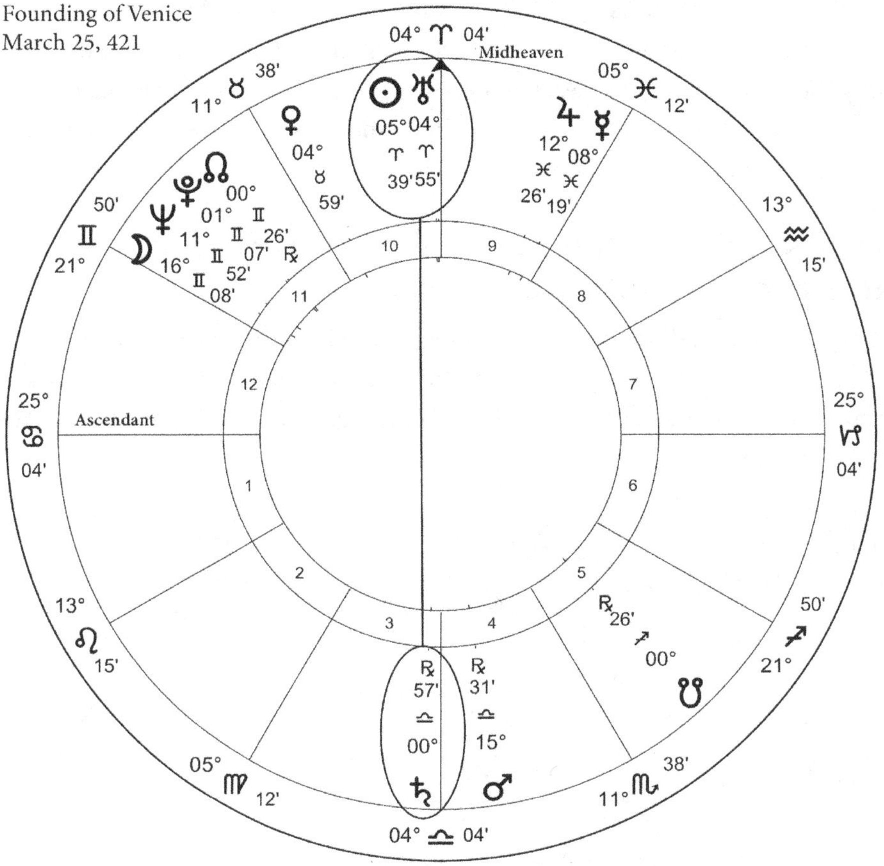

Sun and Uranus in Aries, ruled by Mars, indicate an insistence on absolute dominance. That they conjoin the cusp of the tenth house of government and reputation says that Venice would be known as the leader, the dominant participant, in the areas ruled by the houses of this chart associated with the Sun and Uranus. Aquarius/Uranus rules the cusp of the eighth house of foreign currencies, along with assets, taxes, and death, while Leo/Sun rules the second house of banking and the local currency. There couldn't be a better configuration for achieving dominance over global banking and currency trading. Not only are the Sun and Uranus linked by an aspect in longitude, they are in aspect by declination: The Sun is parallel[27] Uranus, and also parallel Saturn, although

27 Two planets are in parallel aspect when they are equidistant from the great circle of the equator projected onto the heavens, regardless of their positions in the zodiac (see the Glossary for more on this).

both the Sun and Uranus oppose (180° angle) Saturn 0°57' Libra.

With the Sun opposing Saturn, yet parallel to it, and Capricorn/Saturn ruling the Descendant of allies, partnerships, and open enemies, Venice is often working both with and against her "allies" and "enemies." This was certainly the case in this chapter of Venice's history.

Saturn-Uranus-Neptune Conjunction in the Charts of Venice and France

The progressions and transits for September 15, 1307 to the chart for the founding of Venice show that the triple conjunction fell on the cusp of the fifth house of speculation—the first indication of a massive, long-term, risky trade executed by the Venetians.

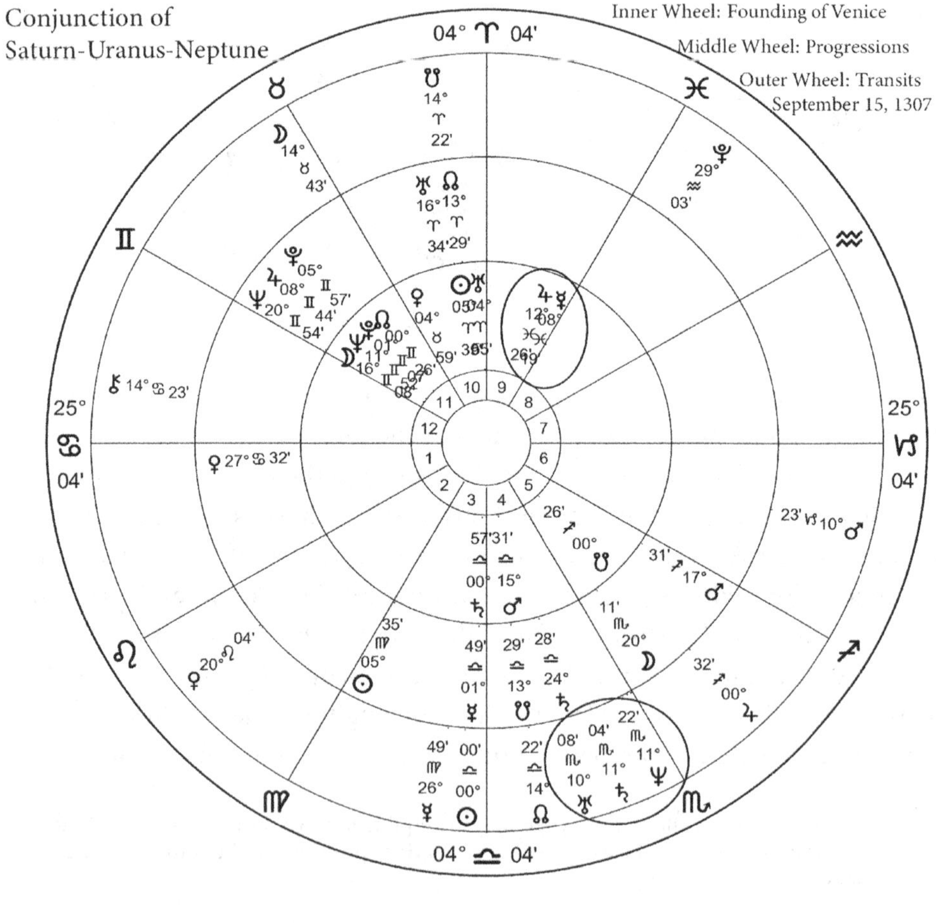

But Venice was accustomed to taking such risks in international trade, as shown by natal Jupiter squaring natal Neptune. Venice would succeed despite the high risk because of her control, not only of her own currency, but the currencies of others—a potential shown by natal Sun conjoining natal Uranus, ruler of the eighth house of foreign currencies and assets.

Uranus, Saturn, and Neptune are trine (120° angle) natal Jupiter 12°26' Pisces in the ninth house of overseas commerce and shipping. Note that the planets of the triple conjunction—Saturn, Uranus, and Neptune—rule the seventh, eighth, and ninth houses, respectively, of Venice's natal chart. Furthermore, transiting Uranus in Scorpio and transiting Pluto in Aquarius are in mutual reception, so they will act as if they are conjoined, giving almost total control over international currency trading to Venice due to Uranus as ruler of both the eighth house and transiting Pluto.

This quadruple conjunction by mutual reception in Scorpio, affecting the area of foreign currencies and finance (areas naturally ruled by Scorpio), was a major factor not only for Venice, but for all of Europe. This particular conjunction also indicated that the trend of emerging territorial states had reached a serious obstacle to development due to the strength of Venice's position.[28]

France had been the foremost of the emerging territorial states, but during this time, Philip IV made a strategic blunder that set the French economy back substantially: The Champagne fairs, which had been an economic center for over a century, had begun to decline around 1284[29] due to the absorption of Champagne into the Royal Domain when Philip IV married Queen Joan I of Navarre. Then, Philip kicked out the Lombards and Jews from the Champagne fairs during 1306 and 1307, which contributed even more to their growing insignificance due to new land and sea trade routes that began to open.[30]

Philip felt he was protecting his interests because he was in debt to both the Jews and Lombards, but the further decline of the fairs shifted the center of economic power away from France. This was a decisive setback to the continued development of territorial states in Europe.[31]

---

28 Fernand Braudel, *The Perspective of the World Volume III: Civilization and Capitalism 15th–18th Century* (University of California Press, 1992), p. 116

29 https://en.wikipedia.org/wiki/Champagne_fairs

30 Fernand Braudel, *The Perspective of the World Volume III: Civilization and Capitalism 15th–18th Century* (University of California Press, 1992), pp. 115–116

31 Ibid., pp. 115–116

How does the Uranus-Saturn-Neptune conjunction of 1307 affect the chart of France?

Looking at progressions and transits for September 15, 1307 to the chart for Philip IV becoming king on October 5, 1285, three configurations stand out. The first was Uranus, Saturn, and Neptune conjoin the progressed Sun

Conjunction of Saturn-Uranus-Neptune

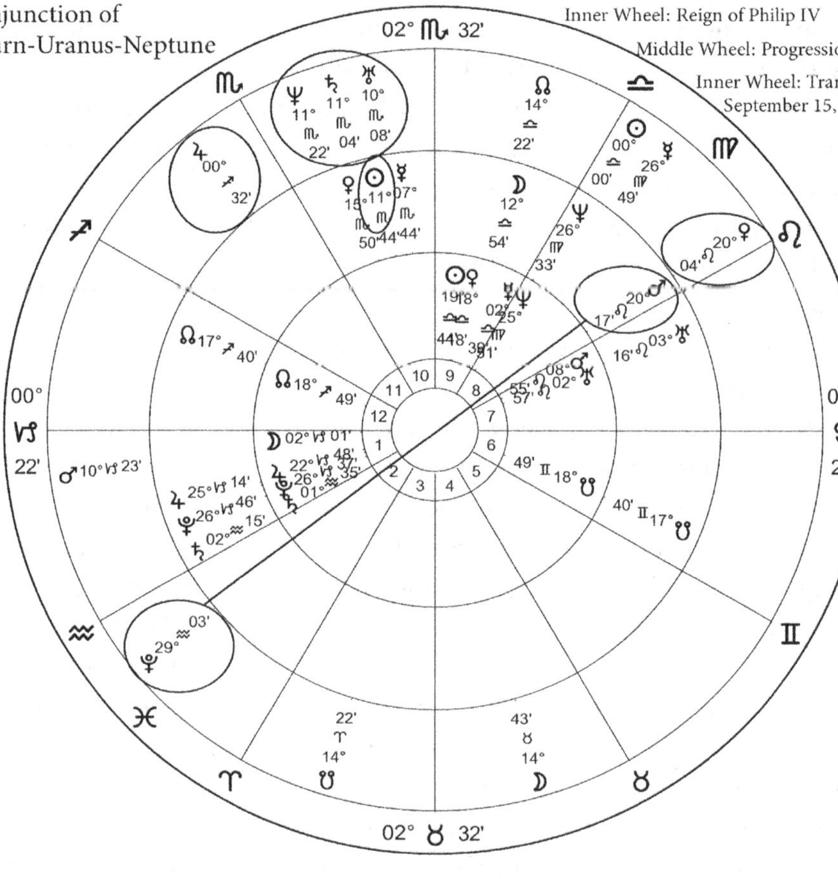

Inner Wheel: Reign of Philip IV
Middle Wheel: Progressions
Inner Wheel: Transits September 15, 1307

11°48' Scorpio, a major indication of suffocating, claustrophobic circumstances befalling France. This conjunction occurs in the tenth house (for rectified chart with time of 12:35 pm for Paris), emphasizing the king and his leadership, which proved to be faulty at this time, at least with regard to France's economic future.

The configuration of transiting Venus opposing transiting Pluto links to progressed Mars, with both transiting Venus and progressed Mars at 21° Leo. This opposition forms a wide T-square with the square between transiting Jupiter 0°32' Sagittarius and Pluto 29°03' Aquarius, indicating that the role of

France as an economic center in Europe is clearly compromised. This transiting T-square affecting Mars, the ruler of Scorpio, the sign of foreign finance and credit (and the sign of the Uranus-Saturn-Neptune conjunction), refers to Philip's disastrous decision to kick out the Jews and Lombards (the financiers offering credit) from the Champagne fairs. Although this may have seemed like a good idea to Philip at the time, as he was in debt to both camps, this action hastened the end of the fairs, which had already been in decline for some time. Philip IV did not comprehend that the Champagne fairs were the main economic component linking France to the overall European economy. France sank into relative obscurity and thus lost her chance to develop the region of Champagne into a major economic player, and in doing so, strengthen her development as a territorial state.[32]

Thus, it was the shortsightedness of the French king which led to a long period of second-class status for the economy of France. The competition to become the economic center of Europe became a rivalry between cities, not states. As noted above, Venice had the advantage in this contest and decisively won it, as indicated by her power in financial markets.

Although the triple conjunction in 1307 signaled that the level of debt was reaching the breaking point, it took until 1324–1325 for conditions to develop that would trigger the collapse of the Florentine banks. But it wasn't until 1343–1346 that the collapse actually happened.

Collapse of the Florentine Merchant Bankers: 1343 Uranus conjunct Pluto

The 1307 Saturn-Uranus-Neptune conjunction indicated that the debt being taken on by the monarchies of England and France had reached the breaking point, and it signaled the impending collapse of European society and severe weakening of the financial system. And although from 1300 to 1325 the Florentine bankers were on a roll, this was because they were profiting from the debt buildup.

The Florentines provided funds for France and England to finance their armies in exchange for those monarchies pledging a portion of the revenue that they collected from issuing licenses for the production of commodities. But, as commodity production declined in this period, partially due to the Hundred

32 Ibid., pp. 114–116

Years War and partially due to the Florentine and Venetian bankers' control of trade and speculation in commodities, the scene was set for debt overload and defaults.[33]

The crux of the problem for the Peruzzi and other Florentine bankers was that they held loans denominated in gold florins. Venice had already been driving down the price of gold while raising the price of silver—which now caused the Florentine bankers to lose money on these loans.

The Chiron-Pluto conjunction 7° Aries in 1339–1340 indicated that debts accrued by European monarchies were the Achilles' heel of the financial system at the time, and the institutions which were financing this debt would be vulnerable if there was a shift in the way that currencies were valued or exchanged. The conjunction by Ceres[34] to Chiron and Pluto in 1340 indicated a consolidation of power around such trading; a restoration, yet a vast extension, of the power of a few players in this trade. Venice was thus able to take advantage of the Florentine bankers' vulnerability due to her position as the one controlling the prices of gold and silver across not just Europe, but Asia as well.

The reason Venice had the advantage was due to her unique position in the trade of gold and silver bullion and currencies, and her trade with the Mongol Khans in Asia. Prior to the Mongols' invasion of China and India, the dominant currencies in Asia were minted in gold. The Mongols confiscated the gold currencies, replacing them with silver currencies and paper money. They sold the looted gold to Venice in exchange for silver.[35]

In Europe, whose currencies were minted in silver, Venice was able to buy large quantities of silver from mines in Germany, Bohemia, and Hungary with the gold from the Mongols. As the demand for silver for minting coinage in Asia continued to rise during the late 13th and early 14th centuries, the Venetians were then able to increase the price of silver despite larger quantities of it being mined—with exports of silver from Venice to Asia beginning to accelerate around 1320–1325.[36]

---

33 Frederic C. Lane and Reinhold C. Mueller, *Money and Banking in Medieval and Renaissance Venice, Volume 1: Coins and Moneys of Account* (The John Hopkins University Press, 1985), p. 316

34 Ceres is associated with exchange rates.

35 Frederic C. Lane and Reinhold C. Mueller, *Money and Banking in Medieval and Renaissance Venice, Volume 1: Coins and Moneys of Account* (The John Hopkins University Press, 1985), p. 373

36 Ibid.

Thus, Venice took advantage of her position with the Mongols during the 1320's and began reversing the precious metal standards for currencies of the two regions for her own profit. Venice would buy silver from European mines and hold it, thus reducing the amount available for minting currencies in Europe, then sell that silver to the Mongols in exchange for gold, which made gold available in Europe, so that the pattern was reversed. Venice first maneuvered the devaluation of the silver currencies of the Holy Roman Empire and Byzantium, and then reduced the value of the Florentine gold florin, leading to the collapse of the Florentine bankers such as the Peruzzi and Bardi.[37]

A major shift in asset values and the balance of currency standards was indicated in late 1324 by transiting Uranus 23° Capricorn passing over the

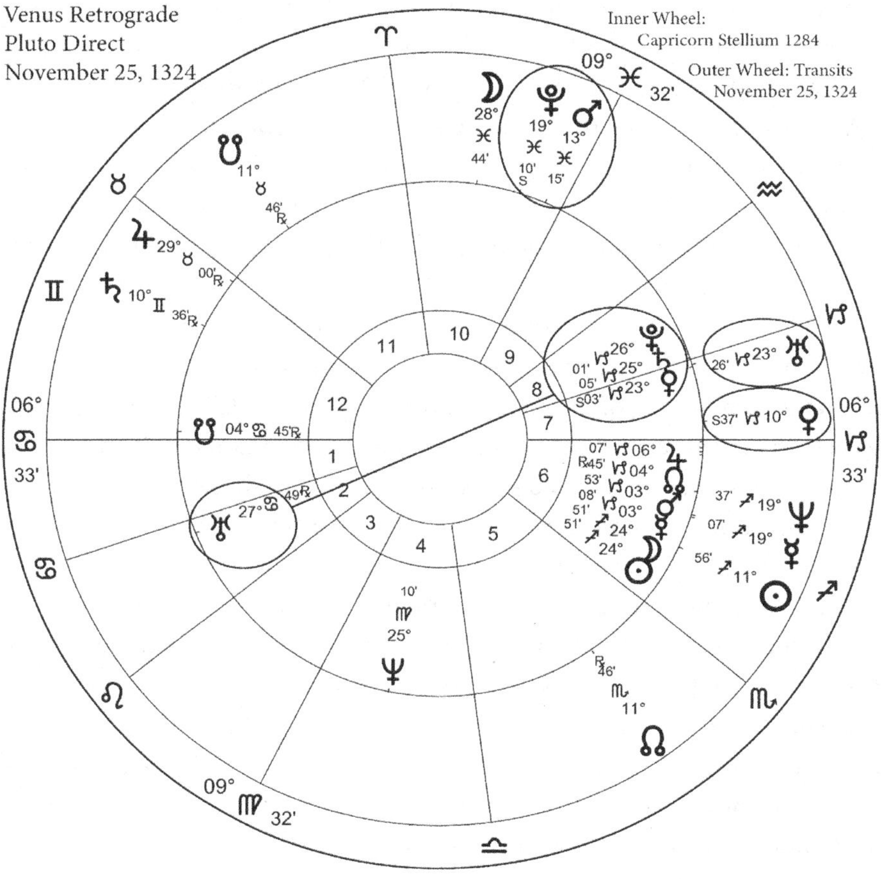

37 Ibid.

position of the stellium planets in the 1284 chart. Thus, Uranus was now opposing (180° angle) its position in 1284, signaling a culmination period in which there was a peak in the profits of the Peruzzi and other Florentine bankers.

On November 25, 1324, transiting Venus in Capricorn (and conjunct transiting Ceres, associated with exchange rates) went retrograde, and on the same day, transiting Pluto in Pisces went back into direct motion. It was around this time period that Venice began to reverse the trend in prices of gold and silver, a shift which would heavily impact the Florentine banking enterprises—especially the Peruzzi.

Overall, that a series of financial institutions would collapse in the 1340's was shown by the major conjunctions in Aries in the 1340's that involved Chiron conjoining Pluto first, and then Uranus conjoining Pluto in 1343 at 11° Aries. As Uranus conjoined Pluto on June 10, 1343, Mars was at 11° Aries as well, resulting in a triple conjunction.[38] Chiron-Pluto indicated serious weakness; then Uranus-Pluto delivered a shocking blow to that weakness.

At the same time as this Mars-Uranus-Pluto conjunction, Saturn 28° Capricorn and Neptune 2° Aquarius were in orb of their conjunction, which occurred at 1°56' Aquarius in January 1344. Both of these outer planet configurations made significant aspects with the chart for the restructured Peruzzi banking enterprise.

The Uranus-Pluto cycle can indicate a systematic attempt to dominate a large group of people by forcing them to accept an ideology, or manipulating their financial situation, or both. The Saturn-Neptune cycle, which can indicate weakness that needs correction, can also indicate corruption that is either in the process of becoming entrenched in a system, or that is already widespread and exposed—resulting in efforts to root out that corruption. It can also indicate the depletion of important resources, or the buildup of debt.

With these two configurations happening simultaneously in 1343–1344, there would be those nations or city-states that would dominate finance and politics—those with a natal chart that had favorable configurations to Uranus-Pluto. And, there would be those nations or city-states that were weaker, more corrupt, or more oblivious to long-term trends that would be annihilated by stronger competitors—those with a natal chart containing detrimental configurations to Uranus-Pluto and Saturn-Neptune.

38 There were three exact conjunctions of Uranus and Pluto in 1343–1344, due to retrograde motion.

★ ★ ★

Overall Astrological Conditions Associated with Debt Buildup, Availability of Capital, Political Shift, and Financial Crisis

The following conditions involve only transiting planets and could apply to the global financial system, but could apply to a regional system as well.

Astrological conditions indicating buildup of debt:

- Saturn conjunct Pluto as part of a stellium in Capricorn.
- Chiron-Pluto and Saturn-Pluto cycles coincide.

Astrological conditions indicating the peak of available capital, or approaching peak buildup of debt:

- Saturn opposing Neptune.

Astrological conditions indicating a shift in the balance of power surrounding a major source of capital in the international (or regional) financial system:

- Grand Trine of Saturn, Neptune, and Pluto.
- Mars interacting with the Jupiter-Neptune and Saturn-Neptune cycles.
- Chiron-Pluto and Saturn-Pluto cycles coincide.

Astrological conditions indicating looming default or severe financial crisis:

- Saturn conjunct Pluto as part of a stellium in Capricorn.
- Aspects by transiting Saturn to the position of the Saturn-Pluto conjunction in Capricorn.
- Chiron-Pluto and Saturn-Pluto cycles coincide.
- Uranus conjunct Pluto.

CONCLUSIONS

From research on the 13th–14th centuries, the following astrological configurations stand out as indicating a financial system collapse.

Transiting Configurations

A Saturn-Pluto conjunction occurring in Capricorn (or possibly a sign in which Saturn is dignified), especially when there is also a stellium in the same sign, indicates that severe problems could develop in the financial system, as well as a looming collapse of part of the system. For a chart calculated at the time of the stellium (usually when Saturn and Pluto are not yet exactly conjunct), when Saturn exactly conjuncts Pluto by progression, issues involving taxation affect the financial system.

A Saturn-Uranus-Neptune conjunction indicates a major long-term disruption to economic conditions, which usually involves the disintegration or massive reorganization of weak economies. Innovations in communications and commerce are often involved.

The Uranus-Pluto cycle indicates disruptions to major areas or major players in the financial system. As most wars are motivated by greed, this economic cycle also indicates times of major conflicts, either military or political, or the introduction of trends that lead to such conflicts.

The coinciding of the Saturn-Pluto and Chiron-Pluto cycles is of major importance for determining a general time frame for financial crises. When Uranus interacts with these cycles, the danger increases.

Saturn opposing or squaring the position of the previous Saturn-Pluto conjunction (that was part of a stellium) often acts as a timer, or trigger, for events related to finance and politics.

Progressed Saturn exactly conjunct progressed Pluto, as calculated for the chart for the date of a stellium that involved other important configurations (such as an eclipse, a planet turning retrograde or direct, etc.) acts as a timer, or trigger, for events related to finance and politics.

CHAPTER 2

LATIN AMERICAN DEFAULTS OF THE 1980'S

Developing countries in Latin America took out huge loans in the 1960's and 1970's to fund industrialization in order to grow their economies, with a climate of low interest rates and a huge influx of capital into the global financial system making it easy—too easy—for these countries to get loans. As debt reached unsustainable levels, the day of reckoning came in the early 1980's when both Mexico and Brazil admitted they could not service their debts.

Due to the fact that Mexico and Brazil were the countries that were the most dramatically affected by this situation, their charts will be examined in detail to determine astrological conditions associated with debt buildup, default, and currency devaluation.

OIL MONEY AND LATIN AMERICAN DEFAULTS

Latin American countries received loans through international development funds such as the World Bank in the 1960's, but after 1973 loans came from private banks[39] that were receiving large amounts of capital deposited by the Organization of Petroleum Exporting Countries (OPEC) countries thanks to two extreme increases in the price of oil.

The first of these increases was in October 1973, which was triggered by an oil embargo declared by OPEC and primarily directed at the United States for its support of Israel in the Yom Kippur War.[40] The second, in 1979, was triggered by a decrease in production due to the Iranian revolution of that year and the Iran-Iraq War which began in 1980.[41]

When the increase in oil prices in the 1970's provided OPEC members, particularly Saudi Arabia, with massive amounts of excess capital that could

39 https://en.wikipedia.org/wiki/Latin_American_debt_crisis

40 https://en.wikipedia.org/wiki/1973_oil_crisis

41 https://en.wikipedia.org/wiki/1979_energy_crisis

not immediately be put to use in their domestic economies, they decided to deposit the money in Western international banks because they considered sovereign debt to be a safe investment. This money was then used for loans to developing countries in Latin American and Africa that needed help growing and strengthening their economies.[42]

With the world economy on a tear in the early 1970's, and real interest rates on short-term loans near zero at that time, it seemed the developing countries that were receiving short-term loans would be able to repay their debt. But while these loans continued to be issued, by 1976 some economists were questioning the sustainability of this practice, noting that Latin American debt to banks in the United States had skyrocketed.[43]

Mexico devalued the peso by 45% in 1976 due to massive capital flight as investors took their money out of the country in response to President Echeverra's erratic fiscal policies (including his support of illegal land grabs by Mexican peasants[44]). New oil discoveries in the Gulf of Mexico which began that same year helped the economy to recover from the devaluation—with Mexico becoming a net exporter of oil after having been a net importer of oil.

As economic growth continued, it meant that Mexico was able to continue getting foreign loans, although the expansion of the oil industry came at the expense of other industries which could not compete in the global economy, causing Mexico to enact protective tariffs. All in all, Mexico's policies continued to put the country in a precarious position in relation to global events outside its control.[45]

But by 1977 as inflation was increasing around the world, and the priority of the Federal Reserve was to contain inflation, interest rates were hiked and the Latin American countries began having trouble repaying their short-term loans—which then had to be rolled over at the higher rates.

By the end of 1978, total debt held by Latin American countries reached $159 billion, from $29 billion in 1970; by 1982 their combined debt totaled $327 billion.[46]

42 https://www.federalreservehistory.org/essays/latin_american_debt_crisis

43 Ibid.

44 https://photius.com/countries/mexico/economy/mexico_economy_1982_crisis_and_reco~473.html

45 Ibid.

46 https://www.federalreservehistory.org/essays/latin_american_debt_crisis

The bubble burst on August 12, 1982 when Mexico announced that it could not service its debts. Then, in 1983, Brazil conceded that it must default on its debt also.

Similarity to the 13th and 14th Centuries

Thus, the situation in the 1970's and 1980's was similar to that of the late 13th and early 14th centuries: An entity with large cash reserves, which they could not put to use, deposited that money with banks which in turn lent it to struggling countries.

In the 13th century, that entity was the Papacy of the Catholic Church, the lending intermediaries were the Florentine bankers, and the recipients were Philip IV of France and Edward I of England (who were interested in building their armies, not their economies). In the 14th century, some banks were allowed to fail, and the economies of France and England were left to limp along.

In the late 20th century, the concern was preventing the failure of the banks, with the best economic interests of the indebted countries being a secondary concern; in essence, they were also left to limp along.

Astrologically, the similarity of these two periods is that both had a stellium that was centered on a Saturn-Pluto conjunction, and it was the triggering of these stelliums that led to financial crises. Note that the signs in which these stelliums occurred both had a strong connection to Saturn: It is the domicile ruler of Capricorn, sign of the 1284 stellium, as well as the exaltation ruler of Libra, the sign of the 1982 stellium.[47]

Overall Astrological Configurations of 1966 to 1983

There are three components of the Latin American debt crisis: Overload of debt due to easy credit and financed by large reserves of an outside entity; capital flight and currency devaluations; and default on loans denominated in a foreign currency.

47 Domicile and exaltation planetary rulers of the signs are part of the system of essential dignities. See the Glossary for an explanation of the system of essential dignities in astrology.

Initial Buildup of Debt

Several long-term cycles coincided in 1965–1966, signaling a buildup of debt in the system as a whole that would result in a financial crisis.

- Uranus was conjunct Pluto in Virgo from June 1964 to June 1968 within a 5° range. From March 1964 through March 1967, Saturn was in Pisces, opposing them by sign. Chiron was also in Pisces at this time.
- From February 1965 to April 1966, Saturn opposed Uranus and Pluto within an 8° range.
- From August 1965 to March 1966, Chiron opposed Uranus and Pluto within a 5° range.
- In the first half of April 1966, Mercury, Chiron, and Saturn 24° Pisces opposed Uranus and Pluto 17° Virgo. Then at the end of April 1966, Venus, Chiron, and Saturn 25° Pisces opposed Uranus and Pluto.

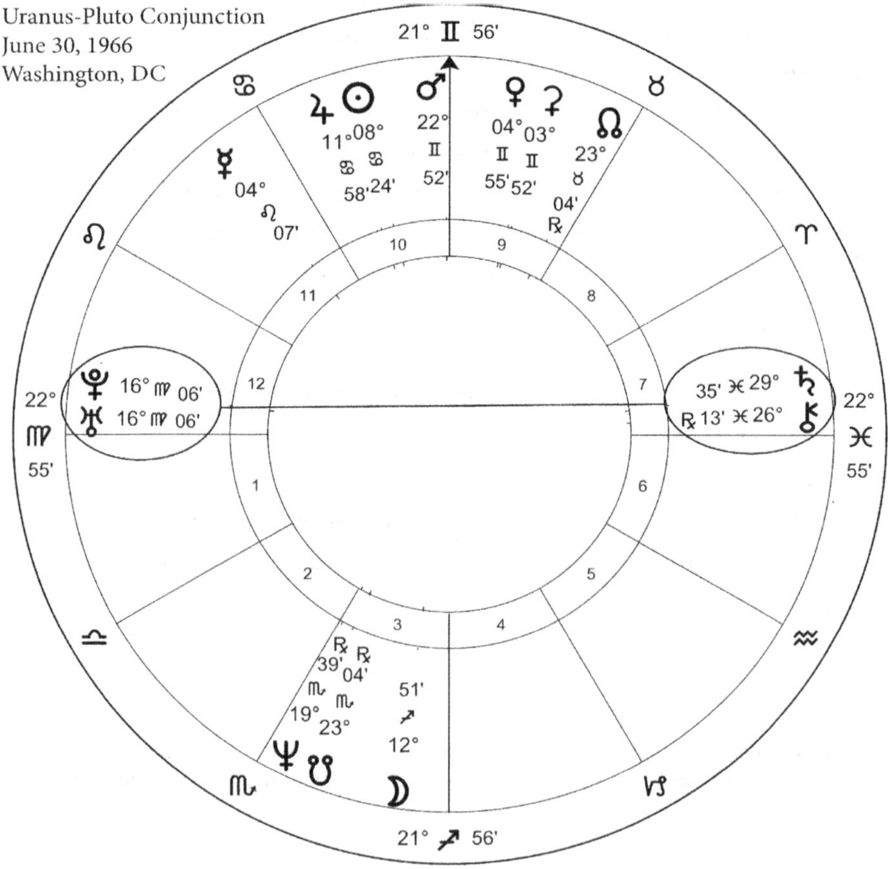

Uranus-Pluto Conjunction
June 30, 1966
Washington, DC

So, the time range when these aspects were close to exact was August 1965 through April 1966, when Chiron-Saturn in Pisces (joined by Mercury and Venus in 1966) opposed Uranus-Pluto in Virgo.

Just as in the 13th and 14th centuries, the Saturn-Pluto and Chiron-Pluto cycles coincided. The final collapse of the Ricciardi bank occurred under the configuration of Saturn opposing Pluto, as both were squared by Chiron, in 1300. The Riccardi were caught in a liquidity trap in 1294–1296, which was the mortal blow that weakened them. The Peruzzi bank was restructured in 1300, and was one of the Florentine banks that replaced the Riccardi in their role of handling Church revenues. The Peruzzi went bankrupt in the early 1340's under the influence of the Chiron-Pluto conjunctions in Aries, followed by the Uranus-Pluto conjunction in 1343 near the same degree of Aries, all of which were trine Saturn in Sagittarius.

In 1966, the Saturn-Pluto and Chiron-Pluto cycles coincided with the Uranus-Pluto cycle once again. As Uranus and Pluto were forming a conjunction, one cycle was ending, and another was about to begin. For the situation in Latin America at the time, these coincident cycles indicated the peak in borrowing from international development funds. As the new Uranus-Pluto cycle unfolded, Latin American countries would shift to getting loans from private investment banks which were flush with petrodollars from the increase in the price of oil.

Jupiter moving through Cancer formed a Grand Trine with Neptune in Scorpio, and Saturn and Chiron in Pisces, also in 1966. And, as in 1295 when the Grand Trine of Saturn, Neptune, and Pluto signaled an impending shift in the balance of power—particularly the waning political power of the Church, and more specifically, the drain on papal reserves that would begin, eventually taking investment capital out of the financial system—the Grand Trine of 1966 indicated an impending power shift that revolved around oil, the energy source of the modern world.

Note that in both cases the source of capital was designated by Neptune: In the 13th century, it was the Church, a spiritual organization; in the late 1960's and 1970's, it was the profits of OPEC countries. (Neptune is associated with spiritual matters and also with oil.)

Influx of Capital into the Financial System

Because the increase in the price of oil in October 1973 merely accelerated the borrowing by Latin America, astrological conditions of that time period should show not only a large existing amount of debt, but also a continuing ramp up in debt. At the same time, conditions should show a change in the price of oil. What were the astrological configurations in the 1970's and 1980's?

- Transiting Neptune was in Sagittarius from January 1970 through November 1984.
- Uranus moved through Libra and Scorpio during that time, and Pluto was in Libra.
- Saturn moved from early Taurus to mid-Scorpio.
- Neptune in Sagittarius alone would indicate sudden spikes in the price of oil, as Neptune rules oil, and Jupiter, ruler of Sagittarius, exaggerates whatever it influences. When Saturn was in Gemini,[48] it opposed Neptune, and then Saturn in Virgo made a waning square to Neptune.[49]

Both of these periods in 1973 and 1979—with transiting Saturn and Neptune in a harsh angle, and in mutable signs,[50]—coincided with a change in the price of oil, and both of these price increases were due to restricted supply, which was the effect of Saturn.

But these oil price increases resulted in more capital being available for investment. At the time of the 1973 oil embargo, Saturn and the South Node in Cancer were in waning square to Pluto in Libra, while Jupiter in Aquarius was trine Pluto. The Saturn-Pluto cycle aligned with the Nodes, showing a shock to the system, although the Jupiter-Pluto trine indicated a silver lining to the situation.

As Pluto rules foreign investment (due to its association with Scorpio), and Jupiter indicates increase, more money was available for investment. Over the course of the next year Jupiter moved from Aquarius to Pisces, and in December 1974 Neptune conjoined the North Node in Sagittarius. Neptune and Jupiter

---

48 Saturn was in Gemini from mid-June 1971 through July 1973, and again from January to mid-April 1974 (due to retrograde motion).

49 Saturn was in Virgo from late July 1978 to late September 1980.

50 Gemini, Virgo, Sagittarius, and Pisces are the mutable signs.

Arab Oil Embargo
1973

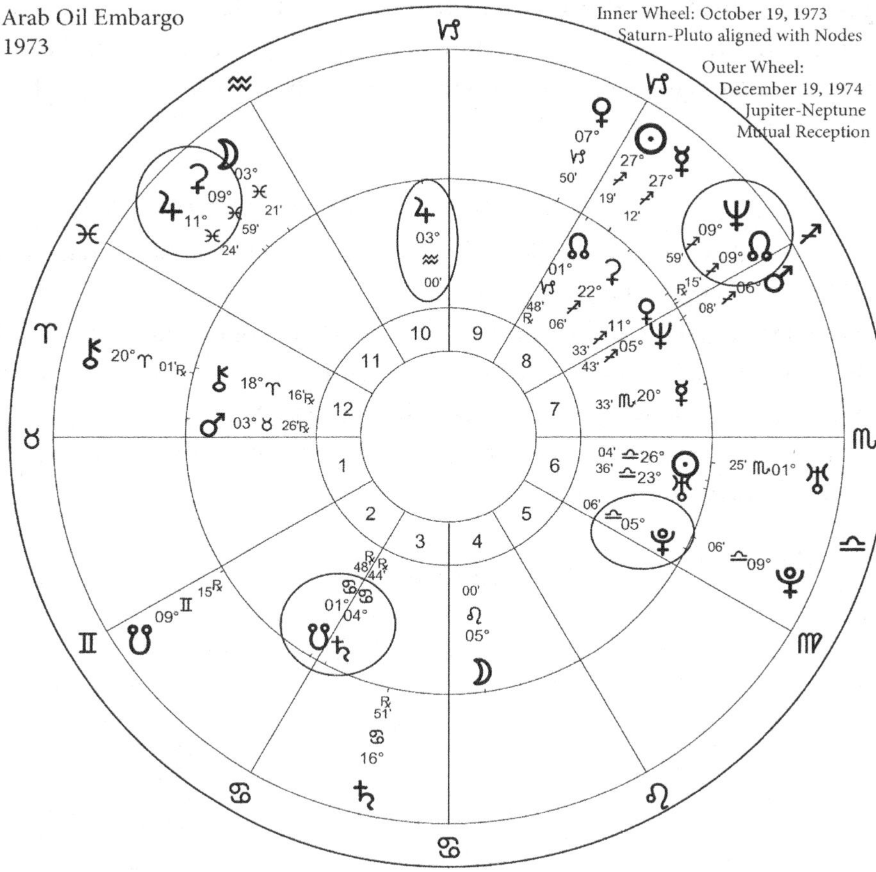

were in mutual reception,[51] however, so it was as if they were conjoined, and also benefiting from the North Node. As this "simulated conjunction" was occurring in Sagittarius, and making a beneficial aspect to Pluto, the indication was that profits from oil would flood into the financial system.

Note, however, that in 1973 the Chiron-Pluto and Saturn-Pluto cycles coincided in a T-square, indicating a major change to some aspect of the global financial system. This change—more investment capital in the system—initially appeared to be beneficial to Latin American countries, but in the long term it was very detrimental.

51 Mutual reception occurs when planet A in is a sign ruled by planet B, and planet B is in a sign ruled by planet A. The two planets will work together as if they are conjoined.

Capital Flight, Currency Devaluation, and Default

As capital flight, currency devaluation, and default are events specific to a country, the astrological conditions for these are examined below in the analyses of Mexico and Brazil.

MEXICO – Potential for Financial Problems

The chart for Mexico's constitution shows the potential for problems related to debt, foreign reserves, and the currency.

Mars 18° Aquarius and Uranus 20° Aquarius are conjoined in the eighth house of debt. This alone is a major indication that debt, especially loans denominated in a foreign currency, could be problematic.

This indication is made even stronger by the positions of both the natural and chart co-rulers of the eighth house.

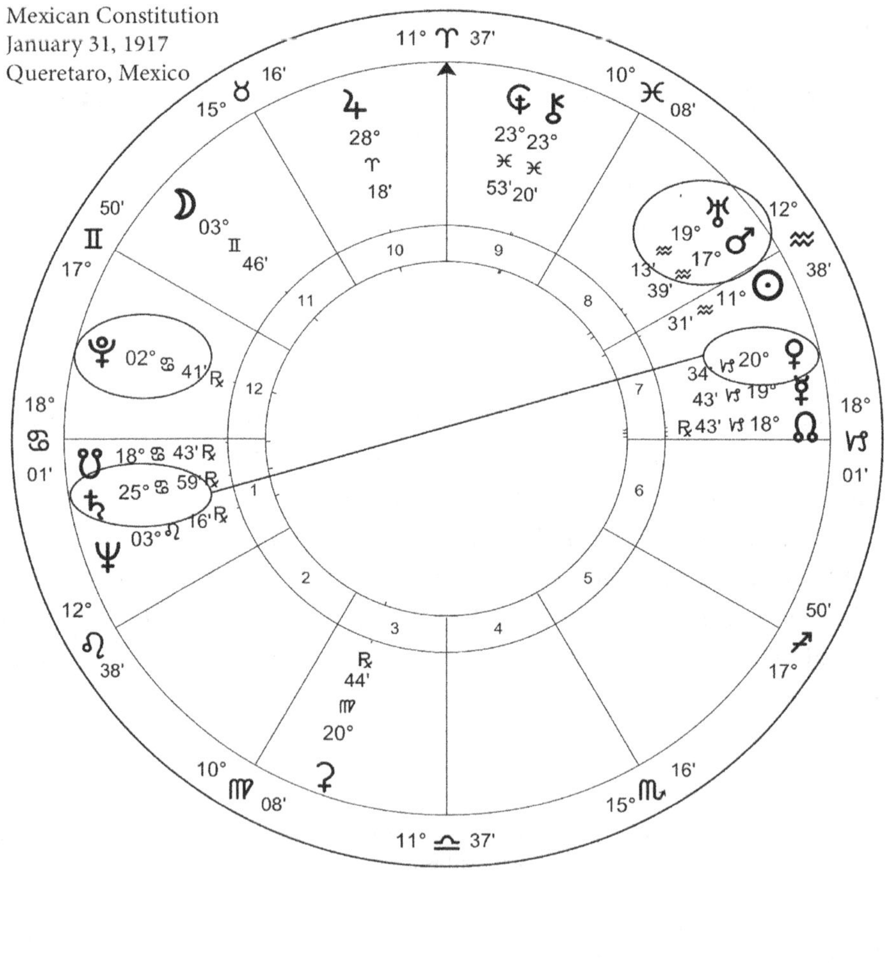

Aquarius is the sign on the cusp of Mexico's eighth house, so the co-rulers of Aquarius—Saturn and Uranus—affect the affairs of that house. Furthermore, Uranus, the most unpredictable planet in its effects, is located in the eighth house.

Scorpio is the sign naturally associated with the eighth house, and its co-rulers are Mars and Pluto. Again, one of those co-rulers, Mars, is in the eighth house. Furthermore, Pluto, in Cancer in the twelfth house of hidden issues and corruption, is sesquiquadrate (135° angle) to Mars and Uranus.

Taken together, these indications revolving around the planets directly associated with Mexico's area of debt and foreign reserves point to serious problems at some point when they are triggered by a transiting and/or progressed configuration.

An indication that problems with debt will affect the value of Mexico's currency is that Venus 20°34' Capricorn opposes Saturn 25°59' Cancer. Venus is the natural ruler of a country's banks, financial system, and currency, so with Venus opposing the co-ruler of Mexico's eighth house (as explained above), there will be issues in Mexico's history that link debt problems to the value of its currency.

MEXICO – Easy Credit, First Oil Price Shock, and Debt Buildup

Mexico's buildup of debt was shown as accelerating from 1966 through 1976 by several outer planet configurations to the chart for Mexico's Constitution. The Uranus-Pluto conjunction in Virgo in 1966 impacted Mexico's chart with this important new cycle encouraging taking on debt for two reasons: The conjunction involved the chart ruler of the eighth house (Uranus) *and* the natural ruler of the eighth house (Pluto); and the conjunction was sesquiquadrate (135° angle) natal Jupiter 29° Aries in the tenth house—a combination of Jupiter-Uranus which encouraged risk.

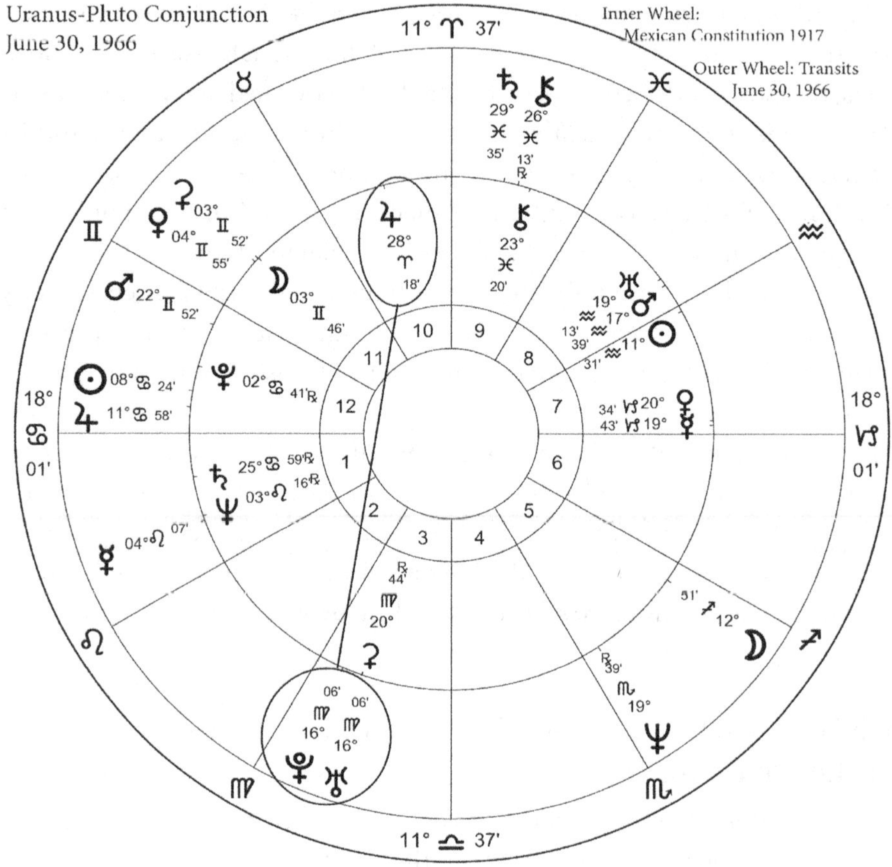

In September 1967, transiting Neptune 20°–24° Scorpio was square progressed Uranus 22° Aquarius, with Aquarius/Uranus ruling the eighth house of debt for this chart, and natal and progressed Uranus residing in the eighth house. Transiting Jupiter 20°–24° Leo was opposing progressed Uranus, forming a T-square with transiting Neptune in a configuration that resides in financial areas of the chart, which are the second, fifth, and eighth houses. In this case, the transiting Jupiter-Neptune square is an indicator of financial excess, centered upon the area represented by the progressed planet, Uranus, in the eighth house of debt—or "other people's money." These configurations show that even at this early stage, poor decisions were being made.

Jupiter-Neptune Square
1967

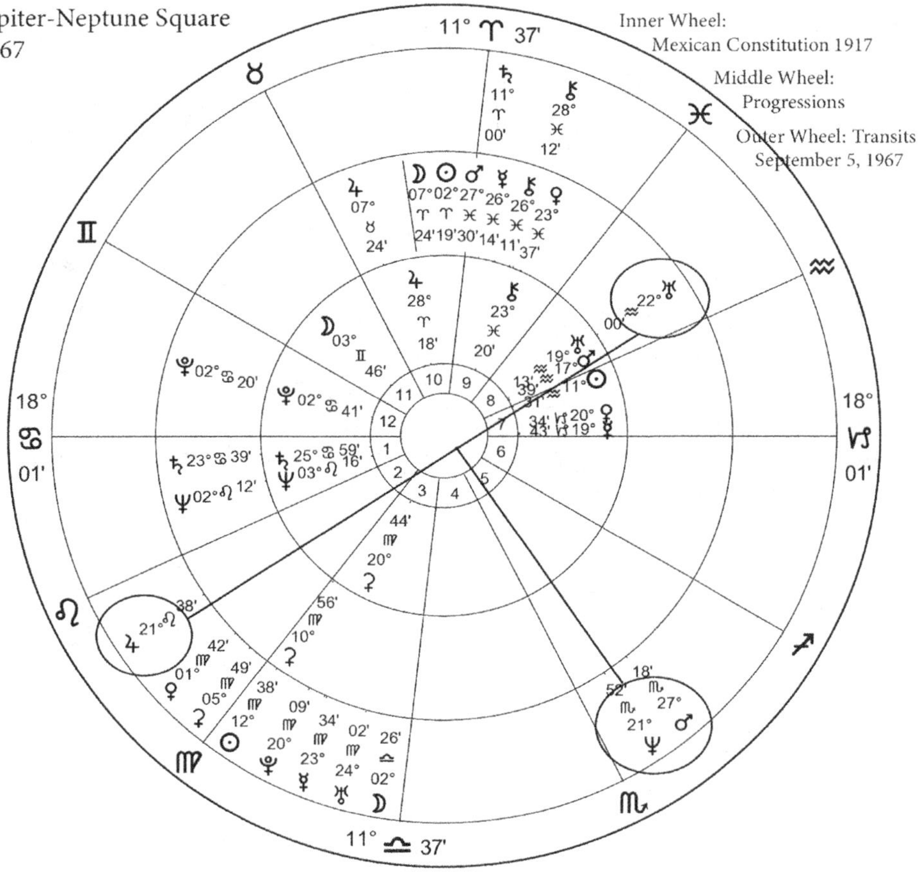

In the fall of 1970, transiting Saturn 20°–23° Taurus conjoined the progressed Moon while squaring progressed Uranus, indicating that although the harsh realities of paying back this debt were being recognized, with transiting Jupiter in Scorpio opposing progressed Jupiter 8° Taurus inspiring an overly confident frame of mind, more debt was taken on.

Thus, in 1973, when OPEC imposed an oil embargo and the price of oil rose considerably, Mexico was able to keep on borrowing money.

Arab Oil Embargo
1973

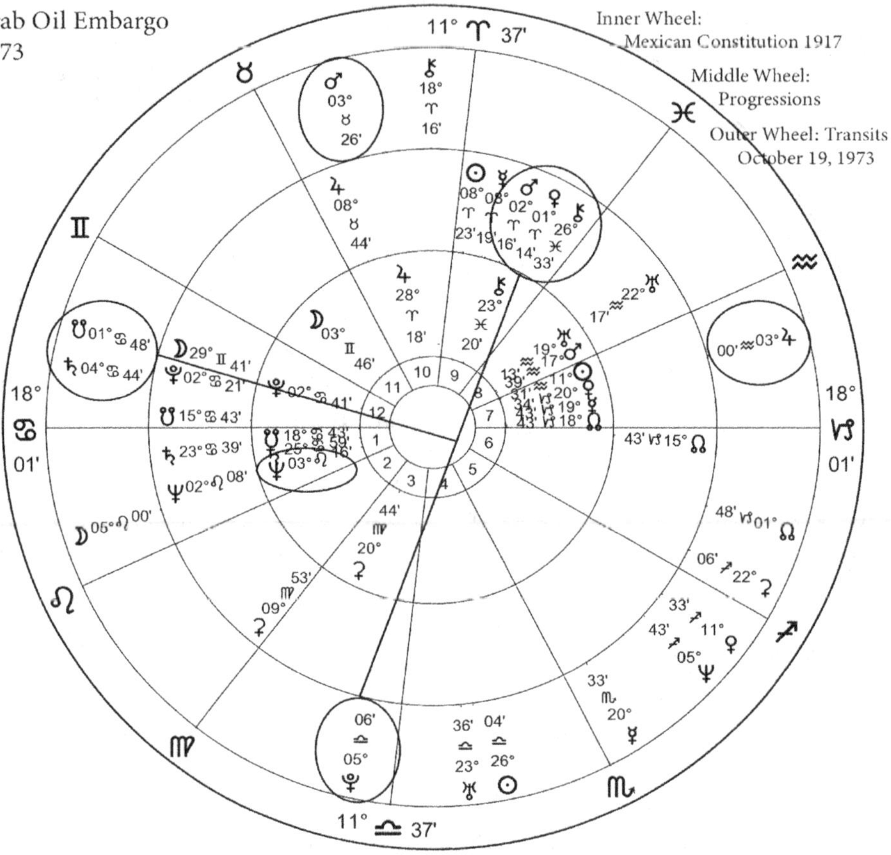

The easy availability of more money in 1973 is shown by the Grand Trine of transiting Neptune 5° Sagittarius trine natal Neptune 3° Leo and progressed Venus and Mars 2°–3° Aries.

But the downside of that easy credit—heavy restrictions in the future, with possible consequences to the currency—is indicated by the T-square of transiting Pluto 5° Libra opposing progressed Venus and Mars[52] in Aries, with all squaring Saturn and the South Node 2°–5° Cancer. As Saturn and the progressed Moon 29° Gemini are in the twelfth house, the consequences of current actions (Saturn) are hidden at this point because it is still developing (the action of the twelfth house). Also, Saturn conjoins natal Pluto 3° Cancer, an important indication of having to face the difficult consequences of past actions.

52 Venus is the planet associated with a country's currency; Mars is associated with foreign currencies and debt.

In 1970 transiting Saturn 22° Taurus squared progressed Uranus of this chart for Mexico, while in 1973 transiting Hades 22° Taurus[53] squared progressed Uranus. These two slow-moving indicators, both destructive in their influence, made a harsh aspect to Uranus from fall 1970 to fall 1973.

That Saturn and Hades would work insidiously to undermine Mexico's currency is shown by the configuration that each formed with natal planets when they were at 22° Taurus, which put them in a Grand Trine with natal Venus 20°34' Capricorn and natal Ceres 20°44' Virgo.

That more risk would be taken despite the situation is shown by the T-square configuration involving Jupiter, Mars, and natal Neptune. Mars in an angle with Jupiter is impulsive, and since it was also in a harsh angle with Neptune, reality was disregarded. Transiting Neptune in Sagittarius trine natal Neptune in Leo had made it easy to gloss over the terms of these loans because Neptune rules Pisces, which rules the ninth house in this chart, the area of the chart associated with these terms.

MEXICO – Capital Flight and 1976 Peso Devaluation

Reality finally began to hit in 1976 when capital flight was accelerating throughout the spring and summer due to excessive government spending and policies which repelled investors.[54] Then, on August 31, 1976 Mexico was forced to devalue the peso by 45%.

First, that the peso was overvalued, and a devaluation inevitable, is shown by transiting Jupiter and Pluto in a complex configuration with progressed Uranus (again!), and progressed Venus and Mars.

Transiting Pluto was at the apex of a triangular configuration with transiting Jupiter and Hades, and progressed Uranus (a triangle formed by 135°–135°–90° angles)—a particularly stressful configuration that demands relief. In late June–early July when transiting Jupiter near 22° Taurus formed this configuration with Pluto and progressed Uranus, capital flight began to drain the country of foreign reserves. Although Mexico was allowed by the Federal Reserve to draw down the $360 million available to it in a swap agreement to compensate for the loss of reserves, capital flight accelerated.[55]

---

53 Hades is not an actual body in space here, it is the calculated Transneptunian point (see the Glossary).

54 http://nsarchive2.gwu.edu/NSAEBB/NSAEBB115/index.htm

55 Ibid.

This capital flight is shown by transiting Ceres in Leo in the second house of finances and currency, moving to oppose natal and progressed Uranus. And because Ceres impacts the movement of assets or people across borders, Ceres in the second house was motivating the Mexican people to protect their savings by moving their money outside of the country.

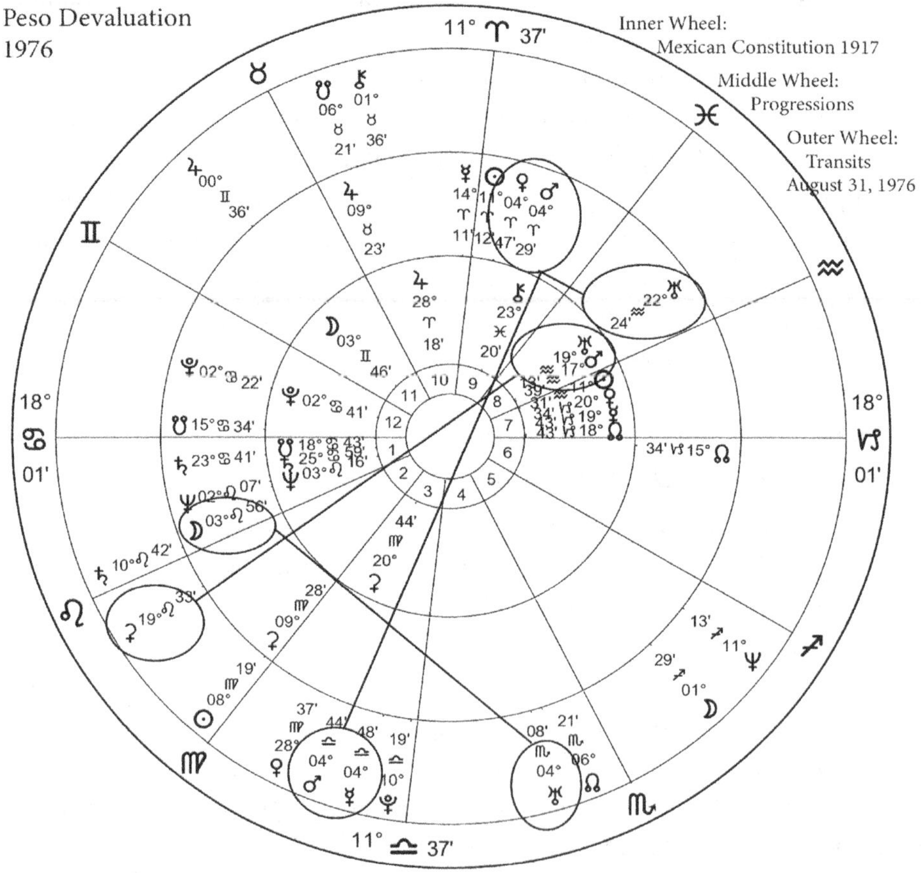

That this situation was building is shown by the semi-square (45° angle) between progressed Venus and Mars[56] and progressed Uranus. Venus and Mars are the natural rulers of the second and eighth houses, respectively (currency, foreign reserves, debt), and here they are making a stressful angle with the chart ruler of the eighth house of foreign reserves. The progressed Moon 3°56' Leo

56 Progressed Venus and Mars were now almost exactly conjunct in Aries (Venus at 4°47' and Mars at 4°44').

conjoining natal Neptune 3°16' Leo in the first house indicated the growing fear of loss of savings by the general population; that they increasingly chose to move their money outside of the country was indicated by transiting Ceres trine progressed Venus and Mars when she moved over the early degrees of Leo in July 1976. The pressure on the peso came to a head in late August when the progressed Moon and Uranus 4° Taurus (ruler of the eighth house) moved into a close square (90° angle) with one another.

This complex interplay of planetary energies triggered the devaluation of the peso on August 31, 1976, the day that transiting Mercury and Mars, conjunct at 4°44' Libra, exactly opposed progressed Venus and Mars, sending shock waves throughout the entire configuration.

Other configurations were in play that confirmed a currency devaluation: Leo rules the second house of the currency for Mexico's chart, so the Sun, the body associated with the sign Leo, should be in a detrimental configuration. Both the natal Sun and the progressed Sun are in harsh angles with restricting planets: Transiting Pluto 11° Libra opposed the progressed Sun 11°12' Aries, while transiting Saturn 11° Leo (in the second house of the currency, but co-ruler of the eighth house of foreign reserves and debt) opposed the natal Sun in Aquarius in the eighth house. With the natural ruler (Pluto) and chart co-ruler (Saturn) of debt and foreign reserves in the actualizing angle of 180° opposition to the chart ruler (Sun) of the currency, the peso could not help but be affected by the buildup of debt, and in turn, that debt was now unsustainable because of lack of foreign reserves.

MEXICO – Admission of Default

Mexico devalued the peso again in 1980, as well as three times in 1982. But the most dramatic event, which impacted other Latin American debtor countries, was Mexico's announcement on August 12, 1982 that it could not service its foreign debt.

The Saturn-Pluto cycle was the main force at work. Saturn combined with Pluto results in harsh measures that impose discipline, and they were conjunct at 27°31' Libra in November 1982, a position linked to the positions of several other important astrological events in 1981 and 1982. Mexico's default and the situation that led to it were shown by a complex interweaving of astrological configurations to its chart that converged in the last half of 1982, linked to the eighth house of debt, and centered upon transiting Saturn and Pluto.

One of these events was a cluster of planets (another stellium) in Libra in 1981. In October 1981, the Sun, Mercury, Ceres, Jupiter, Saturn, and Pluto were all in Libra. All of these planets were ending synodic cycles[57] with each other, and beginning new cycles. Of particular note is the Jupiter-Pluto conjunction at 25° Libra, which occurred on November 2, 1981. Jupiter and Pluto squared the Nodes 27° Cancer/Capricorn in the same time period, and also squared Mexico's natal Saturn 26° Cancer. The unfolding of the new Jupiter-Pluto cycle had much to do with the unfolding of Mexico's debt default in 1982.

This new cycle was under the influence of Venus, which is the domicile ruler of Libra, but it was also under the influence of Saturn, which is the exaltation ruler of Libra—thus the new cycle of Jupiter and Pluto would be operating under the influence of Venus and Saturn. They are in a harsh aspect in Mexico's chart (as explained above), and they are linked to the eighth house which translated into a severe restriction related to debt and foreign reserves.

The stellium in Libra repeated in the fall of 1982, and at the same time there was a stellium in Sagittarius. In October 1982, the Sun, Mercury, Venus, Saturn, and Pluto were in Libra, with all but Mercury clustered in a tight band of 25°–30° Libra. The stellium in Sagittarius consisted of Uranus, Ceres, Mars, and Neptune, with Mars conjunct Neptune 24° Sagittarius. Mars and Neptune were sextile (60° angle) the cluster of planets in Libra.

The 1981–1982 stelliums in Libra were definitely the major trigger for the culmination of Mexico's debt binge, for these stelliums occurred with the ending of the Jupiter-Pluto and Saturn-Pluto cycles. Venus conjoined Saturn and Pluto in late October of 1982, and this triple conjunction of Venus, Saturn, and Pluto tells the story: Lack (Saturn) of currency (Venus) to make loan payments due to depletion (Saturn again) of foreign reserves (Pluto).

Transiting Saturn went retrograde at 22°14' Libra in January 1982, with transiting Mars also going retrograde in February of that year, at 19°10' Libra. These retrograde station positions were very close to the positions where the new Jupiter-Pluto cycle began, and fell in the fourth house of Mexico's chart which rules national security, real estate, mines, and weather events. The fourth is also considered the house of endings, as it is at the bottom of the chart. With the Jupiter-Pluto and Saturn-Pluto cycles ending (beginning) in Libra in Mexico's fourth house, a new approach to handling foreign financing of the economy through loans was about to begin.

---

57 See the Glossary.

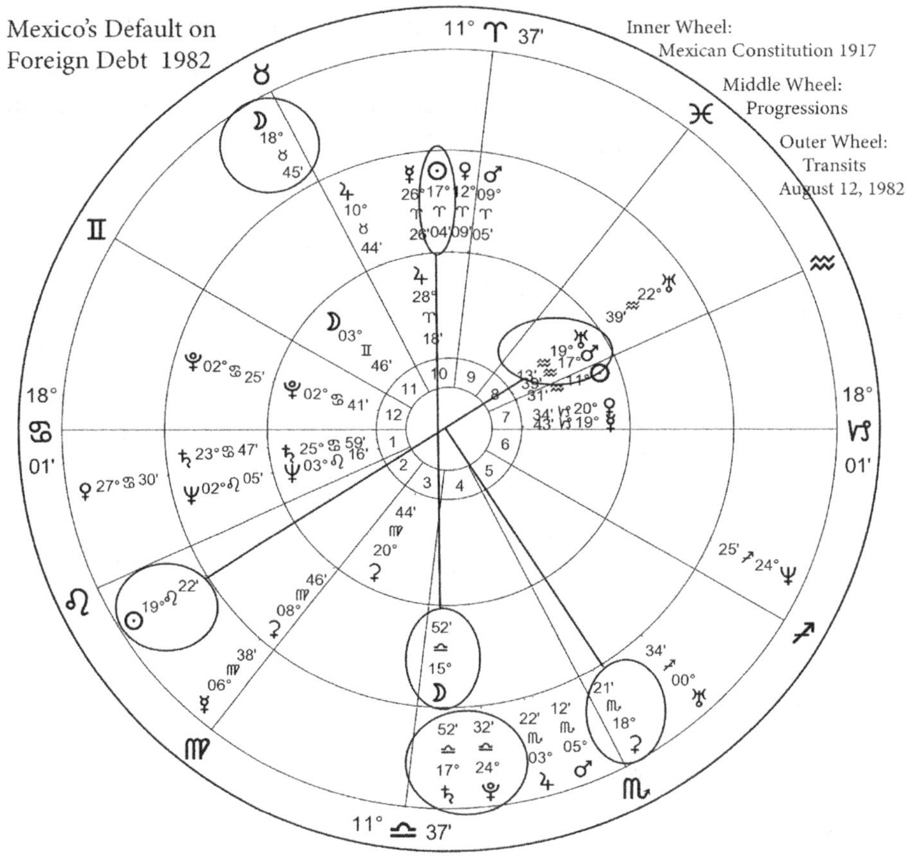

That Mexico would face a decisive event related to its debt obligations between mid-July and mid-August of 1982 was knowable ahead of time by noting two astrological configurations.

The first was that transiting Saturn, moving from 17°00' to 17°59' Libra, opposed Mexico's progressed Sun 17°04' Aries. This opposition formed a Grand Cross with Mexico's Ascendant/Descendant axis, so the effect would be keenly felt. As all of the 1982 stellium planets had passed over 17° Libra in July 1982 (except Pluto, which had done so years earlier), the momentum for a decisive event had been building. Leo/Sun rules the second house of Mexico's financial system and currency, so this aspect signaled a halt to cash flow—as indeed there was, due to President Portillo's nationalization of all private banks in Mexico, and strict currency controls being enacted.[58] The pressure to default became

58 https://historicaltextarchive.com/sections.php?action=read&artid=330

overwhelming when the transiting Sun 19°23' Leo opposed natal Uranus and Mars on August 12, and the transiting Moon formed a T-square to them.

The second configuration was the partial solar eclipse on July 20, 1982 at 27°43' Cancer, which was an important trigger of that "new approach" to stimulating the economy with foreign loans because it was square to the position of the Saturn-Pluto conjunction at 27°35' Libra that occurred on November 7, 1982.

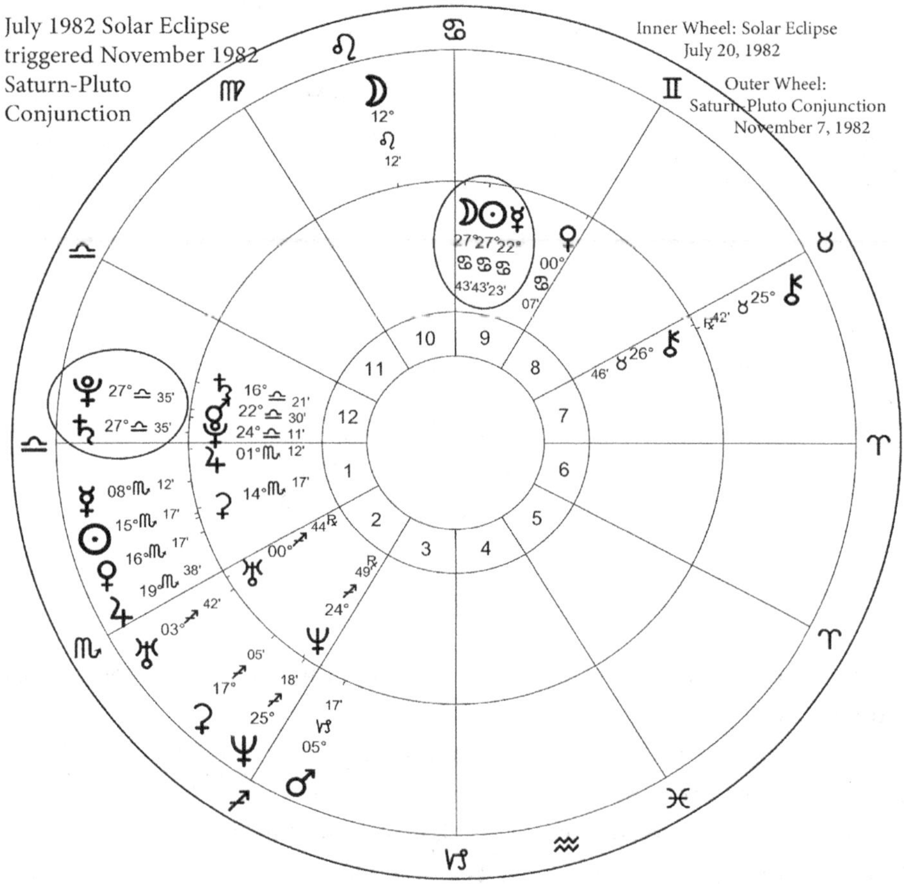

In Mexico's chart, the eclipse point was conjunct natal Saturn 26° Cancer, and squaring natal Jupiter 29° Aries. On the day of the eclipse, transiting Mars 23° Libra was triggering not only this square configuration and the July 20 eclipse, but also the stellium of October 1982 and the Saturn-Pluto conjunction of November 1982.[59] This eclipse signaled the climax of an extreme drain of foreign reserves, and by July, 1982 some $14 billion had been transferred to foreign bank accounts, with another $25 billion invested in US real estate.[60]

On August 12, the actual day of the announcement of Mexico's default, a square of transiting Venus 27°31' Cancer (right on the July 20 eclipse point) to transiting Pluto 25° Libra, aligned with Mexico's natal Jupiter-Saturn square in Aries and Cancer.

MEXICO – Summary

What mattered most for Mexico's chart was the Uranus-Pluto conjunction in the 1960's, for these are the planets associated with its eighth house of debt. The unfolding of events involved progressed Uranus, progressed Venus, progressed Mars, and transiting Pluto, along with the new Jupiter-Pluto and Saturn-Pluto cycles that began in 1981 and 1982 interacting with natal Saturn, and the position of a solar eclipse triggering Mexico's default.

In addition, aspects to Mexico's progressed Venus-Mars conjunction by progressed Uranus (in the eight house) and transiting Mercury and Mars, indicated capital flight from the country and the massive devaluation of the peso in 1976.

59 Although there is a gap of three months between the stellium date and the eclipse date, due to Mars' retrograde motion in 1982, Mars did *not* trigger this stellium before July 1982.

60 https://historicaltextarchive.com/sections.php?action=read&artid=330

BRAZIL – Potential for Financial Problems

The chart for Brazil's independence shows the potential for fiscal irresponsibility and mismanagement.

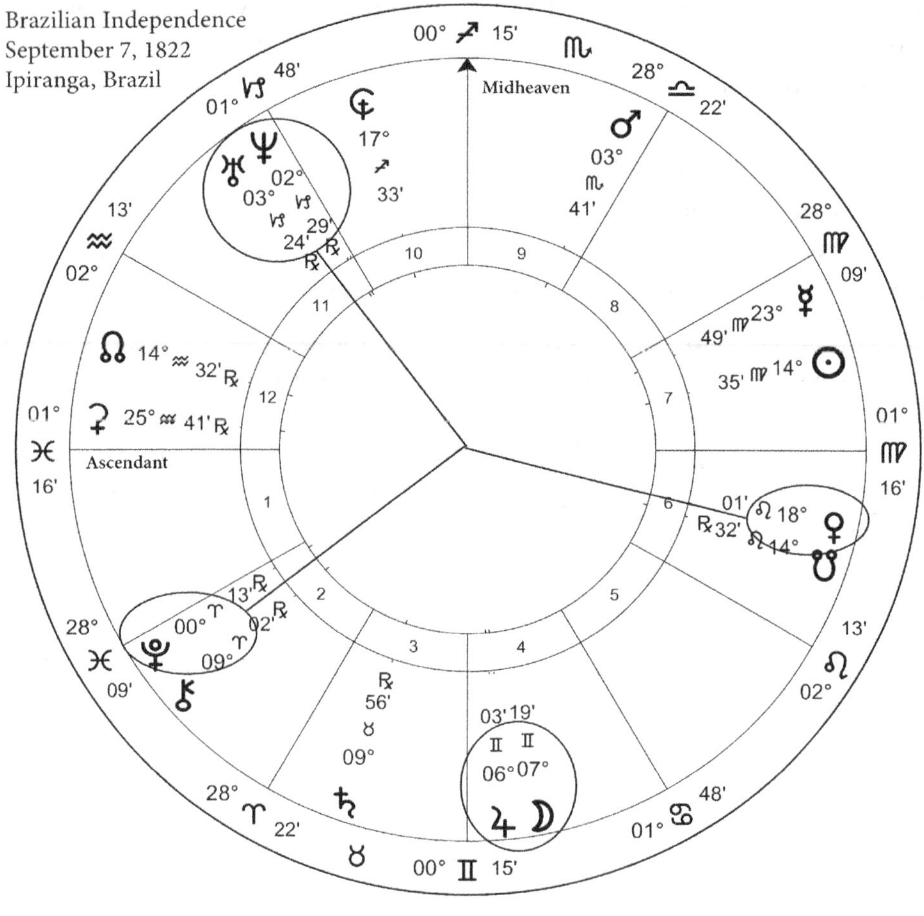

That financial instability and corruption would likely hound Brazil's finances is indicated by Pluto 0° Aries in the second house of finance and currency, squaring Neptune 3° Capricorn, the chart ruler of the second house (Pisces, ruled by Neptune and Jupiter, is on the cusp, or boundary, of the second house). Furthermore, Uranus 4° Capricorn conjoins Neptune, and thus also squares Pluto.

All of this is enough to indicate that some very difficult situations would arise in relation to the country's finances. But Venus, the planet naturally associated with money, forms a 135°–135°–90° triangle with the Pluto-Uranus/Neptune square, indicating complex negotiations to keep the ship afloat.

Not that the Brazilians couldn't handle that, due to the Moon-Jupiter conjunction in Gemini—a wheeler-dealer aspect to the extreme. As Jupiter is co-ruler of the second house, a "free and easy" approach to management of finances seems to be the norm, and all the signs of looming financial problems can be clearly visible yet just as clearly ignored.

BRAZIL – Dynamic Growth, Current Account Deficit, and Debt Buildup

Brazil experienced rapid growth from 1968 to 1973, benefiting greatly from the Uranus-Pluto conjunction of 1966 that occurred at 16° 06' Virgo on June 30, 1966. It conjoined Brazil's progressed Moon 17° 55' Virgo in the seventh house of foreign allies and enemies—as well as partnerships.

Then, only four days later, the transiting Sun and Jupiter at 13° Cancer were conjunct in the fifth house of speculation, making a sextile (60° angle) to the natal Sun 14° 39' Virgo. The sign of Cancer is ruled by the Moon, and as Brazil's chart has the Moon conjunct Jupiter in Gemini in the fourth house of security and natural resources, these transiting aspects supported and expanded the positive potential of the Moon-Jupiter configuration in the natal chart.

And while this meant beneficial partnerships involving finances, particularly the massive amounts of foreign capital invested in the country, with progressed Mercury 25° 56' Aquarius (ruler of the eighth house of debt and foreign reserves) moving to square progressed Jupiter 26° 39' Taurus, taking on too much debt from foreign banks was definitely a potential liability.

Uranus-Pluto Conjunction
June 30, 1966

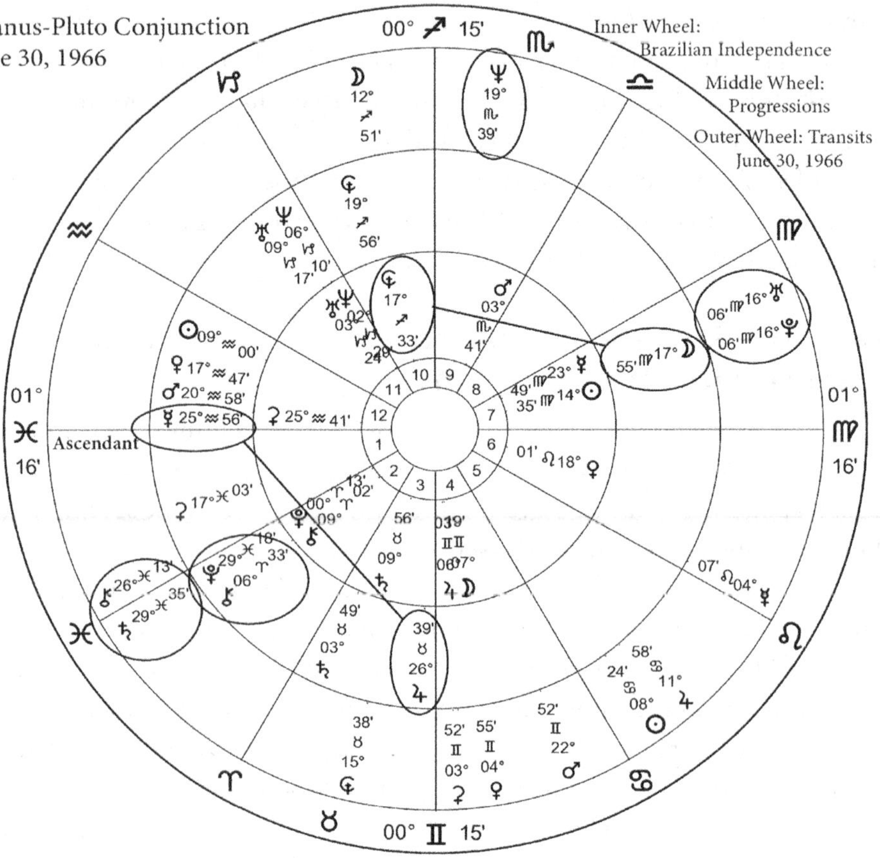

Brazil increased its exports during this time period, as shown by transiting Neptune in Scorpio in the ninth house of international commerce, along with the progressed Mercury-Jupiter square—although they imported more than they exported, as shown by transiting Saturn 29° Pisces conjunct progressed Pluto (both ruled by that Neptune in Scorpio) in the second house of finances. And while this led to a trade deficit, the foreign capital flowing into the country counterbalanced the shortfall, creating a surplus in Brazil's balance of payments accounting.[61]

Although everything looked good on paper, it was really anything but, as indicated by the fact that transiting Neptune would move to the late degrees of Scorpio in subsequent years to form a T-square with the progressed Mercury-Jupiter configuration—which eventually caused considerable angst.

61 https://en.wikipedia.org/wiki/Economic_history_of_Brazil

The Ascendant 1°16' Pisces, the most sensitive point in the chart, is ruled by Neptune. At the time of the configurations noted above, transiting Neptune 19° 39' Scorpio was sextile transiting Uranus and Pluto, and the progressed Moon and natal Sun, bringing even more favorable conditions to Brazil. However, with Neptune in Scorpio, it would in subsequent years move into Sagittarius and then oppose the natal Moon and Jupiter at 7° Gemini. With Neptune opposing these natal planets in 1973–1974, rather than sapping away the easy money (Pisces/ Neptune rules the second house of finances as well), it actually increased Brazil's access to easy credit due to the flow of petrodollars into the global financial system with the first oil price shock in 1973 due to the OPEC oil embargo (see below). Thus, in spite of the fact that the immediate effect of Neptune opposing the natal Moon and Jupiter was an increased inflow of borrowed money, the long-term effect was very detrimental and led to Brazil having to default on its loan payments.

Brazil's currency was extremely overvalued in the early 1970's,[62] which was easy to see ahead of time as transiting Neptune and Jupiter (co-rulers of Pisces, sign of the chart's second house of the currency) conjoined three times in 1971; during their January 27, 1971 conjunction in Sagittarius, they also conjoined transiting Mars. With all three planets conjoining the Midheaven, the cusp of the tenth house of government and business, they affected the general population and the currency, as both the first and second houses are ruled by these planets in this chart. Progressed Venus and Mars were conjunct during the early 1970's, and they were squaring progressed Jupiter, indicating Brazil's overvalued currency, the real. That this was causing problems for Brazil's exporting industries was indicated by transiting Saturn now in Taurus and moving to conjunct progressed Jupiter while squaring progressed Venus and Mars 24°–25° Aquarius. (Venus and Mars rule the third and ninth houses of this chart, the areas of the chart denoting domestic and international commerce, imports and exports.)

Note that a triple conjunction of Mars, Jupiter, and Neptune also occurred in 1293 but in the sign of Libra, which indicated a shift in the amount of investment capital available in the financial system due in part to a looming political conflict between two countries, France and England. It was this triple conjunction of the same planets in 1971 that led to a change in the amount of capital available due to a looming conflict between Israel and other Middle Eastern countries.

---

62 Ibid.

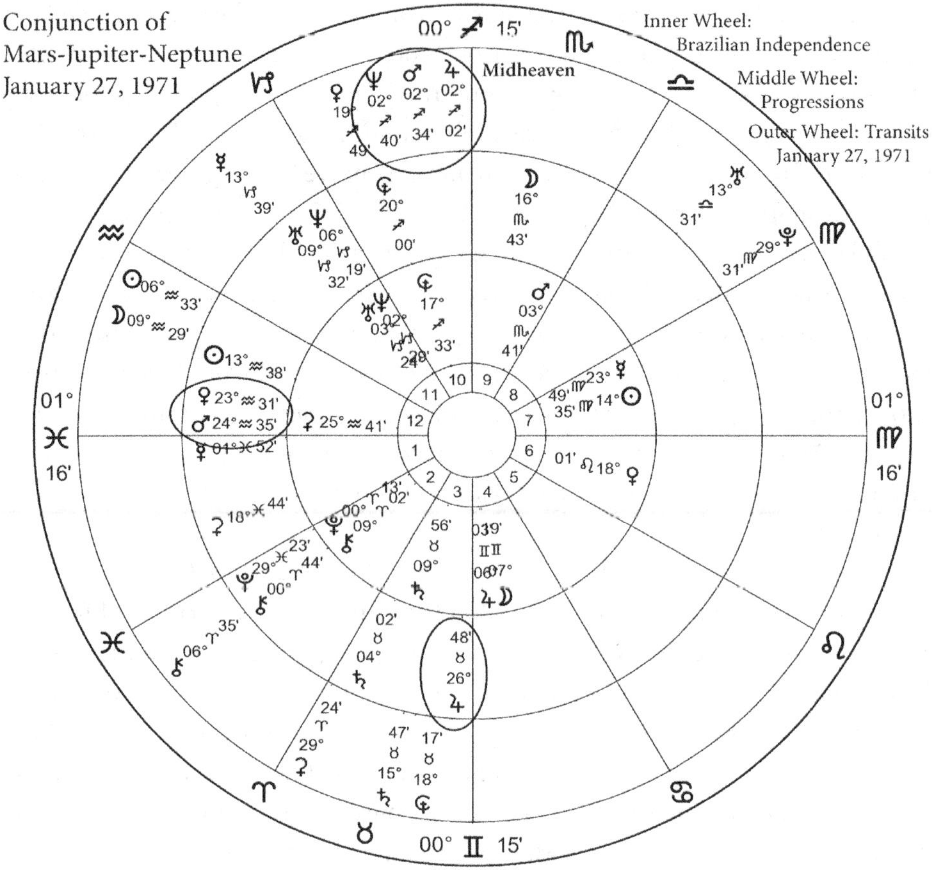

With the oil price shock of 1973, Brazil's trade balance and currency came under even more pressure as higher oil prices increased that country's import bill. While Brazil stuck with its high-growth strategy, which increased the growth of the economy, this came at the cost of increasing Brazil's current account deficit. Although Brazil was able to finance this deficit by taking on more loans from foreign banks, the ability to increase its debt to foreign banks was only partly due to its growth: In reality, these loans continued to be offered mainly because of the influx of cash into the global financial system from Saudi Arabia and other OPEC countries, which bankers were eager to lend.[63]

Several configurations in Brazil's chart for October 19, 1973 (the day the oil embargo began) indicate that a sudden increase in payments for imports—specifically for oil—would hurt Brazil's trade deficit. The most immediately

63 Ibid.

obvious is transiting Neptune 6° Sagittarius opposing natal Moon and Jupiter in Gemini (as mentioned on page 53). Transiting Venus had just conjoined Neptune, so the combination of these planets pointed to an extreme change in Brazil's cash flow that had to do with commodities extracted from within the earth (natal Moon and Jupiter in the fourth house)—which in this case was oil. By now, progressed Mercury had moved to 4°21' Pisces, forming a T-square with this opposition. Thus, as Virgo/Mercury rules the eighth house of debt, Brazil's debt situation was severely impacted.

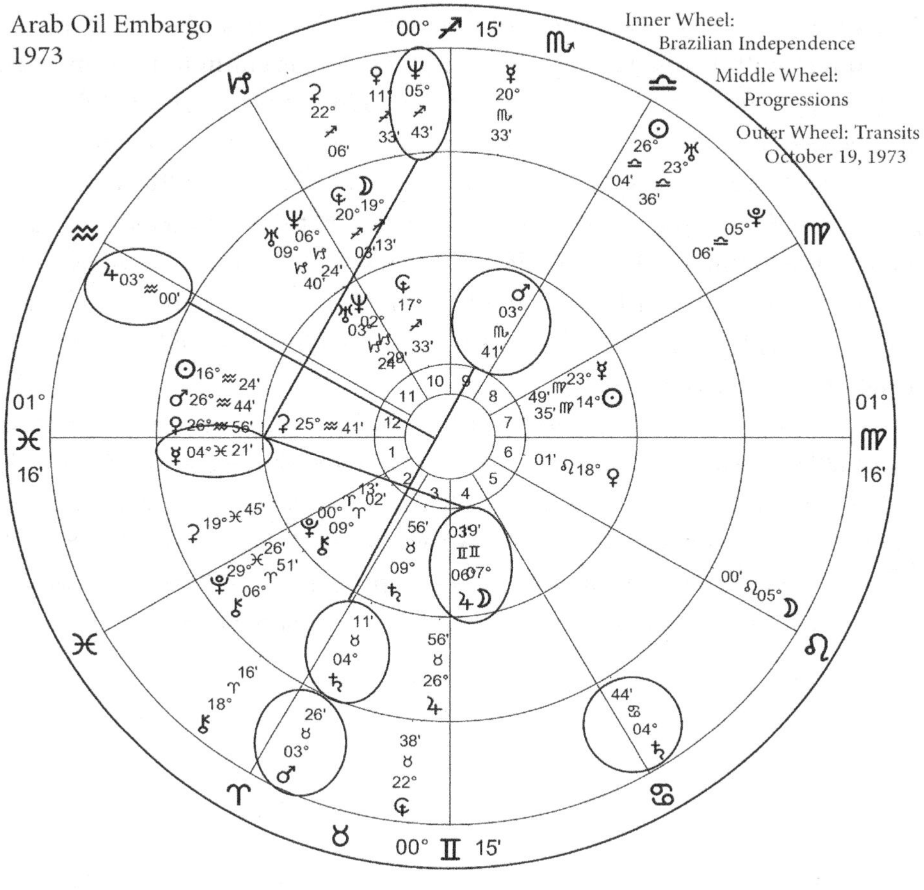

That progressed Venus and Mars in Aquarius squared progressed Jupiter 26°56' Taurus, and progressed Venus squared it exactly, was another indication that an increase in commodity prices would affect Brazil—which could have been known in advance from these astrological configurations.

The decision to take out more loans was shown by two other configurations, with the quick answer to the country's cash flow problem residing in Mercury, which rules Virgo, the sign of the eighth house of debt.

The first configuration was progressed Mercury 4°21' Pisces forming a T-square with transiting Neptune 6° Sagittarius opposing the natal Moon and Jupiter, indicating exaggerated emotions seemed to play their part, along with Brazil's inherent lighthearted attitude toward debt due to the natal Moon and Jupiter as explained above.

The second configuration is transiting Mars conjoining progressed Saturn 4° Taurus, with these two planets opposing natal Mars 3°41' Scorpio forming a T-square with transiting Jupiter 3° Aquarius. This configuration meshed with the first, for transiting Mars was at the midpoint of the trine (120° angle) of progressed Mercury and transiting Saturn. Mars wants action, and when goaded by Jupiter, he wants it fast *and* he wants it excessively. The element of progressed Saturn indicated policymakers felt that the country's status as a rapidly developing economy needed to be preserved, or at least made to look that way. And with transiting Jupiter trine (120° angle) transiting Pluto in the eighth house, there may have been some self-serving financial advice being dispensed by foreign bankers.

The Chiron-Pluto cycle figured prominently in the oil embargo situation for Brazil's chart, with that cycle also coinciding with the Saturn-Pluto cycle just as in the 13th and 14th centuries. Note that when the modern state of Brazil was formed (as defined by the date of its chart, in 1822), Chiron and Pluto, both in Aries, were just separating from a conjunction. In 1973, Chiron was back in Aries, but Pluto was now in Libra, and they were separating from an opposition.

Arab Oil Embargo
1973

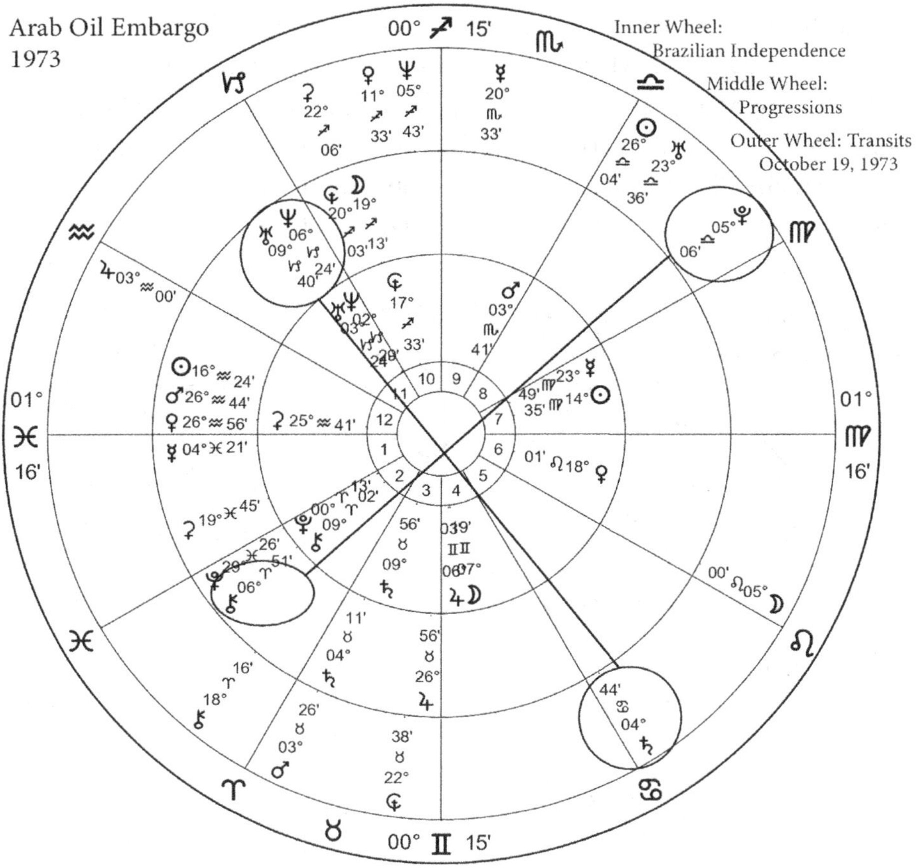

Progressed Neptune 7° Capricorn and progressed Chiron 7° Aries in Brazil's chart were in a very long-term square configuration, and in October 1973 they formed a Grand Cross with transiting Saturn 5° Cancer squaring transiting Pluto 6° Libra, with Pluto in the eighth house of debt. This Grand Cross falls in the financial houses of the chart associated with banking, currency, debt, and foreign reserves, as well as in investment, stocks, speculation, and savings.

The long-term prognosis was an economy wounded by unrealistic expectations of the effects of government policies, with the band aid of more debt from foreign sources being the immediate fix. But with natal Neptune and Uranus conjoined in early Capricorn also influenced by this Grand Cross, the full consequences of the decision to take on more debt to feed growth would be delayed until the early 1980s, when Brazil's debt reached unsustainable levels and interest rates were rising.[64]

64 Ibid.

Reality became obvious under the Jupiter-Saturn conjunction of December 31, 1980 at 9°29' Libra, which occurred in Brazil's eighth house of debt. Jupiter and Saturn opposed natal Chiron 9° Aries; and a Sun-Mercury conjunction the same day at 10°03' Capricorn conjoined progressed Uranus, forming a T-square with the Jupiter-Saturn/progressed Chiron opposition—a T-square that indicated investors were becoming fully aware of Brazil's problems in paying off its debt.

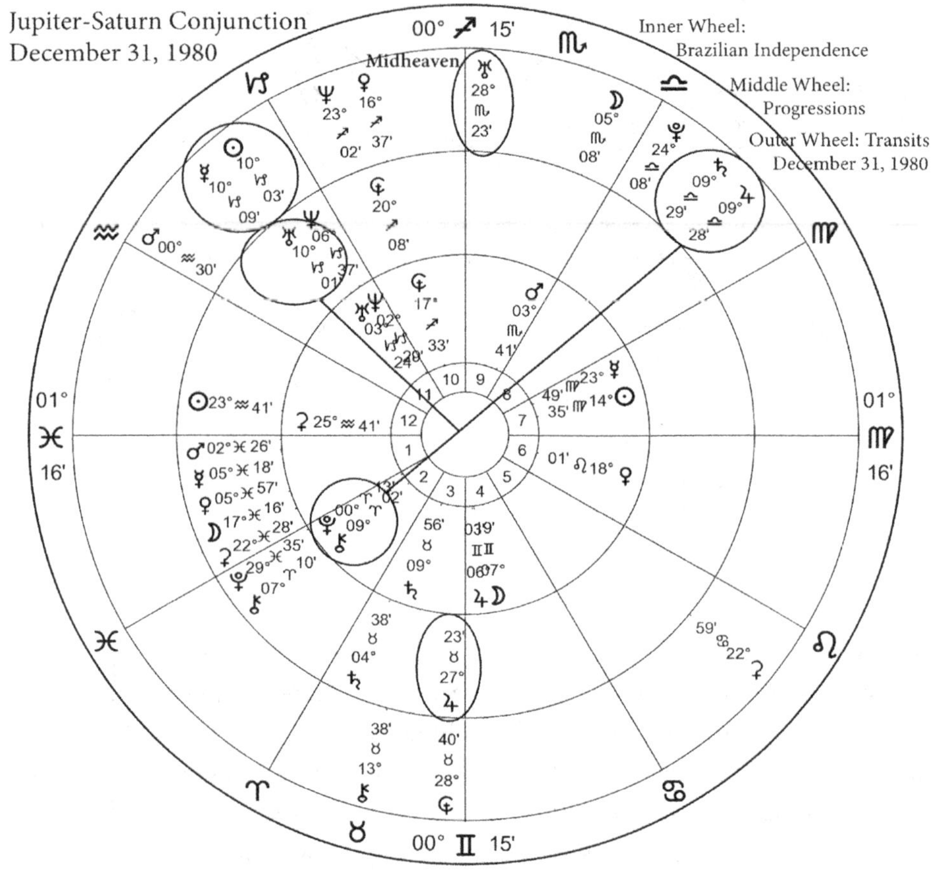

Another indication of a big shift occurring at this time was transiting Uranus in the late degrees of Scorpio, opposing progressed Jupiter 28° Taurus, with Uranus about to pass over the Midheaven. The extent of the problem, which had been glossed over for years, was now being publicized in a big way.

BRAZIL – THE EFFECT OF MEXICO'S DEFAULT ON BRAZIL

Mexico's admission in August 1982 that it could not meet its loan payments affected all emerging market countries with foreign loans, and it was Mexico's default which ended Brazil's access to credit through foreign banks.

That Brazil was in a precarious position was shown by two major configurations to its chart: Transiting Chiron was exactly conjunct progressed Jupiter 27°31' Taurus on August 12, 1982, the day that Mexico made its announcement of default, with this Chiron-Jupiter pair translating the upcoming October 1982 Libra and Sagittarius stelliums by forming a *yod* (a configuration of imbalance) with the planets positioned in a triangle of 150°–150°–60° angles. Chiron and Jupiter were inconjunct (150° angle) the October 1982 positions of Neptune and Mars 24° Sagittarius, and Venus, Saturn, and Pluto 25°–27° Libra. With the co-rulers of the second house of finances, Jupiter and Neptune, both involved with Chiron, a painful financial and economic adjustment was indicated.

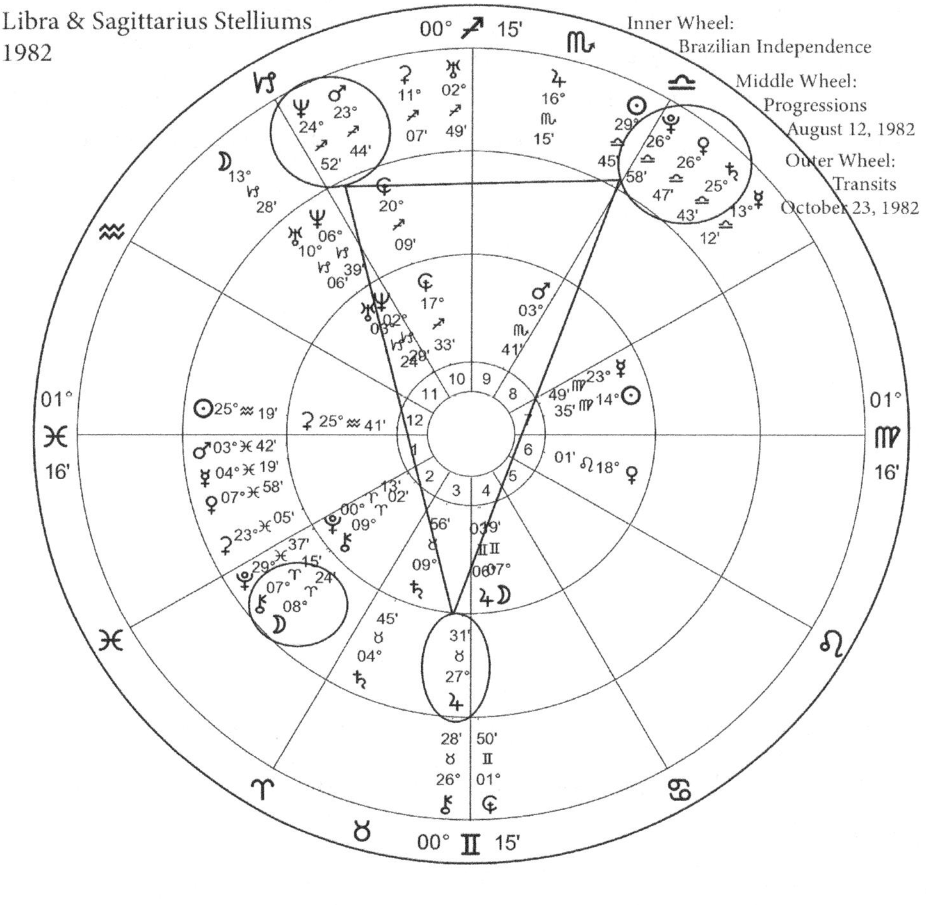

To make this yod even more precarious, transiting Uranus was opposing transiting Chiron and progressed Jupiter,[65] triggering the abrupt end of Brazil's continuous borrowing from foreign lenders. Transiting Chiron's effect was magnified by the progressed Moon conjoining progressed Chiron 8° Pisces in the second house, intensifying the pain. Further emphasizing the negative effects, Uranus at this time was also opposing transiting Hades 2° Gemini.

Brazil had been carrying a trade deficit for some years, but had begun to build a trade surplus in order to meet its loan payments (one of the conditions of an austerity program imposed by the IMF in 1979),[66] a switch indicated by transiting Mars in 1979 and 1982. At the time of the January 1979 oil price increase, transiting Mars 4° Taurus was conjunct progressed Saturn and transiting Chiron 5° Taurus, while opposing natal Mars 3°41' Scorpio, involving the third and ninth houses of trade and commerce. Transiting Chiron was also the cattle prod for difficult change in this case.

By the time of Mexico's default in 1982, transiting Mars had completed one and a half cycles around the zodiac and was now conjunct natal Mars, along with transiting Jupiter. Progressed Mars 3°42' Pisces was exactly trine all of them, indicating an acceleration of the need to develop a trade surplus, which Brazil was able to do, although only by forfeiting GDP growth and igniting inflation.[67]

65 Transiting Uranus had recently passed over the Midheaven 0°15' Sagittarius, and went direct only three days earlier at 0°34' Sagittarius.

66 https://en.wikipedia.org/wiki/Economic_history_of_Brazil

67 Ibid.

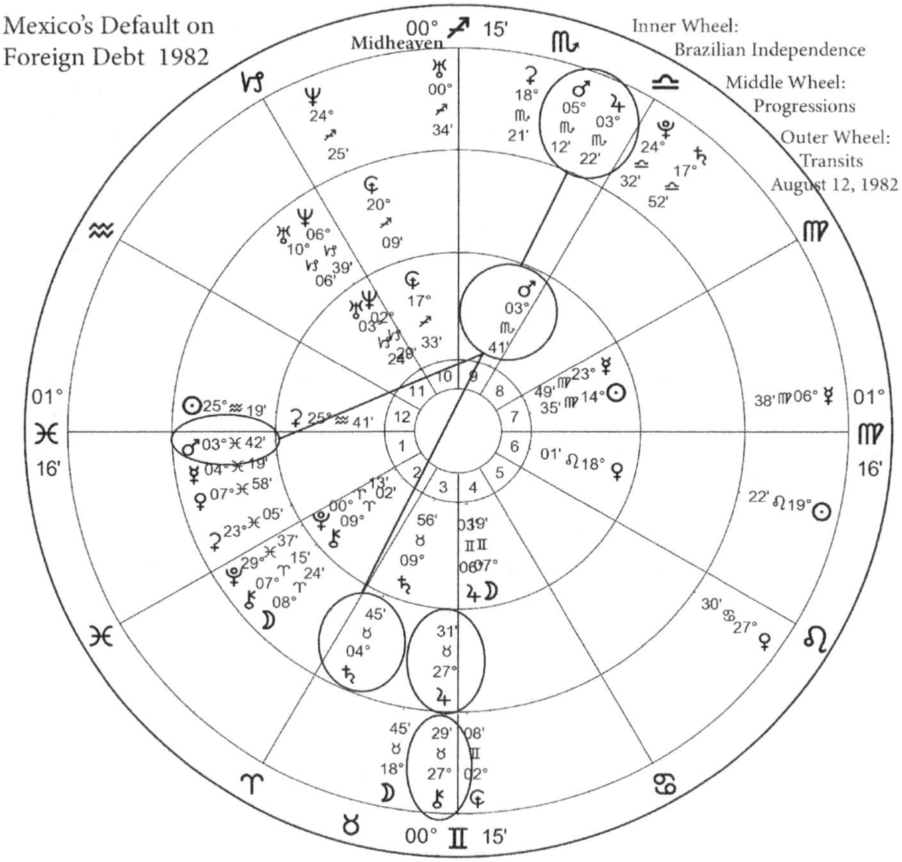

BRAZIL – Brazil's Admission of Default

Brazil announced that it could not service its debts on August 24, 1983. The opposition between transiting Chiron and transiting Uranus hit Brazil's chart again, as Uranus 6° Sagittarius (conjoined by transiting Jupiter 2° Sagittarius) exactly opposed natal Jupiter 6°03' Gemini and the natal Moon 7°19' Gemini. With transiting Chiron and Hades, both at 3° Gemini, conjoined the natal Moon and Jupiter, this big cluster of planets in opposition formed a T-square with the ruler of the eighth house of debt, progressed Mercury 3°29' Pisces, and the natural ruler of the eighth house, progressed Mars 4°31' Pisces.

Brazil's Default on
Foreign Debt 1983

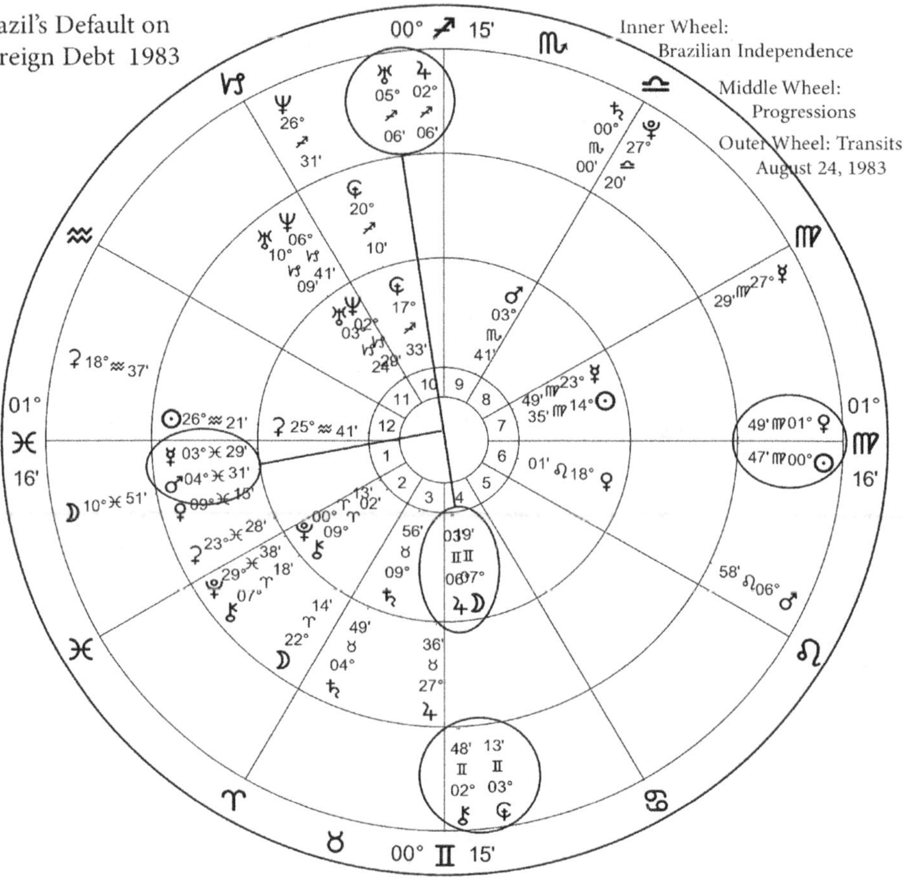

There could be no doubt that the inevitable default would be triggered in this time period due to the transiting Moon in early Pisces, the transiting Sun having just entered Virgo, and transiting Venus 1° Virgo being retrograde. This Full Moon opposition formed a Grand Cross with the configuration described above. The Sun and retrograde Venus were responsible for triggering the default, as these two transiting bodies opposed progressed Mercury and Mars.

Furthermore, the progressed Moon had been in the range of 18°–22° Aries in the second house of finance in the summer of 1983 opposing the 1981 stellium in Libra, another indication that this time period would be important for Brazil's debt situation.

BRAZIL – SUMMARY

Brazil benefited from favorable configurations to its chart at the time of the Uranus-Pluto conjunction in the 1960's. Progressed Mercury, ruler of Brazil's eighth house of debt, was probably the most important indicator over the course of the 1970's and 1980's—it was in the late degrees of Aquarius, and then the early degrees of Pisces, forming a square aspect first to progressed Jupiter, and then to natal Jupiter.

At the same time, transiting Neptune moving through late Scorpio and then Sagittarius formed a T-square configuration with these planets, all indicating an unrealistic attitude toward mounting debt. Brazil's default occurred when progressed Mercury, ruler of the eighth house of debt, formed a T-square with transiting Uranus opposed transiting Chiron and the natal Moon-Jupiter conjunction.

It was also at this time that Brazil's progressed Venus and Mars were conjunct in the late degrees of Aquarius from 1970 to 1975, squaring progressed Jupiter in Taurus, indicating that Brazil's currency was overvalued.

★ ★ ★

Overall Astrological Conditions Associated with Debt Buildup, Availability of Capital, and Financial Crisis

The following conditions involve only transiting planets, and could apply to either the global financial system or to a regional system.

Astrological conditions indicating buildup of debt:

- Saturn-Pluto and Chiron-Pluto cycles coincide.
- Saturn-Pluto and Chiron-Pluto cycles coincide with the Uranus-Pluto cycle.

Astrological conditions indicating a shift in the balance of power surrounding a major source of capital in the international (or regional) financial system:

- Grand Trine of Jupiter, Neptune, and Saturn/Chiron.

Astrological conditions indicating a flood of capital into the international financial system:

- Jupiter trine Pluto, followed by Jupiter and Neptune either conjunct or in mutual reception, with the North Node in the same sign.

Astrological conditions indicating default or severe financial crisis:

- Saturn conjunct Pluto as part of a stellium, in one of the following signs: Capricorn, Libra, or Taurus (and possibly Scorpio).[68]

MEXICO – Astrological Conditions of Debt Buildup, Currency Devaluation, and Default

From the above analysis, the following astrological conditions for Mexico's chart were associated with *debt buildup:*

- Chart and natural ruler(s) of the eighth house in conjunction by transit (in this case, Uranus and Pluto), in a harsh aspect to natal Jupiter: This encouraged taking on too much debt.
- Transiting Jupiter square Neptune, making a harsh aspect to the natal or progressed position of the ruler of the chart's eighth house (in this case, Uranus), and preferably at least one of the planets in this configuration also resides in the second or eighth house: An indicator of financial excess.
- Transiting Jupiter opposing progressed Jupiter, and these planets occupy either the signs of Taurus and Scorpio, or the second and eighth houses: More debt is accrued.
- Transiting Jupiter and Mars in a configuration of harsh aspects to natal or progressed Neptune, *at the same time* that transiting Saturn makes a harsh aspect to natal or progressed Pluto: Inspires rash and sloppy fiscal decisions that ignore reality and lead to grave consequences.

The following astrological conditions for Mexico's chart were associated with *capital flight leading to a drain of foreign reserves and the necessity of a currency devaluation:*

- Transiting Pluto and transiting Jupiter (and possibly Hades in the mix) forming a 135°–135°–90° triangular configuration (or possibly also a T-square) with the natal or progressed ruler of the eighth house (in this case, Uranus).

68 Saturn is the domicile ruler of Capricorn, and it is the exaltation ruler of Libra. Venus is the domicile ruler of Taurus and Libra. Pluto is the domicile co-ruler of Scorpio. See the Glossary for an explanation of the system of essential dignities in astrology.

- Progressed Venus conjunct progressed Mars, and both in a harsh aspect with the natal or progressed ruler of the eighth house.
- Natal and/or progressed positions of the ruler of the second house (in this case, the Sun) in a harsh aspect with transiting Pluto, or transiting Saturn, or the transiting ruler of the eighth house.
- Transiting Ceres in the second house of finances and currency, moving to oppose any natal or progressed planet in the eight house, especially if that planet is the chart or natural ruler of the eighth house.
- Transiting Mercury conjoining transiting Mars, with both either conjunct or opposing a progressed Venus-Mars conjunction, or both conjunct or opposing the natal or chart ruler of the eighth house: A trigger configuration that can closely (and often exactly) time the date of a currency-related event.

The following astrological conditions for Mexico's chart were associated with its *default on its foreign loans:*

- Natal Venus in a harsh aspect with natal Saturn, when there is harsh configuration of transiting outer planets forming that involves the signs of Capricorn, Libra, or Taurus.
- Transiting Saturn opposing the position of the progressed ruler of the second house (in this case, the Sun).
- Transiting Saturn forming a harsh aspect (including conjunction) to the Ascendant of the chart.
- Cycles of transiting Jupiter-Pluto and/or Saturn-Pluto ending/ beginning in the fourth house.
- An eclipse (preferably solar) whose position makes an aspect to a harsh configuration involving either the chart ruler of the eighth house, the position of a Saturn-Pluto conjunction, or the position of a stellium (in Mexico's case, it was all three).

BRAZIL – Astrological Conditions of Debt Buildup, Trade Deficit, Overvalued Currency, and Default

From the above analysis, the following astrological conditions for Brazil's chart were associated with *debt buildup:*

- Progressed ruler of the eighth house (in this case, Mercury) in a harsh aspect with progressed Jupiter: Encouraged taking on too much debt.
- Transiting Neptune in a mutable sign, opposing natal Jupiter: Encouraged increasing the debt load under unfavorable circumstances due to availability of easy credit (the oil embargo of 1973).
- Progressed Neptune in a harsh aspect with progressed Chiron (Chiron in Pisces or Aries[69]) and in a harsh configuration with transiting Saturn and/or transiting Pluto, with some link to the eighth house of debt.

The following astrological conditions for Brazil's chart were associated with a *trade deficit:*

- Transiting Saturn conjoining natal or progressed Pluto in the second house, with favorable aspects to the transiting ruler of the second house (in this case, Neptune) going through the ninth house: Increased both exports and imports, but led to a trade deficit.
- Transiting Neptune and Venus opposing natal or progressed ruler of the second house, *at the same time* that progressed Venus was conjunct progressed Mars, with both squaring the progressed ruler of the second house (in this case, Jupiter, the other ruler of Pisces): Increased the cost of imports.

69 Chiron takes approximately fifty years to go around the zodiac, but it spends half of that time in the signs of Pisces and Aries, which seems to cause financial crisis conditions especially when in this portion of its orbit around the Sun.

The following astrological conditions for Brazil's chart were associated with an *overvalued currency:*

- Progressed Venus conjunct progressed Mars, with both squaring the progressed ruler of the second house (in this case, Jupiter): Indicated Brazil's overvalued real.

The following astrological conditions for Brazil's chart were associated with *recognition of looming problems but still accruing more debt:*

- Transiting Jupiter conjunct Saturn in the eighth house of debt, both making a harsh aspect to natal or progressed Chiron.
- Transiting Uranus near the Midheaven and opposing natal or progressed Jupiter.
- Progressed ruler of the eighth house (in this case, Mercury) in a harsh configuration with transiting Neptune and natal or progressed ruler of the second house (in this case, Jupiter).
- Progressed Saturn either conjoining or opposing natal Mars, in a harsh configuration with transiting Mars and/or Jupiter, with some link to the eighth house.

The following astrological conditions for Brazil's chart were associated with *cutoff of access to foreign loans and looming default:*

- Transiting Chiron conjoining natal or progressed Jupiter.
- Transiting Uranus near the Midheaven and opposing a conjunction of natal or progressed Jupiter with transiting Chiron.

The following astrological conditions for Brazil's chart were associated with its *default on foreign loans:*

- Transiting Uranus exactly opposing natal or progressed Jupiter and transiting Chiron (and possibly including Hades), forming a T-square with a conjunction of progressed Mars with the progressed ruler of the eighth house (in this case, Mercury).
- Transiting Venus opposing progressed Mercury and Mars: A trigger configuration that can closely (and often exactly) time the date of a currency-related event.

CONCLUSIONS

The general time frame in which a financial crisis is likely to happen can be determined by configurations formed by transiting planets alone. However, in order to know which countries will be the source of the crisis—or will be most affected by it—*and* to closely pinpoint the time of the crisis, configurations forming with natal or progressed planets in a country's chart must be considered.

Transiting Configurations

The coinciding of the Saturn-Pluto and Chiron-Pluto cycles is of major importance for determining a general time frame for financial crises. When Uranus interacts with these cycles, or when the Jupiter-Uranus cycle reaches a phase at the same time of these cycles, the danger increases.

Transiting Neptune in a mutable sign seems to add an element of instability and debt overload that can affect the entire financial system.

A Saturn-Pluto conjunction occurring in Capricorn, Libra, or Taurus, especially when there is also a stellium in the same sign, indicates severe problems in the financial system and looming "collapse" of part of the system.

Specific Country Chart Configurations

As with all of the separate analyses in this work, a country's natal chart *must* show the potential for financial crisis. Those that do are most likely to be those that suffer the most in a global crisis.

Progressed Venus conjunct progressed Mars in a nation's chart has a high probability of affecting the nation's currency or triggering a finance-related event, especially when in hard aspect with either the ruler of the second house, the ruler of the eighth house, or Jupiter (natal or progressed).

Within a nation's chart, aspects to the *progressed* ruler of the eighth house are extremely important, and transiting Neptune making an aspect to this progressed planet will especially weaken the country's position in a financial crisis. If this progressed planet makes a harsh aspect to natal, progressed, or transiting Jupiter, it leads to financial excess.

Transiting Neptune opposing natal Jupiter is a classic configuration in an individual's chart that denotes a poor financial decision which drains resources. This is just as true for a country as it is for an individual.

Transiting outer planets making a harsh aspect to progressed Chiron also weaken the country's position. This is especially pronounced if a conjunction of transiting outer planets occurs in the eighth house and makes a harsh aspect to Chiron.

Transiting Uranus conjoining or opposing natal or progressed Jupiter can lead to a sudden, dramatic financial event as a climax to a situation that had been worsening for years. If this configuration also makes an aspect to the progressed ruler of the eighth house, the probability of a financial crisis is increased.

An eclipse, especially a solar eclipse, can trigger extreme financial events when it interacts with a planetary configuration between natal or progressed planets. The effect is even more pronounced if the Saturn-Pluto cycle has, or will, interact with the same planetary configuration.

CHAPTER 3

Collapse of the British Pound in 1992

After World War II, European countries wanted to integrate themselves together more cohesively, in the hope that by creating economic interdependencies, catastrophic war could be avoided by providing an incentive to maintain peace. Prior to creation of the European Union, the European Exchange Rate Mechanism (ERM) was created in 1979 as a way for European countries to coordinate their currencies' values according to exchange rates, thus keeping all of their currencies within a defined range without having to give up their individual currencies.[70]

Being part of the ERM required that each country keep their currency's exchange rate within a trading band with respect to the German deutschmark, which was the strongest currency in Europe at the time.

British Pound Added to the European Exchange Rate Mechanism

In October 1990, the British pound was added to the currencies in the ERM. Britain now had to maintain the exchange rate for the pound within a trading band of 6% higher/lower of a fixed rate relative to the deutschmark.

But when recession hit in 1992, Britain faced problems with maintaining this exchange rate, and it became very obvious by May of that year that the pound had been admitted into the ERM at too high of a rate against the deutschmark. Normally, Britain would have lowered interest rates in order to counteract the surge in unemployment and weak demand due to the recession, but they were unable to do this, for they had to keep interest rates high enough to maintain the exchange rate of the pound.[71]

In the late summer of 1992, Bundesbank officials began making public

70 https://priceonomics.com/the-trade-of-the-century-when-george-soros-broke/
71 Ibid.

remarks that sabotaged the position of the pound, and on August 25 council member Reimut Jochimsen said that the currencies within the ERM might need to be "realigned." On September 10, another Bundesbank official said that devaluation of the pound was inevitable, and the pound fell that day.[72]

On September 16, comments made by Bundesbank President Helmut Schlesinger were published in which Schlesinger said that even with a realignment within the ERM, "one or two currencies" might face further stress. Investors and traders interpreted his remarks as meaning that the pound was one of those currencies.[73]

The next day, George Soros and Stanley Druckenmiller shorted the pound aggressively. John Major, the British Prime Minister at the time, at first refused to raise interest rates in order to maintain the ERM exchange rate, but when it became apparent (the same day) that this was the only recourse, rates were raised twice in one day—to 12%, from 10%, and then again to 15%—but with no effect. The following day Britain was forced to devalue the pound by 15% against the deutschmark.[74]

Overall, the reason for this event was that there was a vast amount of capital floating around international markets which could be mobilized much faster than Britain would have been able to raise the same amount to defend its currency.[75] Thus a major underlying issue here is the same as what happened in 1976 and 1982 for Mexico and Brazil: Too much capital in global markets that needed to be put to use for investment in some way, resulting in a series of events with very negative consequences for the currencies of some countries. In the 1970's and 1980's, while events played out slower than in 1992, the pattern remains the same.

Similarity with the 13th and 14th Centuries

Just as in the late 13th and early 14th centuries for Europe, there were large cash reserves in the global financial system which caused Britain to suffer from excess capital sloshing around in the system at the time of the pound's collapse. But it wasn't a drain of this capital from the system that hurt the UK—it was that capital was being mobilized against its currency's value, as Soros and

72 Ibid.

73 Ibid.

74 Ibid.

75 Ibid.

Druckenmiller sought to borrow funds (denominated in pounds) with which to buy deutschmarks and short the pound.[76]

Overall Astrological Configurations of 1992

The Saturn-Uranus-Neptune triple conjunctions occurred in the late 1980's and early 1990's. This meant that there was a Capricorn stellium in effect over those years, but it was always made more pronounced in January of each year when the Sun, Mercury, and Venus were also moving through Capricorn.[77] In January 1992 the stellium included a Mars-Uranus-Neptune conjunction at 16°–18° Capricorn; Uranus and Neptune were due to conjoin exactly in 1993.

By late February 1992, Saturn in Aquarius was within a 10° range of an exact square to Pluto in Scorpio. Thus, the current Saturn-Pluto cycle was at its first critical harsh aspect, indicating potential problems with the global financial system. Chiron was in the early degrees of Leo, and although not within a 10° range of aspect with Pluto, it was in a wide opposition to Saturn. In the summer of 1992, the Saturn-Pluto and Chiron-Pluto cycles were coinciding in a T-square of Saturn opposing Chiron in Leo and both squaring Pluto in Scorpio. And they were in the signs naturally associated with financial matters, the fixed signs of Taurus, Leo, Scorpio, and Aquarius.

Just as in the mid-1960's for Latin America, these coinciding cycles indicated that some part of the global financial system was about to undergo structural change, which in 1992 and 1993 involved the ERM. In 1992, Finland withdrew its peg with the ECU, Britain and Italy were suspended from the ERM, Sweden and Norway abandoned their pegs, and other countries had to devalue their currencies to stay within the currency exchange rate band. The turmoil continued into 1993, with central banks having to pour massive amounts of reserves into maintaining the pegs of the French franc, Belgian franc, Danish krone, Spanish peseta, and Portuguese escudo against speculative short sales. Germany did finally adjust its interest rates, and the exchange rate bands were widened to lessen the incentive for speculation.[78]

---

76 https://priceonomics.com/the-trade-of-the-century-when-george-soros-broke/ Just as this article states, "As it turns out, Margaret Thatcher was right: the UK had no business trying to artificially prop up its currency in an era when a handful of hedge funds could assemble more capital in a few hours than the Bank of England had at its disposal."

77 The Sun, Mercury, and Venus always travel closely together from the perspective of an observer on Earth, so Mercury and Venus will always be either in the same sign as the Sun, the sign before, or the sign after that of the Sun.

78 https://www.tcd.ie/Economics/assets/pdf/SER/1996/Moniel_Wolters.html

So, although the only case analyzed here is that of the British pound, there was actually a serious forced readjustment of the currency exchange rate system in Europe.

In 1966, Jupiter in Cancer formed a waning trine (120° angle) to Neptune in Scorpio; in 1992, it was forming the same configuration with Neptune, only in Earth signs (Jupiter in Virgo and Neptune in Capricorn). This configuration seems to help further refine the timing of the financial system readjustment indicated by the coinciding of the Saturn-Pluto and Chiron-Pluto cycles.

UNITED KINGDOM – Potential for Financial Problems

1801 Act of Union Chart

The standard chart for the United Kingdom is based on the date of the Act of Union, January 1, 1801, when Ireland was united with Great Britain.

This natal chart shows the potential for financial turmoil due to the kind of extreme pressure that causes an imbalanced situation to finally collapse. Pluto 2°42' Pisces is at the apex of a yod configuration (150°–150°–60° triangle) with Jupiter 1°51' Leo and Uranus 1°53' Libra (note that the Jupiter-Uranus sextile is almost exact). Pluto rules Scorpio, the sign of the second house of the country's finances and currency, and it resides in the fifth house of speculation.

United Kingdom
Union with Ireland
January 1, 1801

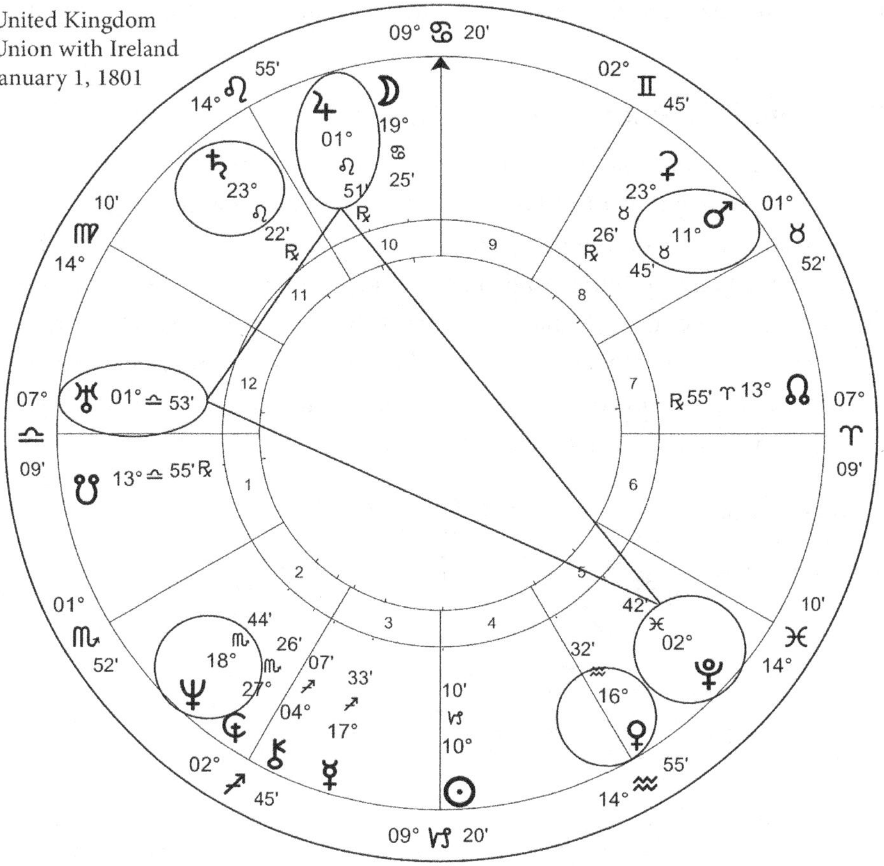

More evidence of problems related to finance, currencies, and investment is shown by the Grand Cross configuration formed by Venus in Aquarius opposing Saturn in Leo,[79] and Mars in Taurus opposing Neptune in Scorpio. These planets are located in the financial areas of the chart—the second, fifth, eighth, and eleventh houses. Furthermore, they are in the signs naturally associated with financial issues.

The most troubling aspect of this Grand Cross is Saturn 22°23' Leo squaring Neptune 18°44' Scorpio, and Neptune resides in the second house of the currency. These two planets that can depress and drain resources are in a harsh aspect, and they are in a harsh aspect with Mars 11°45' Taurus in the eighth house. Venus 16°32' Aquarius, the planet naturally associated with a country's currency, is overwhelmed here by her harsh aspects with these planets; and Venus is in the

79 Venus opposes Saturn in Mexico's natal chart also.

fifth house of speculation, indicating that speculators could negatively affect the pound.

1922 United Kingdom Reorganization

An important alternate natal chart for the United Kingdom is the Reorganization of 1922 chart (when part of Ireland split from the United Kingdom).[80]

Dramatic upsets surrounding currency issues are indicated by Venus 25°51' Scorpio forming a 135° harsh angle to Pluto 10°39' Cancer, and squaring Mars 27°08' Aquarius. Venus is the natural ruler of the second house of the currency, and she makes harsh aspects to the natural rulers of the eighth, Mars and Pluto. The progressed positions of the planets in this configuration were all triggered in 1992, as pressure mounted on the pound.

United Kingdom
Reorganization
December 7, 1922

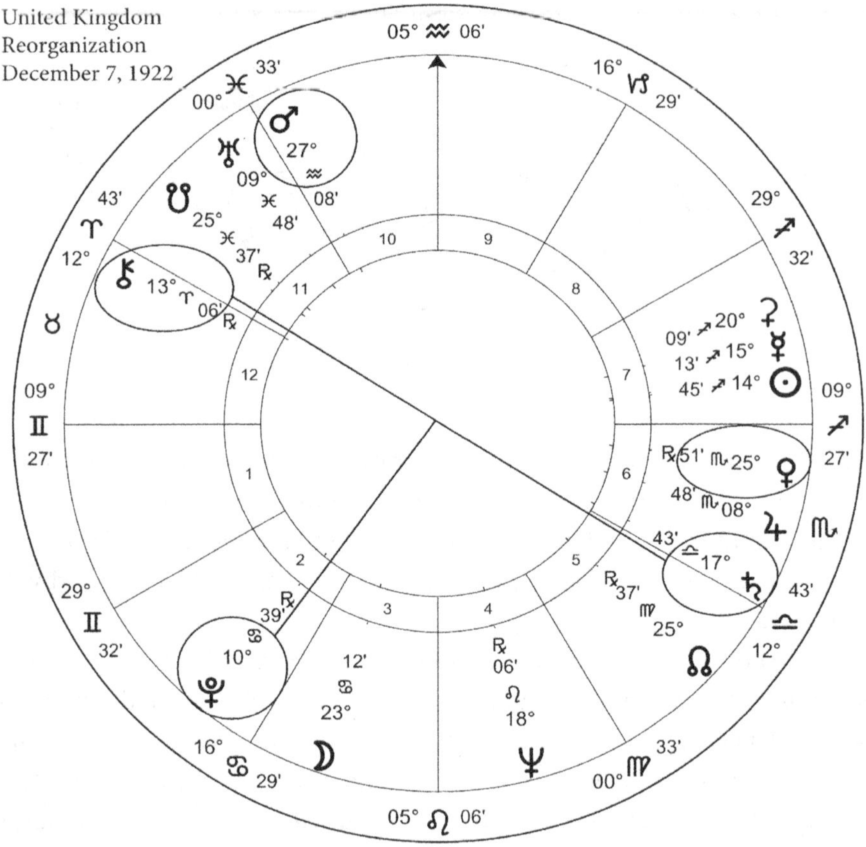

80 The houses are displayed as equal sectors to make the planetary positions easier to see, but some houses cover 60° and others only 17°.

This chart has the Saturn-Pluto and Chiron-Pluto cycles coinciding: Saturn 17°43' Libra opposes Chiron 13°06' Aries, and they form a T-square with Pluto in Cancer. The Venus-Pluto aspect also plays into this configuration.

Two things within this chart show potential for currency devaluations: First, Venus is retrograde in Scorpio, ruled by Mars, and Venus is squaring Mars, her sign ruler. In addition, Saturn is exalted in Libra, and thus functions strongly, but it is ruled by Venus, which is debilitated.[81]

Both Venus and Saturn changed direction by secondary progression for this chart prior to 1992. Natal Venus turned direct by secondary progression in January 1931 at 24°30' Scorpio, and natal Saturn turned retrograde by secondary progression in January 1976 at 20°06' Libra.

These points of 24°30' Scorpio and 20°06' Libra have become sensitive points for this chart, and as such, they also could pertain to problems with the currency. As Venus affects Saturn in this chart (due to Venus's rulership of Libra), any progressed or transiting planet in a configuration with Venus, or the 24°30' Scorpio position, will affect Saturn and thus also tie into the Saturn-Chiron-Pluto T-square.

UNITED KINGDOM – Pressure on the Pound, Forced Devaluation, and Withdrawal from ERM

1801 UK Chart

Progressions and transits for September 16, 1992 to the 1801 UK natal chart clearly show that a financial event related to the currency was about to occur due to configurations based upon natal aspects involving Pluto, ruler of the chart's second house of the currency.

As mentioned above, the 1992 Capricorn stellium included a Mars-Uranus-Neptune conjunction at 16°–18° Capricorn, which opposed the UK's natal Moon 19°25' Cancer. Thus, the stellium formed a 180°–135°–45° triangle configuration with the natal Moon and natal Pluto, the chart ruler of the second house, with the natal Moon sesquiquadrate (135° angle) to natal Pluto 2°42' Pisces. This configuration indicated a serious disruption to the country—and to government leadership, as the natal Moon falls in the tenth house—through currency-related

81 According to the system of essential dignities, Venus is very debilitated in this position, meaning she is weak and functions in a negative manner. See the Glossary for an explanation of the system of essential dignities in astrology.

events, with John Majors, Prime Minister at the time of the pound's collapse, losing the next election largely due to his advocacy of the UK being part of the ERM.[82]

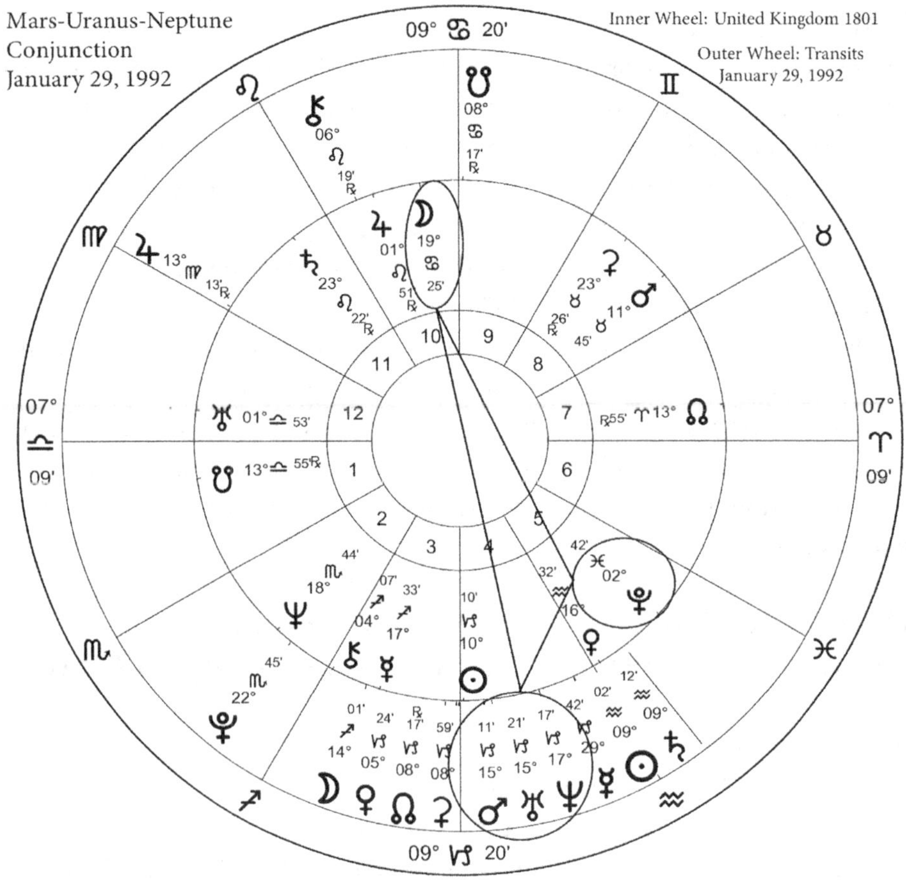

The harsh natal Moon-Pluto aspect was emphasized again in 1993 at the first exact conjunction of Uranus and Neptune at 19°33' Capricorn. They opposed the natal Moon almost exactly. Note also that the Saturn-Chiron and Chiron-Pluto cycles coincided at this time, and aligned with natal Saturn and Ceres.

And transiting Ceres 2°36' Pisces was almost exactly conjunct natal Pluto. With Ceres, the asteroid associated with currency exchange rates, triggering Pluto, chart ruler of the country's currency, a significant and probably detrimental event surrounding the British pound was due to occur between the January 1992 stellium and the February 1993 Uranus-Neptune conjunction.

82 https://priceonomics.com/the-trade-of-the-century-when-george-soros-broke/

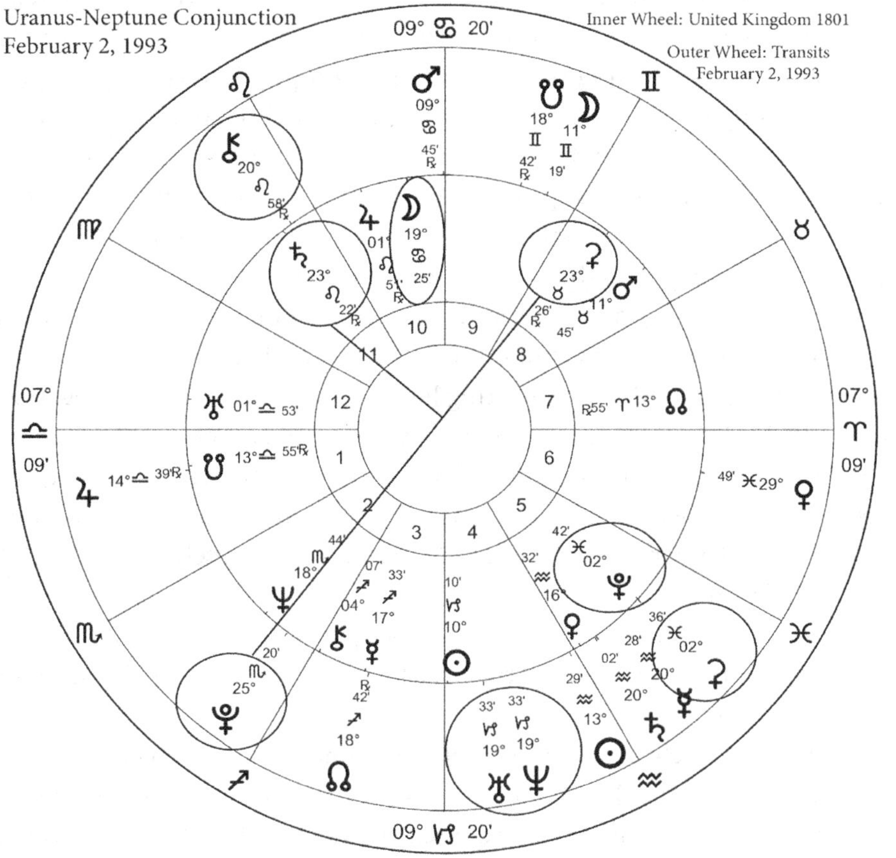

The position of transiting Pluto in 1992 clearly indicated a massive change to the currency was in the works, and throughout the year Pluto 20°–23° Scorpio was moving through the second house of the national currency. On February 24, 1992 transiting Pluto went retrograde at 22°57' Scorpio, squaring progressed Mars and Saturn, which were almost exactly conjunct in Leo at 22°18' and 22°28' respectively. The co-rulers of Scorpio (Mars and Pluto), the sign of the second house for the 1801 chart, are both involved here. However, the square was not exact on September 16.

The interesting thing about the natal position of Uranus at 1°53' Libra is that its contra-antiscion[83] of 28°07' Virgo is almost conjunct it, although out of

83 Antiscion and contra-antiscion points for a planet's position are determined by a system that "reflects" that position with relation to the 0° Cancer-0° Capricorn axis. These points, when triggered, can release the planet's effects. See the Glossary for more explanation.

sign. In 1992, progressed Uranus 28°20' Virgo conjoined this contra-antiscion point. On September 16, 1992, transiting Jupiter, Mercury and the Sun at 25° Virgo were also conjoining this contra-antiscion point, thus triggering the natal yod configuration. The planet of the unexpected (Uranus), the planet of transformational crisis (Pluto), and the planet of exaggeration (Jupiter) were combined in this moment to produce exactly that: A wild, sudden, and deep collapse of the British financial system via currency speculation. (Natal Pluto, ruler of the currency, is in the fifth house of speculation).[84]

It was in late May of 1992 that it became obvious to the markets that the pound had been admitted into the ERM at too high of a rate against the deutschmark, and on May 28 transiting Jupiter 5°45' Virgo opposed progressed Pluto 5°34' Pisces, forming a T-square with progressed Venus 5°48' Gemini. Venus rules the eighth house in this chart, and Pluto is co-ruler of the second house. With these two financial planets in a harsh configuration with transiting Jupiter (in its detriment, being in Virgo[85]), drama was definitely about to unfold in the near future.

Also in May 1992, the progressed Ascendant of the 1801 natal was at 11°52' Taurus—almost exactly conjunct that chart's natal Mars at 11°45' Taurus in the natal eighth house.

The total solar eclipse of June 30, 1992 made important set-up configurations in both UK natal charts. In the 1801 chart, the eclipse at 8°56' Cancer conjoined the Midheaven 9°20' Cancer and squared the Ascendant 7°09' Libra, as well as opposing the natal Sun 10°10' Capricorn. Progressed Mars and Saturn were exactly conjunct at 22°31' Leo on the same day. Taken together, these configurations signaled that a dramatic event related to the areas of the chart ruled by the Sun and Mars[86] was brewing: Mars (and Pluto) rule the second house of the currency, Mars also rules the seventh house of allies, and the Sun rules the eleventh house of associations in the 1801 chart—with the ERM, a currency association of which the UK was a member.

---

84 It would be interesting to see how this yod interacts with Mr. Soros's chart (maybe at another time).

85 See the Glossary for an explanation of the system of essential dignities in astrology.

86 It was also the day of the UK's Mars return.

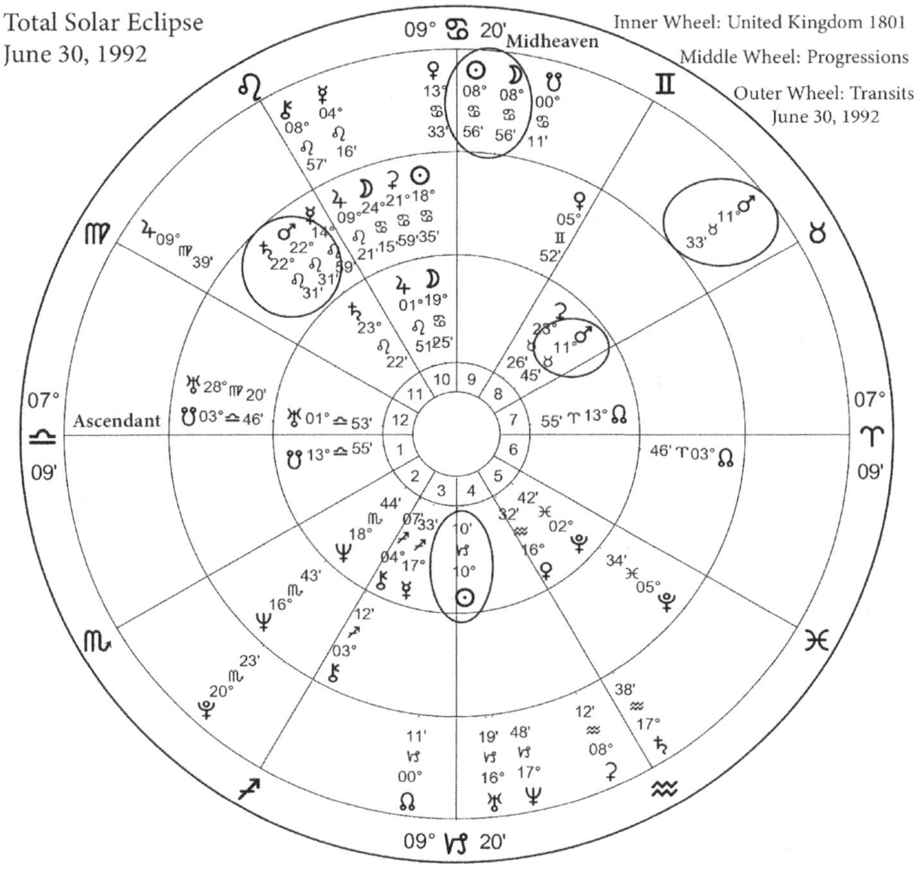

1922 UK Reorganization Chart

The 1922 UK Reorganization natal chart also pointed to a looming financial crisis, and there are several indications in this chart that show the pressure on the pound would reach the breaking point in 1992.

The configuration of transiting Neptune in hard aspect to natal or progressed Saturn of a nation's chart[87] was at work for the UK and the pound in 1992, and the square between transiting Neptune in Capricorn and natal Saturn in Libra intensified the effect of a stellium that occurred in Capricorn in late January 1992. The stellium consisted of the Moon 7° Capricorn, Venus 8° Capricorn, North Node 9° Capricorn, Ceres 10° Capricorn, Sun 11° Capricorn, Uranus 16° Capricorn, Mars 17° Capricorn, and Neptune 18° Capricorn. Note that this stellium involved Ceres, which influences currency exchange rates.

87 See Chapter 4 on the 1997 Southeast Asian currency crisis.

On July 11, 1991 there was a total solar eclipse with the Sun, Moon, and South Node all exactly at 18°58' Cancer, with transits and progressions to the UK Reorganization chart for the moment of this eclipse showing the eclipse point opposing progressed Ceres at 17°31' Capricorn.

On May 28, 1992 transiting Mars and the Moon were conjunct progressed Mars in Aries, intensifying the effect of this eclipse (by being square to the eclipse position), and they opposed natal Saturn 17°43' Libra. This opposition formed a Grand Cross with progressed Ceres 17°51' Capricorn, transiting Uranus 17°29' Capricorn, and transiting Neptune 18°35' Capricorn, all opposing the eclipse point 18°58' Cancer. That same day, transiting Saturn went retrograde at 18°29' Aquarius, conjunct the progressed Moon, initiating the decline of the British pound.

On September 16, the day of the pound's dramatic collapse, transiting Venus was conjunct natal Saturn, interacting with this Grand Cross configuration.

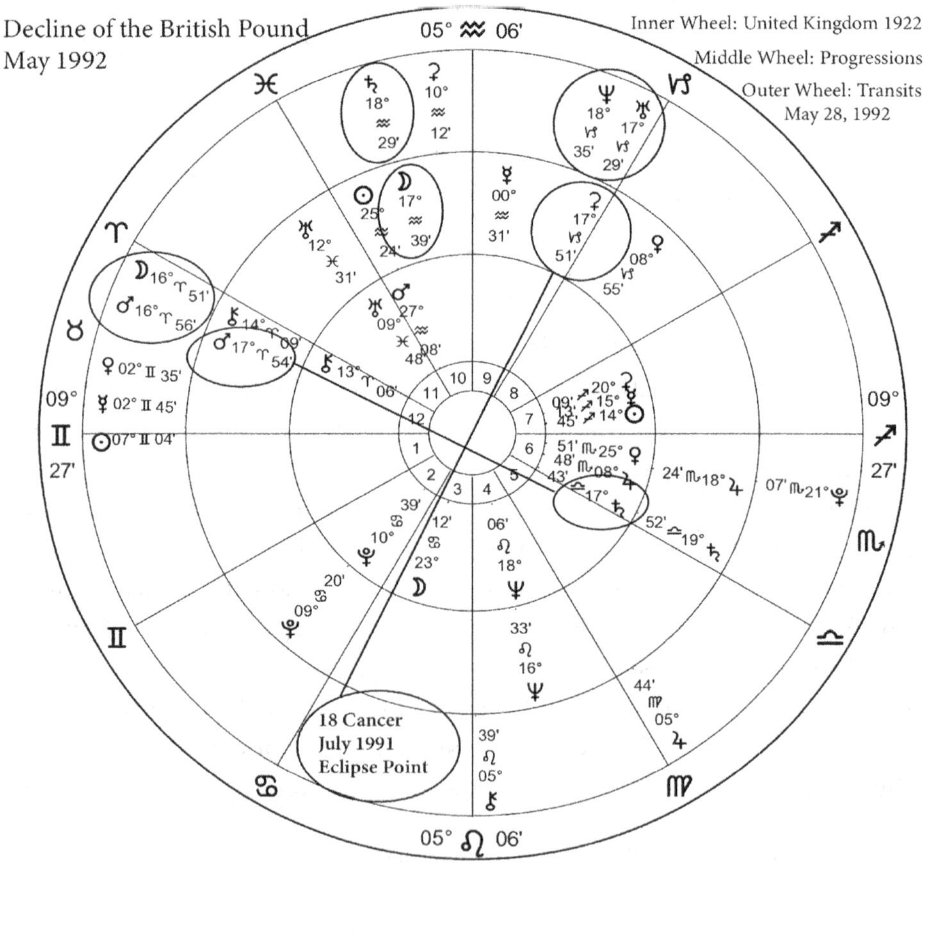

Eclipse Configuration Triggers on the Day of the British Pound's Collapse

Time is not linear in astrology, so an astrological configuration that occurs ***after*** an event could still be part of the build-up, and a trigger to that event. That is the case here for the British pound: The effects of two solar eclipses (one before and one after the event) were triggered exactly on September 16, 1992.

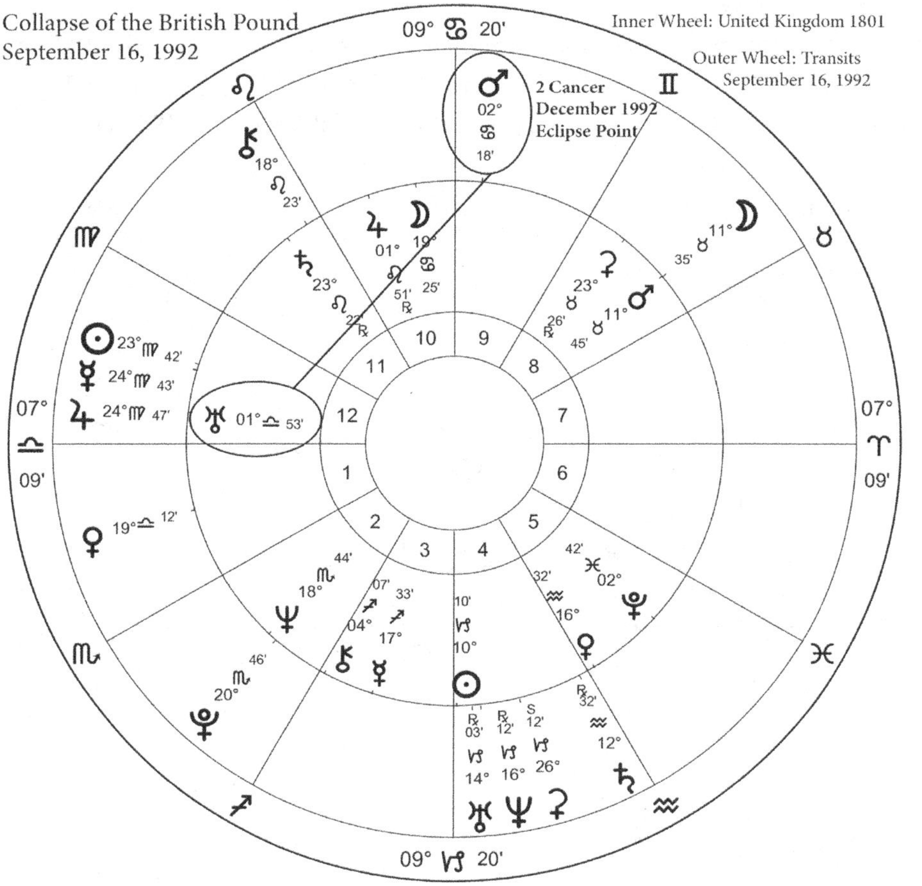

A partial solar eclipse on December 24, 1992 at 2°27' Capricorn squared natal Uranus 1°53' Libra of the 1801 UK natal chart. It was triggered on September 16, 1992 by transiting Mars at 2°27' Cancer (the harsh aspect between Mars and Uranus contributing to the sudden, drastic fall of the pound). The previous eclipse, a total solar eclipse on June 30, 1992 at 8°56' Cancer, had conjoined progressed Pluto 9°20' Cancer and opposed progressed Venus 9°01' of the 1922 UK natal chart, with this harsh aspect between progressed Venus and progressed Pluto accentuating their harsh aspect in the natal chart. At the time of this eclipse the Midheaven[88] was located at 12°06' Cancer. Note that on September 16, 1992 the progressed Moon of this eclipse chart was at 12°05' Cancer, conjoining that natal Midheaven point of the eclipse[89]—with this being the strongest trigger, and resulting in a deeper collapse to the devaluation of the pound which had begun in late May 1992.

To show the importance of this timing technique using the progressed Moon of an eclipse chart, on March 11, 1993 transiting Venus went retrograde at 20°01' Aries, almost exactly opposing the point at which Saturn (in the 1922 UK natal

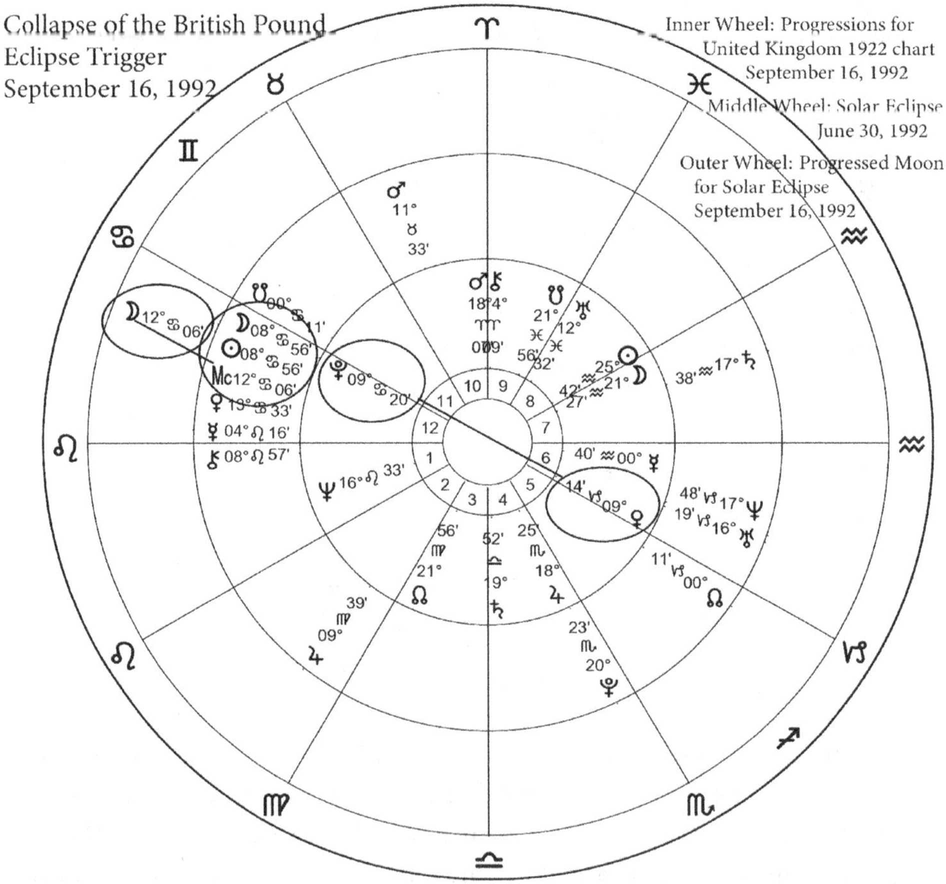

88 The Midheaven at the exact time of the eclipse for the location of Westminster, UK.

89 This is similar to the timing technique used for the 1997 Asian crisis, which also involved the progressed Moon *of the eclipse chart itself.* (See Chapter 4.)

chart) went retrograde by secondary progression. On that day (March 11, 1993) transiting Venus at her retrograde stationary point was squaring transiting Neptune 20°40' Capricorn, forming a T-square with the Saturn secondary progression retrograde point of 20°06' Libra. Neptune drains energy from whatever it influences, and Saturn is depressive, so with these two planets in close harsh aspect with Venus, the natural ruler of finances and a country's currency, a devaluation was indicated. Furthermore, transiting Saturn on that day was at 24°30' Aquarius—exactly squaring the position of 24°30' Scorpio at which Venus in the UK chart went direct by secondary progression.

So why did the pound collapse in September 1992 rather than March 1993? None of the solar eclipses in the 1991–1994 time period had a progressed Moon trigger on March 11, 1993, when Venus went retrograde.

ERM – More Indications of Currency Crisis from the European Exchange Rate Mechanism Charts

When the British pound collapsed in September 1992, it was part of the European Exchange Rate Mechanism, having become subject to this mechanism after being added to the European Monetary System on October 8, 1990. The European Exchange Rate Mechanism (ERM), initiated on March 13, 1979,[90] has a natal chart which shows potential for a sudden breakdown in its functioning.

March 13, 1979 was the day of a lunar eclipse at 22°42' Virgo. At the time that the ERM came into being (midnight), the Moon conjoined Saturn at 10° Virgo in the tenth house of the entity's purpose, opposing the Sun, Mars, and Ceres.

The ERM was all about currency exchange rates, and keeping them aligned. The Full Moon eclipse coincided with Mars and Ceres opposing Saturn, and in the same signs of the zodiac. Mars conjunct Ceres indicates that it would take frantic juggling for some members to maintain that alignment, and that the overall group would be at odds with some of its members is shown by Mars opposing Saturn.

90 https://en.wikipedia.org/wiki/European_Exchange_Rate_Mechanism

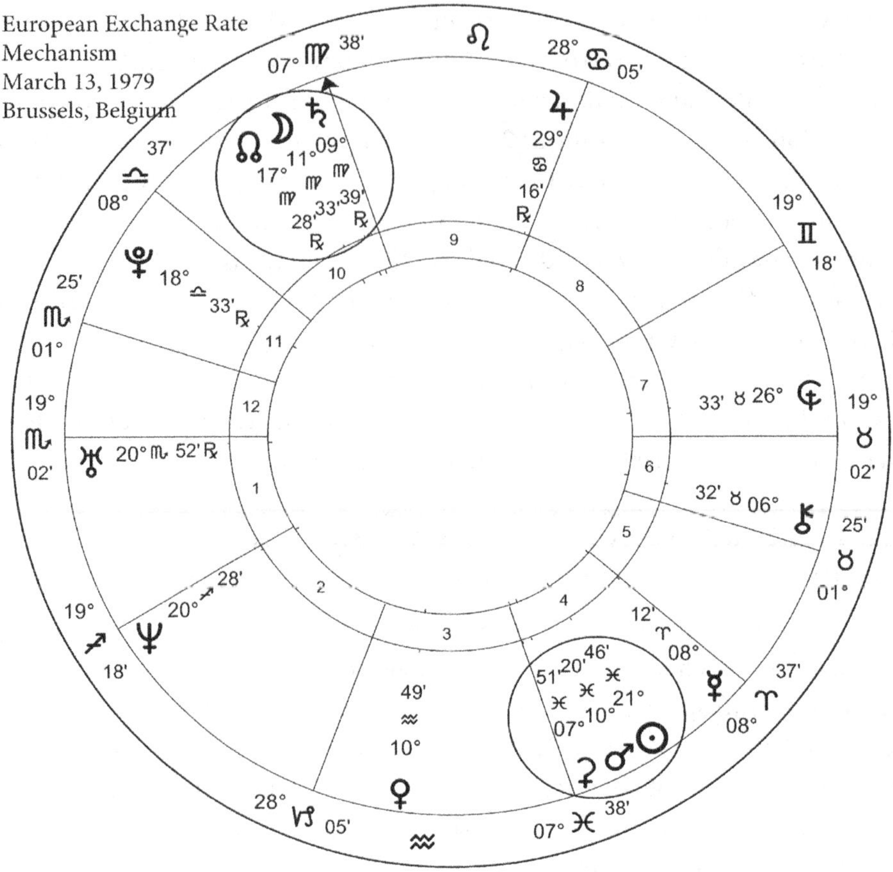

European Exchange Rate
Mechanism
March 13, 1979
Brussels, Belgium

Aries/Mars rules the fifth house of the individual members; Saturn in the tenth shows harsh, and in some cases, out of touch leadership (clinging to outworn attitudes is shown by Saturn conjunct the Moon). Saturn conjunct the Midheaven indicates that a senior member would dominate the group, as was the case: Germany's deutschmark quickly came to be the benchmark currency of the group, due to its strength relative to the currencies of other members.

On September 16, 1992 transiting Sun, Mercury, and Jupiter 24°–25° Virgo were opposing the ERM natal Sun 21°18' Pisces and progressed Mars 20°59' Pisces, thus triggering the Full Moon/Mars-Saturn configuration explained above.

Jupiter is especially important: Not only does it rule the second house of the ERM chart, the house which is directly involved with currencies, but Jupiter went into direct motion by progression on April 11, 1992 at 29°00' Cancer in the eighth house, indicating that important events involving the very purpose of the ERM would occur in 1992.

In 1992, the Chiron-Pluto and Saturn-Pluto cycles coincided by forming a T-square, with transiting Pluto conjoining natal Uranus at 20°46' Scorpio. Uranus rules Aquarius, and progressed Venus at 26°52' Aquarius was triggered by this Pluto transit (both Venus and Pluto indicate currency and finance issues).

The progressed Moon at 12°30' Pisces was conjoining progressed Ceres (associated with currency exchange rates) at 13°04' Pisces—less than one degree apart.

That the currencies within the ERM would undergo a violent shift during the summer of 1992 was shown by transiting Mars passing through 8° to 18° Gemini in mid-August 1992. Mars formed a T-square with transiting Jupiter (ruler of the second house) and natal Moon/Saturn opposing natal Mars, progressed Moon and progressed Ceres. At the same time, transiting Ceres 29° Capricorn opposed progressed Jupiter, still at its stationary direct point of 29° Cancer. As Mars moved forward from 18° Gemini, German officials began making public comments undermining the value of the pound, referring to "potential realignment within the ERM," and George Soros and Stanley Druckenmiller opened large short positions against the pound in August.

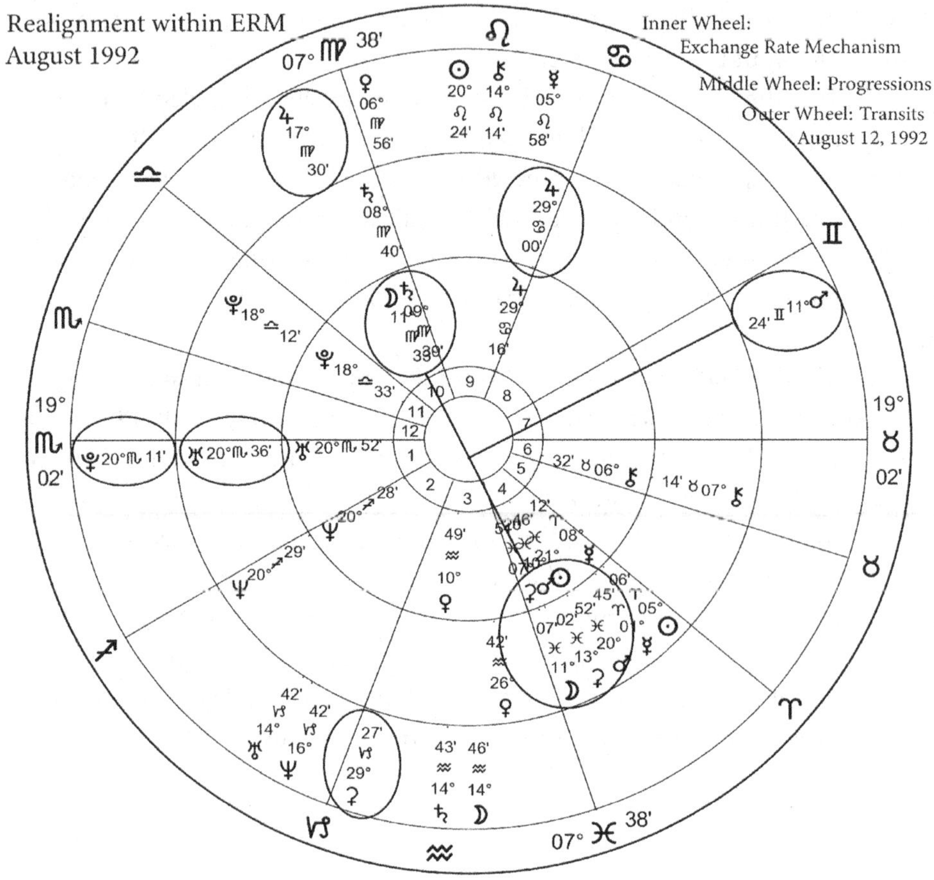

UNITED KINGDOM – SUMMARY

The 1992 Capricorn stellium and the Uranus-Neptune conjunction in 1993 profoundly affected the UK's natal chart (the 1801 Act of Union chart) by linking into the natal Moon-Pluto aspect. As Pluto rules the second house of the currency of this chart, and with transiting Pluto moving through this house, an upset involving the pound was a strong probability. So, with the Moon in the tenth house of the ruling government, the knock-on effect was voters electing for a change of leadership.

Just as for Thailand, Indonesia, and Russia in the 1997 Asian currency crisis, transiting Neptune was making a harsh aspect to natal or progressed Saturn—although in the UK's case, Neptune was squaring natal Saturn, whereas Neptune was conjunct or opposing Saturn in the other cases.

And two solar eclipses in 1992 timed the exact date of the pound's collapse by configurations involving either the progressed Moon of the eclipse chart, or transiting Mars.

★ ★ ★

Overall Astrological Conditions Associated with Financial Crisis

The following conditions involve only transiting planets, and could apply to the global financial system or a regional system.

Astrological conditions indicating severe financial crisis:

- Saturn-Pluto and Chiron-Pluto cycles coincide.
- Uranus and Ceres as part of a stellium, in the sign of Capricorn (or a sign where Saturn is dignified).

Astrological conditions indicating a profound shift in global politics and erosion of established structures:

- Uranus conjunct Neptune.

UNITED KINGDOM – Astrological Conditions of Overvalued Currency and Devaluation

From the above analysis, the following astrological conditions for the UK's chart were associated with *pressure on the currency and severe currency devaluation:*

- Yod configuration in the natal chart involving Uranus and Pluto, where one of those planets is the chart ruler of the second house of the currency, and progressed Ceres then conjuncts that planet: This indicated a time period in which there could be a crisis surrounding the currency.
- Transiting stellium in Capricorn that makes a harsh aspect with the natal position of the chart ruler of the second house (in the case of the 1801 UK chart, it was Pluto): This indicated a serious disruption to the country overall, due to a currency-related event.
- Transiting Neptune in harsh aspect with natal or progressed Saturn: This indicated mounting pressure to maintain a currency trading band.

- Progressed Pluto (or progressed ruler of the second house) closely conjunct progressed Saturn, squaring the transiting ruler (or co-ruler) of the second house while that transiting planet moves through the second house: This indicated a massive change in the value of the currency, most likely a devaluation.
- Progressed Pluto and progressed Venus in a harsh configuration (this occurred with both natal charts analyzed) and possibly being triggered by transiting Jupiter, with either Venus or Pluto (or both) as chart ruler of a financial house (second, fifth, eighth, and eleventh houses), or located in those houses: This indicated the release of pent-up pressure on the currency to be devalued.
- Progressed Ascendant conjunct natal Mars in the eighth house: This indicated that the currency needed to be devalued.
- Progressed Moon of a solar eclipse exactly conjunct the Midheaven of the solar eclipse when the eclipse chart has a link to the country's natal chart: This timed the currency devaluation to the day.
- Transiting Mars exactly conjunct the position of a solar eclipse and making a close harsh aspect to a natal planet: This timed the currency devaluation to the day.

CONCLUSIONS

The general time frame in which a financial crisis is likely to happen can be determined by configurations formed by transiting planets alone. However, to know which countries will be the source of the crisis, or will be the most affected by it—*and* to closely pinpoint the time of the crisis—configurations forming with natal or progressed planets in a country's chart must be considered.

Transiting Configurations

The coinciding of the Saturn-Pluto and Chiron-Pluto cycles is of major importance for determining a general time frame for financial crises.

A stellium in Capricorn (or a sign in which Saturn is dignified) which includes Uranus and Ceres indicates imbalances in the financial system that resolve themselves in a sudden crisis when the stellium is triggered.

Specific Country Chart Configurations

As with all of the separate analyses in this work, a country's natal chart *must* show the potential for financial crisis. Those that do are most likely to be those that suffer the most in a global crisis.

Within a nation's chart, aspects to the *progressed* ruler of the eighth house are extremely important. If this progressed planet makes a harsh aspect to natal, progressed, or transiting Jupiter, it leads to some sort of overvaluation or financial excess.

When transiting Pluto moves through a country's second house of the currency and financial system, and it makes a harsh aspect to the progressed ruler of the second house, it indicates a coming upset in the currency's value. If transiting Pluto, in the second house, makes a harsh aspect to progressed Saturn, this could also indicate an upset, particularly a devaluation.

Related to the above, during the time that the progressed ruler of the second house is closely conjunct progressed Saturn, an upset to the currency or the country's financial system could occur in that time period.

Progressed Venus and progressed Pluto in a harsh aspect, especially if either or both planets have some connection to the second and eighth houses, indicates a major currency-related event is likely. The event can be triggered by a transiting outer planet forming a harsh configuration with progressed Venus and progressed Pluto.

Although the true time of day of a country's "birth" is often unknown or debatable, in the case of the 1801 UK natal chart, **the progressed Ascendant closely conjunct natal Mars** in the eighth house did help to narrow the time period in which the devaluation of the pound would occur.

Transiting Neptune in a harsh aspect with natal or progressed Saturn can indicate a time period in which a currency devaluation is likely. With the 1922 UK natal chart, when transiting Saturn went retrograde and was opposing natal Neptune within a 1° range, this also indicated that a devaluation was imminent.

A stellium in Capricorn, *if it impacts natal or progressed planets of a country's chart,* has been found consistently to indicate some sort of financial crisis. It could be that it is not so much the sign Capricorn, but the fact that Saturn is dignified in that sign (and the signs Libra and Aquarius) that is the important factor.

Several of the analyses of this work show that **eclipse positions *that impact either natal or progressed positions of a country's chart*** can be used to narrow the time period of an important event to within a few days by using the progressed Moon of the eclipse chart in relation to the natal positions of the Ascendant, Midheaven, and nodes (and possibly the planets) of the eclipse chart itself. It does appear that solar eclipses are more important in this regard.

CHAPTER 4

ASIAN CURRENCY CRISIS OF THE LATE 1990'S

In 1997–1998 the countries of Thailand, Indonesia, Malaysia, South Korea, Hong Kong, and the Philippines, among others, experienced a financial crisis that forced them to dramatically devalue their currencies, caused their stock markets to plummet, and wreaked havoc on their economies.

ECONOMIC DEVELOPMENT AND DEBT OVERLOAD IN SOUTHEAST ASIA

From the late 1980's to 1996, these same Asian countries had increased their export base and had impressive annual GDP growth of 6–9%. Not only had exports increased, but the nature of their exports had changed from products made from basic commodities to high tech products such as electronics and automobiles.[91]

The capital coming in from these exports fueled investment in property, with property values rising accordingly, and this rise sparked a development boom in both residential and commercial property. Overbuilding became the norm, and much was financed by loans. As values continued to rise, and exports increased, banks felt comfortable with the added risk of extending more and more loans on the assumption that those investing in industrial projects would be able to repay. This also led to certain wealthy sectors of society, such as the *chaebol* family businesses in South Korea, taking out huge loans in order to establish their dominance in certain industries. And because this was encouraged by the region's governments, it also added to the debt load as they embarked on infrastructure projects.[92]

Most of this expansion was funded by debt denominated in foreign currencies—mainly the US dollar, because of the favorable exchange rate. And

91 http://www.wright.edu/~tdung/asiancrisis-hill.htm

92 Ibid.

although their currencies were pegged to the dollar, most of them had limited reserves of foreign currency.

By the mid-1990's, the tide was shifting. The Thailand property market had excess capacity, and investors were beginning to be concerned about this. In South Korea, the chaebol were investing heavily in semiconductor factories due to a global shortage of memory chips, which drove their price higher. But then oversupply hit the semiconductor market in 1996 and the price plunged, leaving these companies with huge loans, denominated in US dollars, which they were struggling to repay by 1997.[93]

Another condition was also dragging down the Southeast Asian economies: As they shifted to producing and exporting more high-tech products, their imports naturally increased so they would have the necessary components for production. This eventually led to current account deficits across the region,[94] which in turn made it difficult for them to maintain their currency pegs to the US dollar. But they found themselves between a rock and a hard place, for if they did not maintain the peg, the value of their debt, in terms of their local currency, would skyrocket—and loans that were already burdensome would become even more so.

This combination of excess capacity in the property market, more imports yet lower price for exports, currency pegs, heavy US dollar denominated debt funding all types of property investment, and limited foreign reserves set the stage for a financial meltdown.

Overall Astrological Configurations of the 1990's

What astrological conditions were present in the 1990s that indicated that this situation was developing?

Looking only at transiting planetary configurations, there were three noteworthy configurations:

- Intermittently throughout the 1990's, Saturn opposed Chiron within a 10° range.
- In 1993, Uranus conjoined Neptune at 19° Capricorn; the third, and last, exact conjunction of this pair.
- There was a stellium in Aquarius in February 1997 that included Ceres, Jupiter, and Uranus.

93 Ibid.

94 Ibid.

As was explained in the chapter on Latin America, Saturn and Chiron were in the same sign of Pisces in the mid-1960's and were conjunct on April 12, 1966 at 23°51' Pisces. In the 1990's, they had now reached the halfway point of their cycle, the opposition aspect (180° angle). In the case of Latin America in the 1960's and 1970's, this planetary pair's new cycle coincided with an expansion of infrastructure and economic development financed by debt. And their opposition coincided with the same financial situation in Southeast Asia.

In the 1980's, the Saturn-Pluto and Chiron-Pluto cycles had coincided by harsh angles; Saturn was conjunct Chiron, with both opposing Uranus and Pluto. In 1992–1993, these cycles also coincided by harsh angles, with Saturn in Aquarius opposing Chiron in Leo, and both forming a T-square with Pluto in Scorpio. By late 1996 through 1997, these cycles coincided with "soft" angles—Saturn was trine (120° angle) Pluto and Chiron was semi-sextile (30° angle) Pluto. In the 1960's, these cycles indicated the beginning of debt expansion in Latin America; in the 1990's, these cycles indicated the peak of debt overload and the approach of default in Southeast Asia.

The Uranus-Neptune conjunction of 1993 was the last phase of the Saturn-Uranus-Neptune conjunction that began in the late 1980's. As discussed in the chapter on the 13th century, it indicates an erosion of established structures, including natural resources in some cases. In the 20th century, it indicated the dissolution of the Soviet Union, the repression of the Tiananmen Square revolt in China, and the proliferation of the Internet—a new global structure for doing business, but also a powerful way of spreading false information. Overall, this conjunction led to greater control of the many by the few, and in the case of the Asian currency crisis, it indicated the establishment of monopolies by elites over key industries—with the few dominating the masses.

A stellium in Aquarius in the early part of 1997 played a role in triggering the crisis in Southeast Asia. The stellium consisted of Jupiter, Uranus, Mercury, Ceres, Venus, and the Sun; on February 13, there was a conjunction of Jupiter, Uranus, Mercury, and Ceres at 6° Aquarius. The natal charts of several countries involved in the crisis were strongly impacted by the February 13 conjunction, as will be explained below.

This conjunction was an important factor in the currency crisis because it involved Ceres, which appears to influence both currency exchange rates and changes or violations of national borders.

Note that Aquarius is the sign co-ruled by Saturn; other stelliums that were associated with financial crises occurred in signs where Saturn is either exalted or the ruler of the sign.[95]

The total solar eclipse of March 9, 1997 at 18°30' Pisces was a decisive factor in triggering the events of the crisis. Mars conjunct the North Node at 29° Virgo, with both making a trine to Neptune at 29° Capricorn, added to the effects of the eclipse.

The financial meltdown began in Thailand in 1997, so its chart is analyzed first.

THAILAND – Potential for Financial Problems

The chart for the modern state of Thailand shows the potential for problems related to debt, foreign reserves, and the currency.

Thailand
June 24, 1932
Bangkok, Thailand

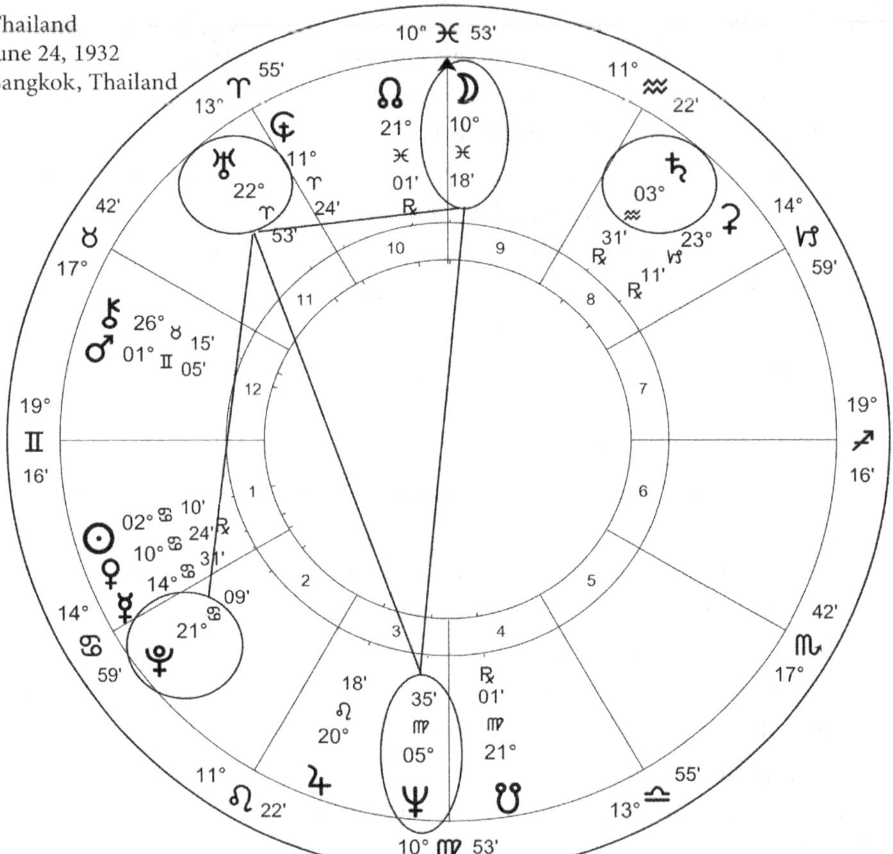

95 "Exaltation" and "rulership" are designations given to planets within the system of planetary dignities. See the Glossary for an explanation of the system of essential dignities in astrology.

The most outstanding indicator is Uranus 22°53' Aries squaring Pluto 21°09' Cancer, with these planets located in finance-related houses, Pluto being in the second house of the currency. Cancer is ruled by the Moon, which is located at 10°18' Pisces and opposes Neptune, the ruler of Pisces, at 5°35' Virgo, so with the ruler of the second house of the currency in a harsh aspect with Neptune, currency-related crises should be expected. With this Moon-Neptune configuration linked to the Uranus-Pluto square, such crises can be expected to spiral out of control and have the potential to both affect, and be affected by, the global financial system.

But with the Moon in Pisces almost exactly trine Venus 10°24' Cancer, the planet naturally associated with currency and finance, the country's banking system runs smoothly enough, although the Moon's opposition to Neptune will intervene at times and create excesses.

The sign Capricorn is on the cusp of the eighth house of debt and foreign reserves. Capricorn is ruled by Saturn, and Saturn 3°31' Aquarius is located in the eighth house. As seen before in the case of Mexico, when the ruler of the eighth house resides in the eighth house the potential for problems related to debt, especially debt denominated in a foreign currency, is increased.

However, Saturn trines Mars 1°05' Gemini. This is helpful for containing debt problems, for not only is Mars the planet naturally associated with the eighth house, it also rules the sign Aries, where Uranus is located. And although Uranus being influenced by Mars is a volatile combination, with Saturn influencing Mars, some prudence enters the picture.

THAILAND – Economic Boom and Increased Foreign Investment

Thailand suffered many economic problems in the 1970's and early 1980's. It devalued its currency, the baht, twice in 1981 and again in 1984. But between 1987 and 1996, Thailand's private sector experienced strong growth due to a new focus on industrialization to increase exports, as well as to foreign investment.[96]

Thailand's progressed planets were impacted by the Saturn-Uranus-Neptune triple conjunction of 1989–1993. These conjunctions[97] fell in Thailand's seventh and eighth houses, areas of the chart related to foreign relations, foreign investment, and foreign reserves.

96 https://en.wikipedia.org/wiki/Economy_of_Thailand

97 There wasn't one exact triple conjunction, but these planets were traveling closely together in Capricorn as each pair formed a conjunction.

Saturn-Neptune Conjunction Novenber 13, 1989

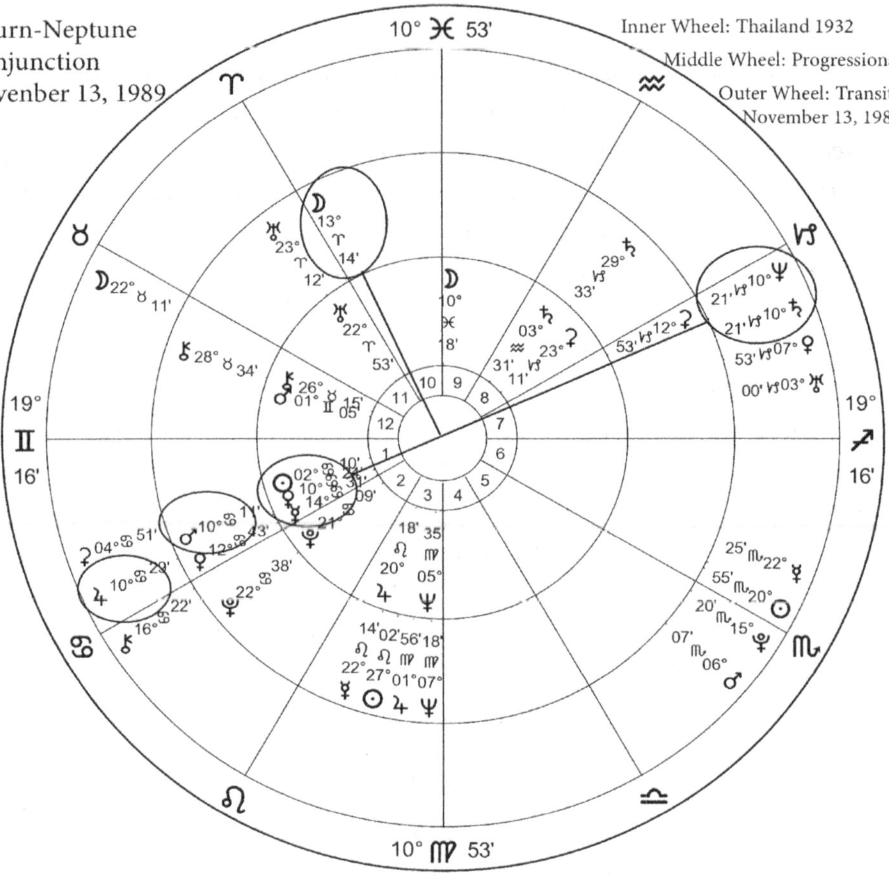

Inner Wheel: Thailand 1932
Middle Wheel: Progressions
Outer Wheel: Transits November 13, 1989

On November 13, 1989, the transiting Saturn-Neptune conjunction at 10°21' Capricorn was almost exactly opposed by transiting Jupiter 10°30' Cancer, progressed Mars 10°11' Cancer, and natal Venus 10°24' Cancer—with these planets forming a T-square to the progressed Moon 13° Aries in the tenth house of government and leadership.

Saturn is the powerful planet here, for it is in Capricorn, the sign which it rules. And Capricorn/Saturn rules Thailand's eighth house of foreign investment and debt. The involvement of Neptune and Jupiter, along with natal Venus, indicated that Thailand's economic growth was garnering much attention by foreign investors. But the opposition aspect indicates excessive debt is a risk, due to all parties being too willing to jump in without thorough investigation of the situation.

Usually a harsh aspect between Venus and Neptune would mean either deception or delusion was driving decisions that might later be regretted. But with progressed Mercury 22°14' Leo moving retrograde to conjunct natal Jupiter, there must have been some exaggeration of the true situation going on, and foreign investors were eager and willing to ignore any warning signs.

THAILAND – Excessive Property Development Loans

The Southeast Asia financial meltdown began on February 5, 1997 with the default on a eurobond by Somprasong Land, a Thai property developer.[98]

Investors had already been nervous about high levels of debt in the Thai property market, but their anxiety reached a peak in early 1997 as transiting Jupiter and Neptune were conjunct in the late degrees of Capricorn in Thailand's eighth house of debt. These planets were also conjunct progressed Saturn, the chart ruler of the eighth house.

With progressed Jupiter 3°30' Virgo exactly inconjunct (150° angle) transiting Uranus and natal Saturn 3°31' Aquarius, investors were nervous and heading for the exits. Jupiter represents foreigners and their interests in this chart, for Sagittarius/Jupiter rules the seventh house of foreigners. Somprasong's default triggered investors' concerns about the entire region, and was the tipping point toward the Thai baht devaluation in July 1997.

Somprasong Land's incorporation chart (dated September 16, 1992) with transits and progressions for February 5, 1997 has the Aquarius stellium planets passing over progressed Saturn at 12°21' Aquarius, and forming an exact trine (120° angle) to natal Hades 12°21' Gemini in the eighth house. Progressed Saturn is in the fourth house, the foundation area of any chart, and as the stellium planets passed over it, they shook the foundations of the company.

98 https://en.wikipedia.org/wiki/Economy_of_Thailand

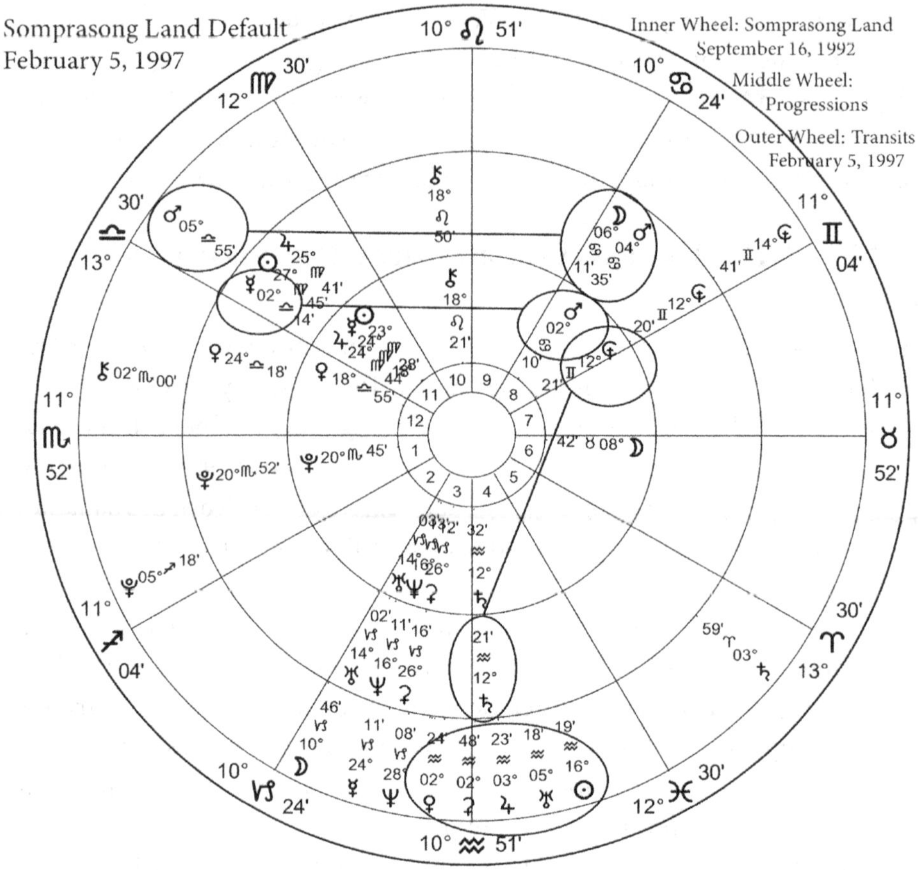

Transiting Mars 5°55' Libra was at its stationary point on February 5 (about to turn retrograde), conjunct progressed Mercury, ruler of the eighth house of bonds and financing, and they were squaring progressed Mars and Moon 5°–7° Cancer in the eighth house. Progressed Mercury 2°14' Libra was just past being exactly square natal Mars 2°10' Cancer.

That Somprasong Land's business model was to fund property development by taking out excessive loans is shown by the natal configuration of the Sun, Mercury, and Jupiter, all conjoined at 24°–25° Virgo. Mercury, the ruler of the eighth house of debt, is involved here; Jupiter expands whatever it touches; and the Sun added energy and executive decision-making to the mix.

And transiting Mars had just passed over this natal triple conjunction. Granted, Mars had done this twice before in the short lifespan of Somprasong

Land,[99] but the difference this time was that Mars turned retrograde in the early degrees of Libra, and thus passed over that triple conjunction three separate times in late 1996 and 1997, dealing a mortal blow.

THAILAND – July 1997 Forced Currency Devaluation

In the months leading up to the 1997 devaluation of the baht, transiting Neptune 29° Capricorn was conjunct Thailand's progressed Saturn in the eighth house of debt and foreign currency reserves. Neptune hides facts, and being in the eighth house of foreign reserves and conjoining the chart ruler of those reserves, this probably indicated what wouldn't become known until later: A Forex trader at Thailand's central bank had committed a large portion of the country's foreign reserves to forward contracts. Thus, although Thailand had $33 billion in reported reserves in the summer of 1997, it really had only $1.14 billion available to prop up the baht.[100]

The February 13, 1997 stellium (transiting Jupiter, Uranus, Mercury, and Ceres) conjoined natal Saturn at 3°31' Aquarius in the eighth house of debt and foreign currency reserves. Thailand's progressed Moon at 10°47' Cancer was conjunct natal Venus, and it was moving to conjunct progressed Mars 14°51' Cancer, right on the cusp, or boundary, of the second house, which rules the country's currency.

---

99 Mars completes a revolution of the zodiac in approximately two years.

100 http://www.wright.edu/~tdung/asiancrisis-hill.htm

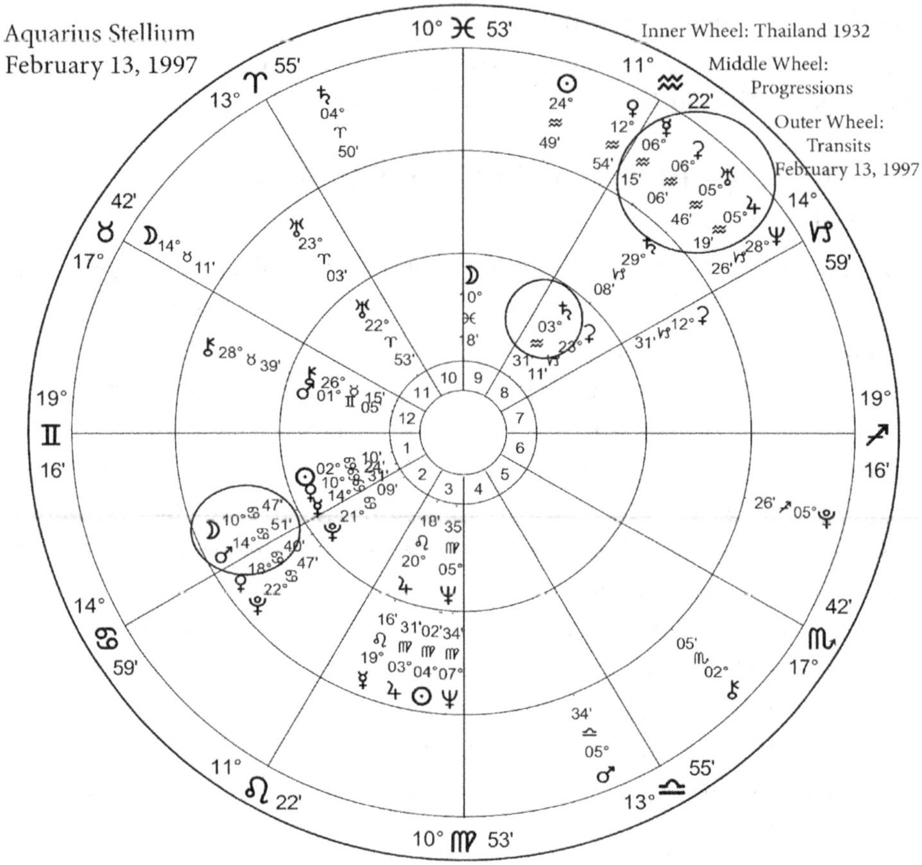

On July 2, 1997, when the Thai baht was allowed to float freely—and it subsequently plunged—transiting Venus was at 5° Leo, opposing the position of the Aquarius conjunction.

In addition to this, the progressed Moon and Mars were conjunct on July 2, 1997, with transiting Mercury having just passed over them when the Thai baht plunged.

Collapse of the Thai Baht
July 2, 1997

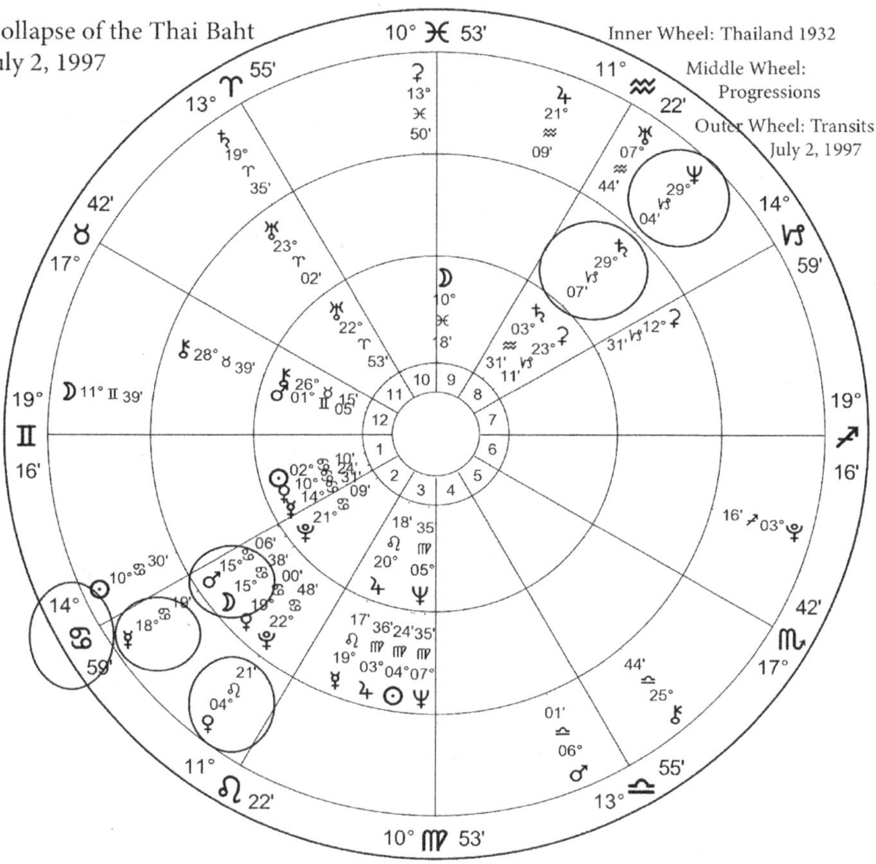

THAILAND – Summary

Thailand's economy prospered in the 1980's and mid-1990's due to factors indicated by the conjunctions of Saturn-Neptune and Uranus-Neptune, both in Capricorn. Due to these configurations falling in the areas of Thailand's chart associated with the perceptions of foreign relations and investments, Thailand was viewed favorably—but transiting Neptune in the eighth house of debt signaled that foreign currency denominated debt would eventually be the source of problems. The unfolding of events involved progressed Saturn, progressed Mars, natal Venus, and transiting Neptune, with the Aquarius stellium of February 1997 bringing the situation to a head.

The conjunction of natal Venus and progressed Mars in the second house of Thailand's currency indicated the sudden, dramatic devaluation of the baht as the progressed Moon also conjoined them.

INDONESIA –
Potential for Financial Problems

Indonesia's natal chart shows not just the potential for debt-related problems, but also that such problems could lead to political instability. Indonesia underwent extreme political upheaval as a result of the debt crisis and currency devaluation of 1997, much as China (whose chart has similarities to Indonesia's chart) looks to be on the verge of a similar upheaval.

Indonesia
December 27, 1949
Jakarta, Indonesia

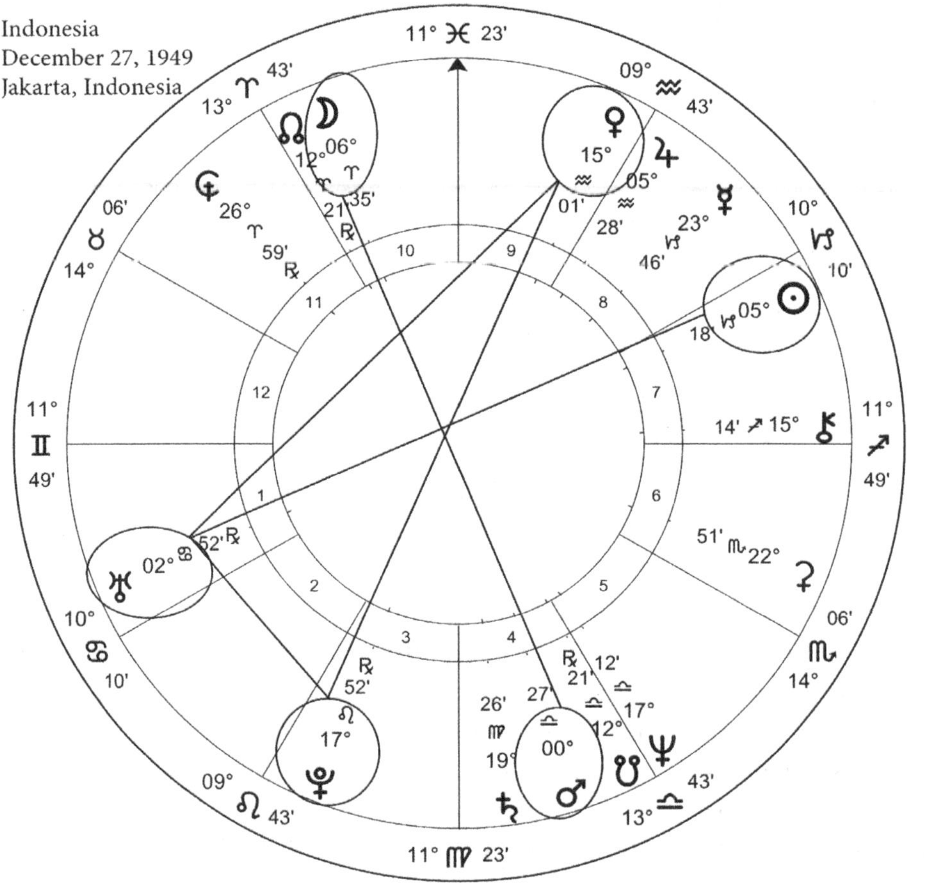

The Moon 6°35' Aries rules the second house of banks and currency through its rulership of Cancer, the sign on the cusp, or boundary, of the second house. The Moon opposes Mars 0°27' Libra, and they form a very stressful Grand Cross configuration with Uranus 2°52' Cancer opposing the Sun 5°18' Capricorn. This Grand Cross indicates the potential for sudden political upsets and military coups due to Mars in the fourth house of opposition to the country's leadership, and Mars indicates Indonesia's military through its association with Scorpio, the sign ruling the chart's sixth house of the armed forces. And although Mars rules Aries, the sign occupied by the Moon, the Moon is in the tenth house of the established leadership and government, which shows there would probably be a lot of shifting of the political winds.

Because Moon/Cancer rules the country's finances and currency, these are also under stress by this Grand Cross, indicating that political and economic instability are interwoven and often trigger one another.

Venus 15°01' Aquarius is in the eighth house of debt, opposing Pluto 17°52' Leo, a natural co-ruler of the eighth house; and she is trine (120° angle) Neptune 17°12' Libra in the fourth house. Venus in Aquarius is co-ruled by Uranus, which is in the first house of the general population and state of the country, whereas Taurus/Venus rules the twelfth house of illicit activity. While this configuration tying together the first and twelfth houses shows potential for corruption and related problems with debt and foreign currency reserves, Venus in a 135° angle to Uranus emphasizes the eighth house, which indicates that any corruption, carried too far, will inevitably lead to a purge at some point.

Chiron 15°14' Sagittarius is in the seventh house of foreign allies, investors, and also enemies. Chiron squares Saturn 19°26' Virgo; Saturn/Capricorn rules the eighth house of debt; and Jupiter 5°28' Aquarius, the ruler of the sign Sagittarius, is located in the eighth house. Foreign investors would have a difficult time with Indonesia's changing political situation under this configuration.

INDONESIA – Crony Capitalism

President Suharto came to power as president under the Uranus-Pluto conjunction of 1966. His predecessor, President Sukarno, had relied on his ability to bring together the Communist Party of Indonesia (PKI) and the army, but on October 1, 1965 six generals were murdered as part of an attempted coup, which General Suharto quickly put down (the official version of events claiming that the PKI was responsible for the coup). This weakened President Sukarno's position considerably, and led to Suharto becoming acting president in March 1967.[101]

The Uranus-Pluto conjunction of June 30, 1966 at 16°06' Virgo conjoined Indonesia's natal Saturn 19°26' Virgo in the fourth house of opposition to the established government. This conjunction was sesquiquadrate (135° angle) to natal Jupiter 5°28' Aquarius. As Pisces is on the cusp of the tenth house of leadership, Jupiter as co-ruler of Pisces denotes the leader of the country. With this harsh aspect coming from the fourth house of opposition, and from such an overwhelming pair as Uranus and Pluto, Sukarno's leadership was doomed.

During the early and mid-1990's, President Suharto promoted a system of crony capitalism (the natal Venus-Neptune-Pluto configuration) in which his family and associates had monopolies in lucrative businesses that were being established at the time—and he insisted that Indonesian banks finance these ventures.[102]

The Saturn-Uranus-Neptune triple conjunctions of 1988–1993 impacted Indonesia's chart, mainly by harsh angles to progressed Uranus 1°26' Cancer and natal Mars in Libra in 1988. At this time, transiting Mars, Saturn, and Uranus were tightly conjoined at 1° Capricorn. Due to Mercury's rulership of Gemini and Virgo, the signs of the Ascendant and fourth house cusp respectively, the trine (120° angle) of progressed Mercury 19°41' Capricorn to natal Saturn indicated that President Suharto's family, friends, and cronies would be the beneficiaries of most of the available investment capital.

---

101 https://en.wikipedia.org/wiki/History_of_Indonesia

102 http://www.wright.edu/~tdung/asiancrisis-hill.htm

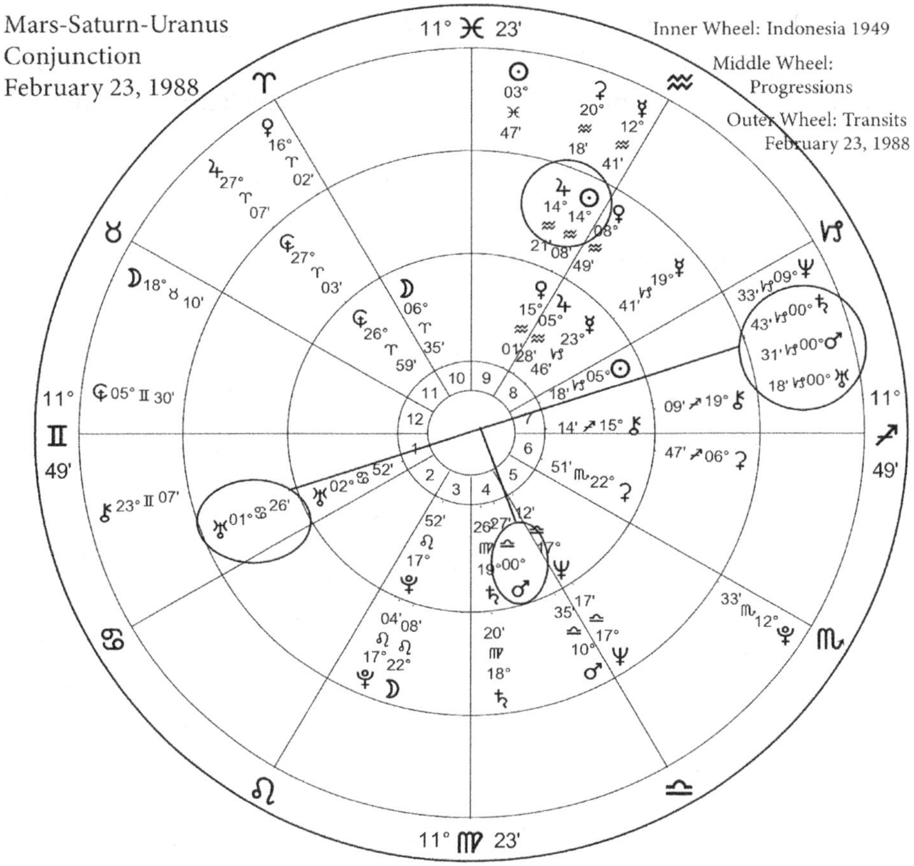

It was the period between 1988 and 1993 in which this crony capitalism flourished. In February 1988, transiting Mars, Saturn, and Uranus 1° Capricorn were semi-square (45° angle) progressed Sun and Jupiter 15° Aquarius. Although Suharto was able to profit immensely (Sun representing the leader, conjoining the ruler of the tenth house of government, Jupiter, which is also expansion and riches) by these arrangements, this corruption was not going unnoticed. By the time of the Uranus-Neptune conjunction at 19° Capricorn in 1993—exactly trine natal Saturn in Virgo—this funneling of money to a few cronies had reached its peak. The 1997 stellium in Aquarius, which conjoined natal Jupiter, signaled the peaking of the buildup of debt and Suharto's resignation under fire in 1998 for his handling of the financial crisis.

Through 1988 to 1997 Indonesia's situation seemed very good at first glance, which was due to progressed Jupiter conjunct natal Venus 15°–16° Aquarius in the ninth house, and progressed Venus conjunct natal Jupiter 5°–6° Aquarius in the eighth house. The country had amassed foreign exchange reserves of over $20 billion and had a healthy banking system, as shown by Venus/Jupiter in the eighth house; and it was running a trade surplus over $900 million, as shown by Venus/Jupiter in the ninth house.

Venus-Jupiter Configurations for Indonesia 1993

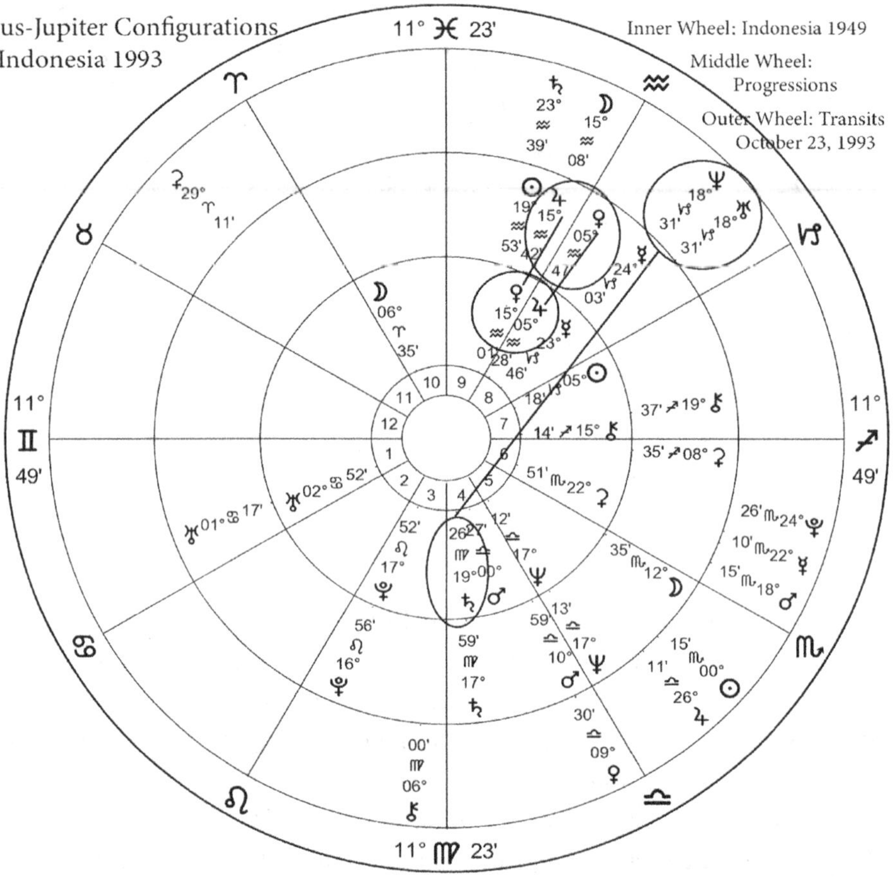

But these conjunctions also show Indonesia's weakness at that time: Both the public and private sectors had a lot of dollar-denominated debt, and these sectors were intertwined in the activities of Indonesia's crony capitalism (Taurus/ Venus rules the twelfth house; Jupiter is natural ruler of the twelfth). This was a favorable arrangement during the 1990's because of the favorable exchange rate. But these planets are in Aquarius, co-ruled by Saturn, and if these planets in Aquarius, or natal or progressed Saturn, suffer any affliction, so will the arrangement. Uranus is the other co-ruler of Aquarius, and it is part of the natal Grand Cross discussed above. If any planet in that configuration is triggered by transiting or progressed planets, the interweaving of corruption and debt will go sour.

So, with the February 1997 stellium planets in Aquarius conjunct natal Jupiter at 6° Aquarius and progressed Venus at 5° Aquarius in the eighth house, it triggered an upset to the precarious balance around the exchange rate.

Adding to the unstable currency conditions was the March 9 eclipse position of 19° Pisces opposing progressed Saturn 18° Virgo, the ruler of Indonesia's eighth house.

INDONESIA – Effect of Thai Baht Devaluation

Indonesia's currency, the rupiah, which was pegged to the dollar, had its trading band widened in July 1997 in response to Thailand's devaluation. This prompted speculators to begin trouncing the rupiah, and as a result it was allowed to float freely on August 14, 1997.

During July and August of 1997, transiting Saturn passed over 20°–21° Aries and went retrograde on August 2 while opposing progressed Neptune 17°10' Libra.

As with Thailand, transiting Neptune was passing through the eighth house; in Indonesia's case, it was conjunct progressed Mercury at 27°58' Capricorn. On August 13, the day before the rupiah's devaluation, they were exactly conjunct, and they squared transiting Chiron 27°56' Libra.

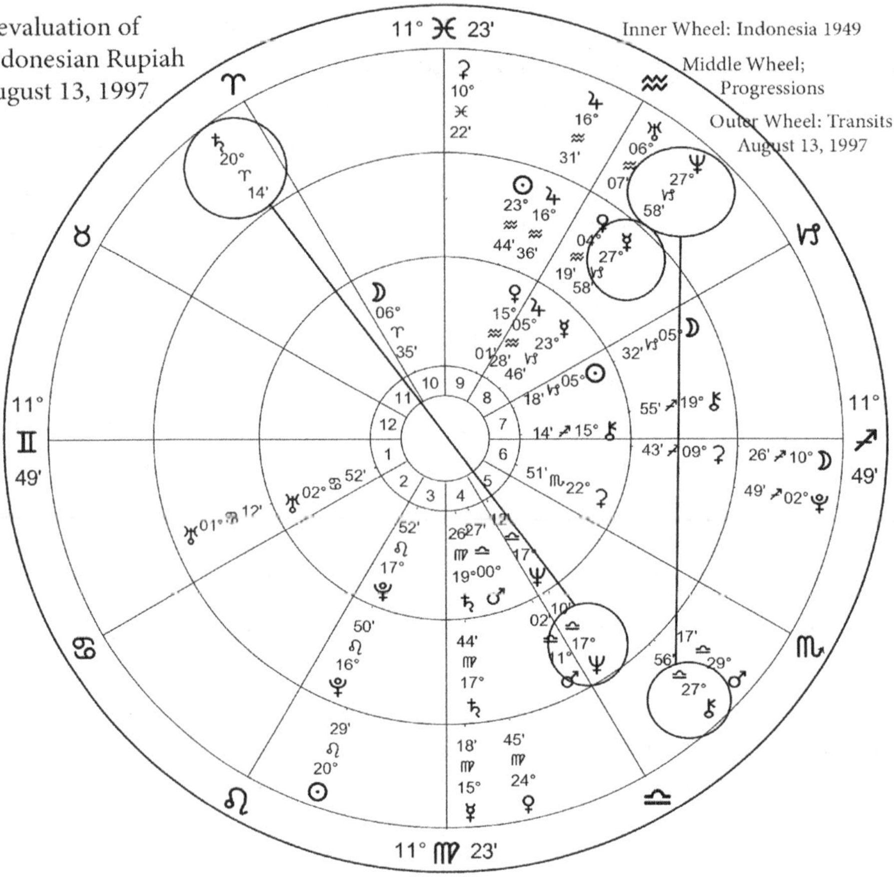

Devaluation of Indonesian Rupiah August 13, 1997

Inner Wheel: Indonesia 1949
Middle Wheel; Progressions
Outer Wheel: Transits August 13, 1997

Transiting Neptune conjunct progressed Mercury triggered the effect of Saturn because progressed Saturn in Virgo, ruled by Mercury, was in mutual reception with progressed Mercury in Capricorn, ruled by Saturn. Furthermore, the progressed Moon was at 5°32' Capricorn, conjunct the natal Sun, triggering the natal Grand Cross. All of these elements involving Saturn combined to result in an extreme drain of foreign currency reserves, as Capricorn/Saturn is the chart ruler of the eighth house of foreign reserves.

INDONESIA - Summary

The Saturn-Uranus-Neptune triple conjunctions of 1988–1993 were a major influence in the events of the late 1980's and 1990's for Indonesia—particularly the crony capitalism that was fostered by Present Suharto—due to the fact that they formed configurations with Indonesia's natal and progressed Saturn. Transiting Neptune moving through the eighth house of debt indicated that the debt edifice would collapse, which was the same influence that had been at work in Thailand's case.

The double Venus-Jupiter configurations (progressed Jupiter conjunct natal Venus, and progressed Venus conjunct natal Jupiter) were indicative of an economic buildup that was "too good to be true." The Aquarius stellium brought this situation to a head as it conjoined natal Jupiter and progressed Venus in the eighth house of debt.

Progressed Saturn played a role not only in the events leading to Indonesia's debt problem, but was also involved in triggering devaluation and economic collapse, as it was almost exactly opposed by the March 9, 1997 solar eclipse.

SOUTH KOREA – Stock Market Plunge of November 1997

The crisis accelerated across the region in November 1997, with South Korea's stock market plunging on November 7–8.

South Korea's chart is not examined in detail, but it is included here because the way it was affected by the March 9, 1997 solar eclipse illustrates an important timing technique.

That this time period would affect South Korea's stock market, and especially on November 7, was indicated by the *progressed Moon of the March 9 eclipse*, now at 29° Pisces. That progressed Moon was now within 1° of exact conjunction with the South Node's position at the time of the eclipse, and it was opposing the Mars-North Node conjunction of the eclipse chart.

The 29° Pisces point falls in South Korea's fifth house of speculation and the stock market. On November 7–8, transiting Mars at 28° Sagittarius opposing South Korea's natal Uranus at 29° Gemini formed a Grand Cross with the eclipse progressed Moon opposing the eclipse chart's Mars-North Node, which triggered South Korea's stock market meltdown.

South Korea
Stock Market Crash
November 7, 1997

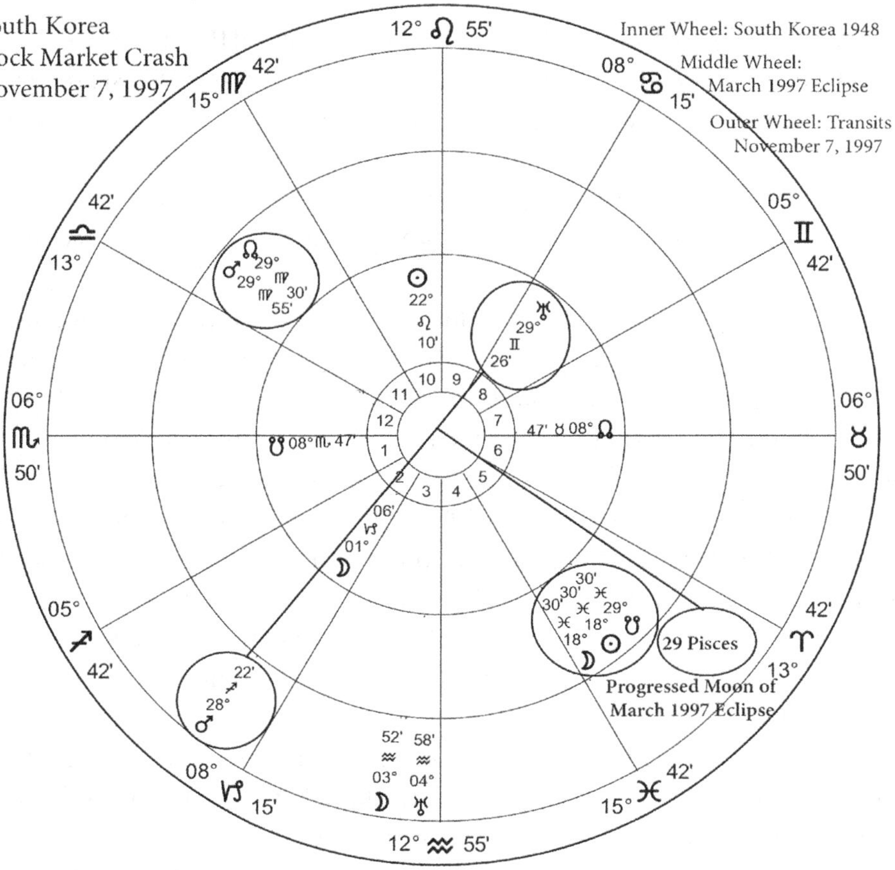

CHINA – Effect of Thai Baht Devaluation

China did not fare so badly in 1997 and 1998 because it had the means to shore up its currency—probably with some hidden resources, as transiting Neptune was in China's twelfth house, conjunct progressed Jupiter at 28° Capricorn. (Jupiter-Neptune-Pisces rules the second house in China's chart, which is analyzed in Chapter 5.) Also, transiting Jupiter in Aquarius was forming a trine (120° angle) to the natal planets in Libra in the eighth house, offering protection to the currency.

In October 1997, this conjunction formed a T-square with China's progressed Moon at 29° Libra in the ninth house of international commerce, opposing natal Hades 28° Aries, indicating that foreigners were willing to extend a hidden helping hand because they had so much at stake: Foreign-held assets in China at that time were in the form of factories and could not be easily liquidated.[103]

In China's chart, the February 1997 stellium planets conjoined the natal Moon at 3°03' Aquarius and the natal Ascendant at 1°44' Aquarius, with all forming a trine to the natal Sun 7°46' Libra. As Jupiter was part of the stellium, its trine to the natal Sun helped to avert disaster through successful negotiations with foreign allies (Leo/Sun rules natal Mars and Pluto in the seventh house of alliances).

China maintained their currency peg to the US dollar, which protected their currency, although their economic growth slowed. That China was taking on more debt to get through the crisis could be seen by transiting Jupiter, which due to its retrograde and then direct motion was in the range of 16°–23° Aquarius squaring progressed Mercury 23° Scorpio, ruler of the eighth house (and also squaring natal Venus 19°26' Scorpio), from April to August 1997, and again from November 1997 to January 1998.

103 https://en.wikipedia.org/wiki/1997_Asian_financial_crisis

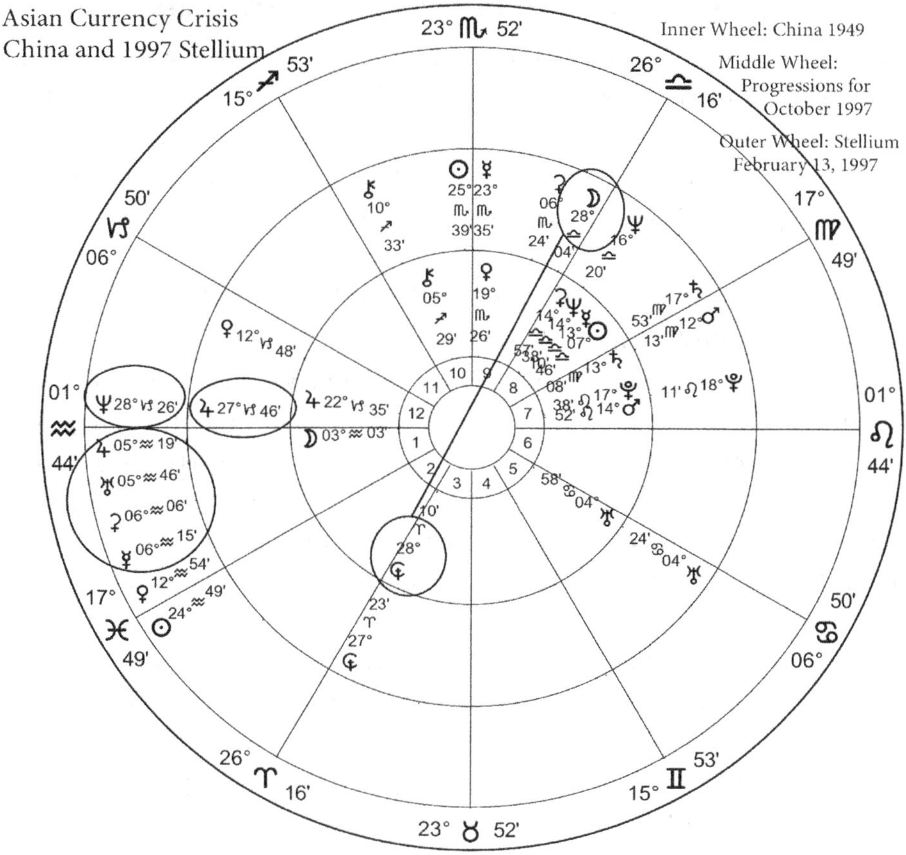

Another indication that China would continue to amass debt—yet remain unscathed at the time— was the transiting North Node 18° Virgo, conjoining progressed Saturn and the cusp (boundary) of the eighth house. This gave China some measure of control over their debt situation, and also meant that they felt confident to take on more.

Although China's problem of massive debt was exposed at this time, it has not been addressed seriously enough since then, and later chapters will examine how this pattern of piling on debt is approaching the breaking point for China.

RUSSIA – Potential for Financial Problems

The current state of Russia evolved from the meltdown of the Soviet Union in the late 1980's, so there are two natal charts to examine: The chart for the Soviet Union, which is considered as beginning with the Bolshevik revolution of 1917; and the chart for the current state of Russia, which is considered as having been established upon Gorbachev's resignation in 1991.

1917 Bolshevik Revolution Chart for the Soviet Union

The November 8, 1917 natal chart has Libra on the cusp of the second house, so Venus is especially strong in her rulership of the country's finance and currency. Venus 0°50' Capricorn in the fourth house of real estate and mines, opposes Pluto 5°19' Cancer; because Pluto rules the extraction of oil, this configuration definitely shows that the petroleum industry would become the major engine of the nation's economy. Venus in Capricorn has Saturn as her ruler, so Saturn 14°13' Leo conjunct Neptune 7°06' Leo also points to oil (Neptune rules oil) as being important for the nation's survival.

Venus is trine Mars 2°58' Virgo, so the rulers of the chart's second and eighth houses, both important to the nation's finances, are in a beneficial relationship; and they are in Earth signs, which are associated with material prosperity and security. But Mars in Virgo has Mercury as his ruler, and Mercury 17°35' Scorpio is squaring Uranus 19°49' Aquarius. As Mercury rules the Ascendant 14°10' Virgo and the Midheaven 6°26' Gemini, the two most sensitive positions of any chart, its square to Uranus indicates boom and bust periods. In addition, with Mercury also squaring Saturn in Leo it affects Venus, and thus the stability and continued viability of the economy and the financial system.

Russian Revolution
November 8, 1917
Leningrad, Russia

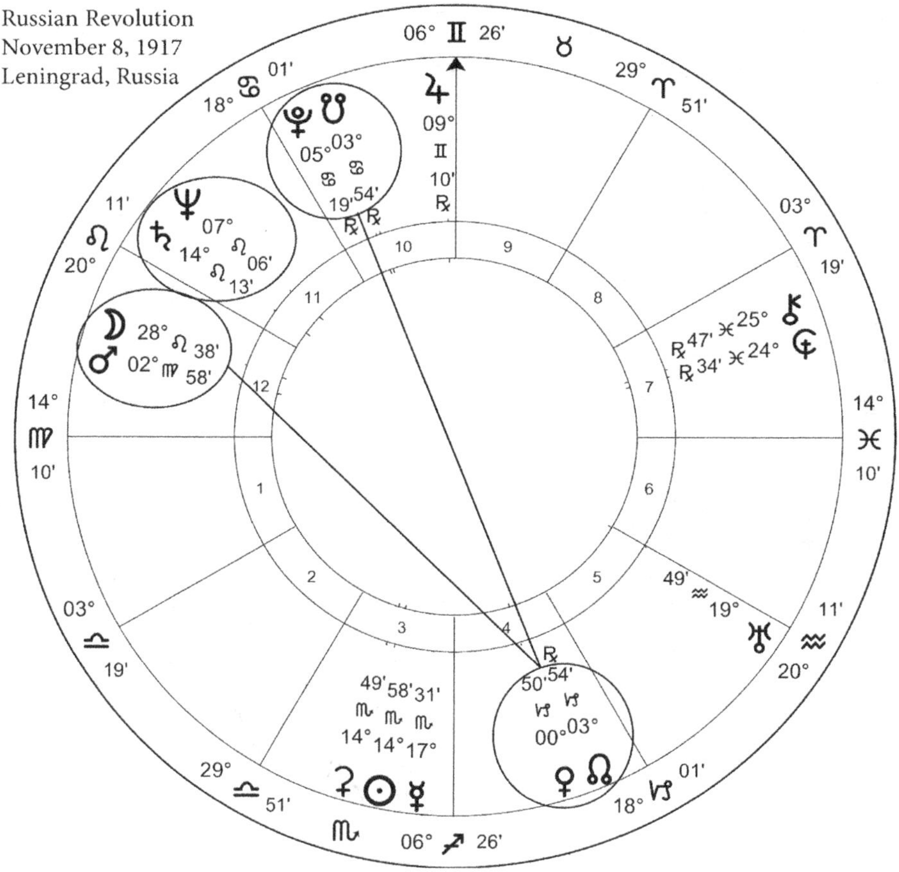

With the Moon conjunct Mars in the twelfth house of hidden problems and corruption in the 1917 natal chart, and Aries (ruled by Mars) on the cusp of the eighth house of debt and foreign reserves, there was potential for ongoing, unresolved problems concerning how large of a portion of the national budget would go toward national security.

1991 Chart for Russia

The December 25, 1991 natal chart for Russia also shows that oil is foundational to the country's economy. Venus conjoins Pluto 22°–23° Scorpio in the fourth house, indicating again how the extraction of oil drives the economy. This is reinforced by Mercury 11°27' Sagittarius ruling the second house of finances by its rulership of the sign Virgo in mutual reception with Jupiter 14°35' Virgo in the second house, which also shows a dependence on oil.

Modern Russia
December 25, 1991
Moscow, Russia

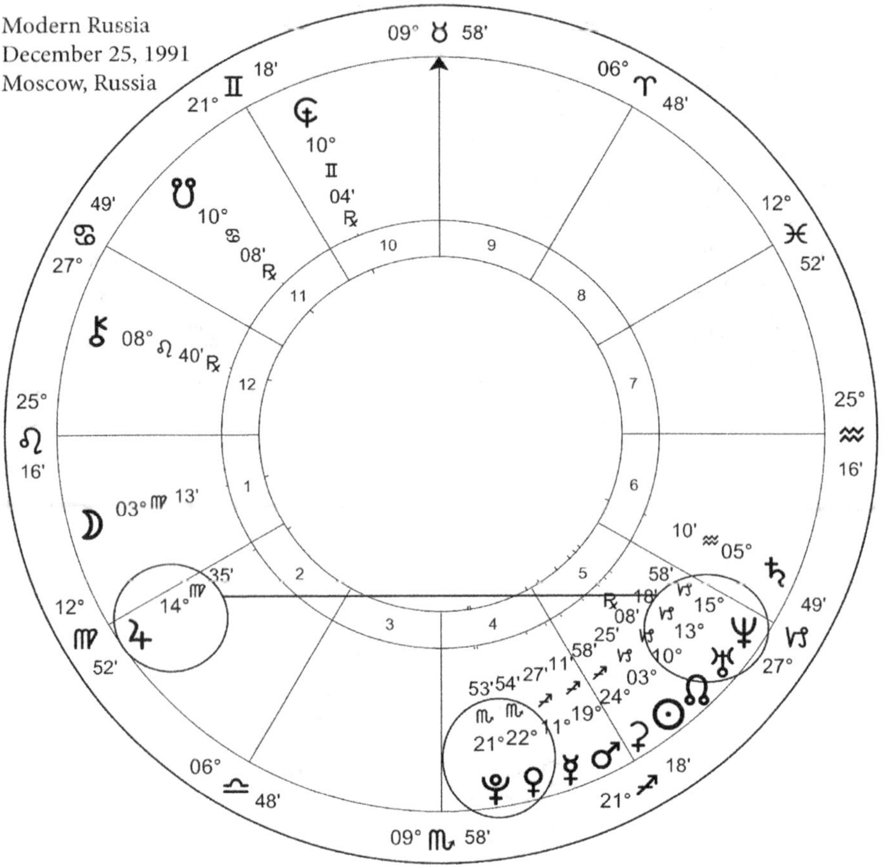

Pisces rules the eighth house of debt and foreign reserves. Jupiter 14°35' Virgo and Neptune 15°58' Capricorn, the co-rulers of Pisces, are forming a trine (120° angle), which indicates that profits from oil keep the boat afloat, even during times of sudden upsets, due to Uranus conjoining Neptune. This configuration also shows that foreign sanctions have an impact on the country, although it does manage to pull through.

SOVIET UNION – Dissolution of the Union of Soviet Socialist Republics

The natal chart for the 1917 Bolshevik Revolution was dramatically impacted by both the Uranus-Pluto conjunction of 1966 and the Saturn-Uranus-Neptune triple conjunctions of 1988–1993. Only the latter will be analyzed here, but note that the Uranus-Pluto conjunction in 1966 at 16°06' Virgo was conjunct the Soviet Union's Ascendant, the most sensitive point in the chart, at 14°10' Virgo. This Uranus-Pluto cycle affects the Russian people until the next Uranus-Pluto conjunction in April 2104 at 7°35' Taurus.

In 1988, satellite members of the Soviet Union began to seriously press for independence. On February 20, 1988, the Regional Soviet of Azerbaijan voted to secede from the Soviet Union and merge with Armenia; between February 20 and 25 there were large protests in Azerbaijan and Armenia, and the protests turned violent in Azerbaijan.[104]

Estonia and Latvia also began serious efforts to secede from the Soviet Union after Gorbachev replaced their Communist Party leaders during the spring and early summer of 1988. On November 16, 1988, the Supreme Soviet in Estonia declared national sovereignty and made laws of the Soviet Union subordinate to Estonian law.[105]

It was during 1988 that the Mars-Saturn-Uranus conjunction at 1° Capricorn strongly impacted Russia's 1917 natal chart, with this conjunction occurring on February 23, 1988 at the time of the protests in Azerbaijan and Armenia. These planets conjoined natal Venus and the progressed North Node at 1° Capricorn, in the fourth house of opposition to the ruling government. All were opposing natal Pluto 5°19' Cancer, and this opposition formed a T-square with progressed Mars 1°17' Libra, indicating strength and determination behind the efforts to secede.

But this was just the beginning of secessionist movements throughout the Soviet satellite republics, which spread through Ukraine, Belarus, Uzbekistan, and Kazakhstan.[106] That the movement to dissolve the Soviet Union would accelerate in 1989 was indicated by transiting Jupiter in early Cancer, conjunct natal Pluto and opposing transiting Uranus, which was back at 1° Capricorn because of retrograde motion.

---

104 https://en.wikipedia.org/wiki/Dissolution_of_the_Soviet_Union

105 Ibid.

106 Ibid.

Mars-Saturn-Uranus
Conjunction
February 23, 1988

Inner Wheel:
Russian Revolution 1917
Middle Wheel:
Progressions
Outer Wheel: Transits
February 23, 1988

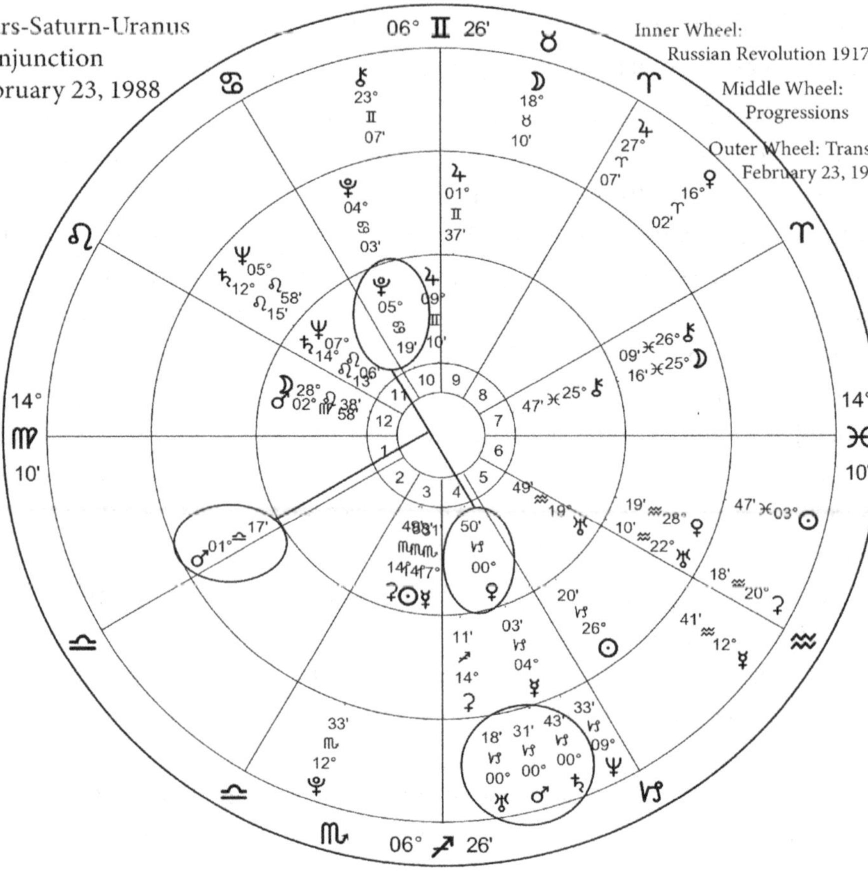

By the time the Soviet Union was officially dissolved in late December 1991, transiting Jupiter 14°35' Virgo had just passed over the Ascendant of the 1917 chart, as it was trine (120° angle) transiting Uranus and Neptune 14°–16° Capricorn—indicating victory for those advocating a new foundation (Jupiter rules the fourth house) for the country.

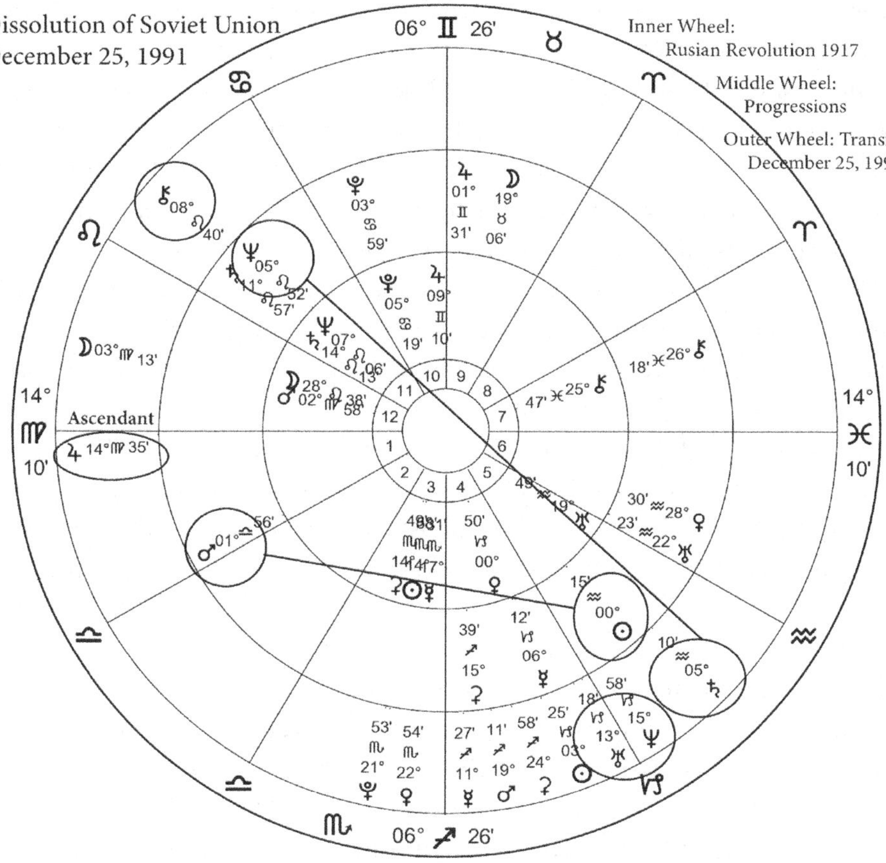

Dissolution of Soviet Union
December 25, 1991

Inner Wheel:
Rusian Revolution 1917
Middle Wheel:
Progressions
Outer Wheel: Transits
December 25, 1991

Transiting Saturn 5°10' Aquarius was opposing progressed Neptune and transiting Chiron in Leo. With the ruler of the sign of Leo being the Sun, and that the progressed Sun 0°15' Aquarius was trine progressed Mars in Libra, these configurations signaled that corruption and rule by elite interests was not going away—in fact, it would become more rampant and insidious, as Leo rules the twelfth house of corruption and hidden influences.

RUSSIA – 1998 Drain of Foreign Reserves and Ruble Devaluation

The following analysis uses only the 1991 natal chart for Russia.

It was not until 1998 that the Russian ruble, as well as Russian stocks and bonds, began to collapse. In late November and December 1997, configurations involving Jupiter and Neptune indicated a drain of foreign reserves (with Pisces on the cusp of the eighth house of foreign reserves, Jupiter and Neptune are the co-rulers of that house). The transiting North Node in Virgo was conjoining natal Jupiter 14°35' Virgo in the second house of the currency,[107] and transiting Neptune 29° Capricorn was semi-square natal Mercury 11°27' Sagittarius (Mercury, as ruler of Virgo, rules the second house of this chart). At the same time, the progressed Moon had moved to conjoin natal Venus and Pluto 22°–23° Scorpio, the two planets naturally associated with currency and debt issues. This configuration with the progressed Moon indicated Russia would burn through a massive amount of foreign reserves to maintain the ruble's peg to the US dollar from January through August 1998.

On August 17, 1998, Russia widened the trading band for the ruble against the dollar. On September 2, Russia abandoned the currency trading band and allowed the ruble to float freely. On August 16, one day before Russia widened the trading band, transiting Saturn went retrograde at 3°37' Taurus. In the 1991 natal chart, it had formed a T-square to transiting Neptune 0°07' Aquarius conjunct natal/progressed Saturn 5° Aquarius (and conjunct the position of the February 13, 1997 stellium), opposing transiting Venus at 5° Leo.

The progressed Moon and progressed Venus were now conjoined in the fourth house at 0°53' Sagittarius (Sagittarius is ruled by Jupiter), and transiting Jupiter, co-ruler of the eighth house, was now moving through the eighth house.

The progressed Venus-Moon configuration ruled by Jupiter was a key to Russia's ability (and luck) in rebounding quickly: Oil prices rose in 1999 and 2000. But it also shows that Russia burned through much of its foreign currency reserves to maintain the dollar peg in the first part of 1998, as the progressed Moon moved away from conjoining natal Venus-Pluto and toward progressed Venus.

---

107 Jupiter was retrograde by progression, and had returned to its natal position in December 1997, so that progressed Jupiter was exactly conjunct natal Jupiter, in the second house of finance and currency.

Collapse of Russian Ruble
August 17, 1998

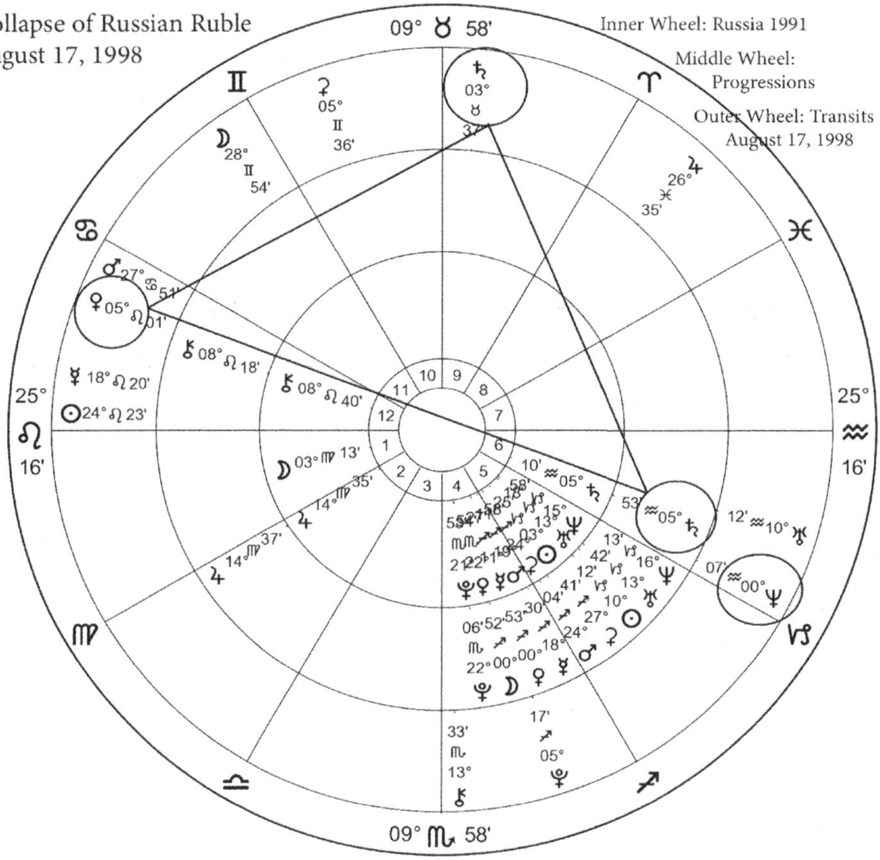

RUSSIA – Summary

The Saturn-Uranus-Neptune triple conjunctions of 1988–1993 are crucial to the 1991 chart for modern Russia, for that "new" state came into being under their influence. Thus, the Uranus-Neptune conjunction in that natal chart will usually have some part in significant events for the country.

Transiting Neptune in 1997–1998 made a harsh angle to natal Mercury, the ruler of Russia's second house of the currency. As Pisces is on the cusp of the eighth house, Neptune rules the eighth house of debt and foreign reserves; with the rulers of the second and eighth houses in a stressful angle, problems with the exchange rate for the ruble were indicated, which would probably result in a drain of foreign reserves. As transiting Neptune moved into Aquarius and conjoined natal Saturn, the situation came to a head.

Progressed Venus played a big role in timing the drain of foreign reserves to maintain the ruble's peg to the dollar in 1998. She was in Sagittarius at the time, a sign ruled by Jupiter, so a combination of Venus-Jupiter was at work for Russia just as in the chart for Indonesia.

★ ★ ★

Overall Astrological Conditions Associated with Debt Buildup and Political/Financial Upheaval

The following conditions involve only transiting planets, and could apply to the global financial system or a regional system.

Astrological conditions indicating buildup of debt:

- Saturn-Pluto and Chiron-Pluto cycles coincide.

Astrological conditions indicating political upheaval and erosion of established structures:

- Saturn-Uranus-Neptune conjunction.
- Mars-Saturn-Uranus conjunction.

Astrological conditions indicating severe financial crisis:

- Saturn-Pluto and Chiron-Pluto cycles coincide.
- Uranus, Jupiter, and Ceres as part of a stellium, in the sign of Aquarius (or a sign where Saturn is dignified).

THAILAND – Astrological Conditions of Debt Buildup and Currency Devaluation

From the above analysis, the following astrological conditions for Thailand's chart were associated with *debt buildup:*

- Transiting Jupiter-Neptune conjunction in the eighth house, conjoining the progressed ruler of the eighth house (in this case, Saturn): This is an indicator of financial excess.
- Progressed Jupiter inconjunct (150° angle) the natal ruler of the eighth house, with one of these planets located in the eighth house: This indicated debt reaching unsustainable levels.

The following astrological conditions for Thailand's chart were associated with *a drain of foreign reserves and the necessity of a currency devaluation:*

- Transiting Neptune moving through the eighth house, conjoining the progressed ruler of the eighth house of debt (in this case, Saturn): This indicated a coming drain of foreign currency reserves.
- A stellium either occurring in the eighth house, or conjoining the ruler of the eighth house (for Thailand, it was both), with transiting Venus opposing the stellium position acting as a trigger for devaluation: This indicated the coming drain of foreign reserves.
- Progressed Mars conjunct natal Venus in the second house of currency, with a conjunction by the progressed Moon triggering a severe devaluation.

INDONESIA – Astrological Conditions of Debt Buildup and Currency Devaluation

From the above analysis, the following astrological conditions for Indonesia's chart were associated with *debt buildup:*

- A configuration combining Venus and Jupiter that affects the eighth house of debt: For Indonesia, this was a double configuration of progressed Venus conjunct natal Jupiter (in the eighth house), along with progressed Jupiter conjunct natal Venus (in the ninth house); this indicated buildup of debt, but also a buildup of foreign reserves, which unfortunately was not enough to maintain the currency's peg to the US dollar.

The following astrological conditions for Indonesia's chart were associated with *a drain of foreign reserves and the necessity of a currency devaluation:*

- Transiting Neptune moving through the eighth house of debt and foreign reserves, conjoining a natal planet which is in mutual reception with the natal planet ruling the eighth house (in this case, Saturn): This indicated a coming drain of foreign currency reserves.
- A stellium occurring in the eighth house and conjoining a natal planet and progressed Venus in the eighth house, with transiting Venus opposing the stellium position acting as a trigger for devaluation.
- The position of a solar eclipse opposing the progressed ruler of the eighth house, (in this case, Saturn): This also indicated a coming drain of foreign reserves.

RUSSIA – Astrological Conditions of Drain of Foreign Reserves and Currency Devaluation

From the above analysis, the following astrological conditions for Russia's 1991 chart were associated with *a drain of foreign reserves and the necessity of a currency devaluation:*

- Ruler of the eighth house of foreign reserves (or both co-rulers, as in this case, Jupiter and Neptune) in a harsh aspect with the ruler of the second house of currency (in this case, Mercury): This indicated that a severe drain of foreign reserves was on the horizon.
- Transiting Neptune conjunct natal and/or progressed Saturn, with transiting Saturn opposing them while at its retrograde station position acting as a trigger for devaluation: This indicated a coming drain of foreign currency reserves.
- A stellium conjoining natal or progressed Saturn, with transiting Venus opposing the stellium position acting as a trigger for devaluation: This indicated the coming drain of foreign reserves.
- Progressed Moon moving from conjoining a natal Venus-Pluto conjunction in Scorpio (the sign naturally associated with the eighth house and foreign reserves) to conjoining progressed Venus, now in Sagittarius, with Jupiter, ruler of Sagittarius, as ruler of the eighth house: This timed the period of the drain of foreign reserves to maintain the ruble's peg to the dollar.

CONCLUSIONS

The general time frame in which a financial crisis is likely to happen can be determined by configurations formed by transiting planets alone. However, in order to know which countries will be the source of the crisis—or will be most affected by it—*and* to closely pinpoint the time of the crisis, configurations forming with natal or progressed planets in a country's chart must be considered.

Transiting Configurations

The coinciding of the Saturn-Pluto and Chiron-Pluto cycles is of major importance for determining a general time frame for financial crises.

A Jupiter-Uranus conjunction occurring in Aquarius, especially when there is also a stellium in the same sign, indicates a sudden, severe problem in the financial system.

Specific Country Chart Configurations

As with all of the separate analyses in this work, a country's natal chart *must* show the potential for financial crisis. Those that do are most likely to be those that suffer the most in a global crisis.

Natal Venus conjunct progressed Mars in a nation's chart has a high probability of affecting the nation's currency or triggering a finance-related event—especially when in the second house, or in hard aspect with the ruler of the second house (natal or progressed).

Natal or progressed Venus conjunct natal or progressed Jupiter in a nation's chart leads to financial excess, especially to excessive debt when the eighth house, or the chart ruler of the eighth house, is involved in some way. This seems to be a configuration of too easy access to credit in some cases.

Within a nation's chart, aspects to the *progressed* ruler of the eighth house are extremely important. Transiting Neptune making an aspect to this progressed planet will especially weaken the country's position in a financial crisis.

Transiting Neptune conjunct or opposing natal or progressed Saturn will weaken the country's position in a financial crisis.

Transiting Neptune conjunct transiting Jupiter in the eighth house, with both conjunct the progressed ruler of the eighth house, leads to financial excess.

Transiting Uranus conjunct natal Jupiter, especially if Uranus is part of a stellium in the same sign, can lead to a sudden, dramatic financial event as a climax to a situation that had been worsening for years.

A configuration centered on a **natal Venus-Pluto conjunction** can indicate problems related to the currency and foreign reserves.

An eclipse, especially a solar eclipse, can trigger extreme financial events when it interacts with a natal or progressed planet. If the progressed planet has some link to the eighth house, the probability is increased.

CHAPTER 5

Analysis of China's Chart and Recent Financial Events

Before looking ahead at 2019 and beyond for China, it would be helpful to see how astrological configurations already identified in previous chapters were repeating for China during the 2015 devaluation of the yuan, as well as during the buildup of debt and the trade surplus in 2017.

CHINA – Potential for Financial Problems

The chart for the moment that the formation of the People's Republic of China was announced publicly shows potential for a drastic transformation of China's financial system at some point.

The main indicator of such a transformation is the Mars-Pluto conjunction in Leo, in the seventh house of foreign allies, competitors, and enemies. Mars and Pluto are the natural co-rulers of the sign of Scorpio, which is always associated with eighth house matters of foreign reserves, debt, foreign exchange rates, and interest rates, regardless of what sign is on the cusp of the eighth house of a nation's chart.

Uranus 4°58' Cancer is in China's fifth house of speculative markets, and this planet has potential to bring its sudden and unexpected moves to China's stock market.

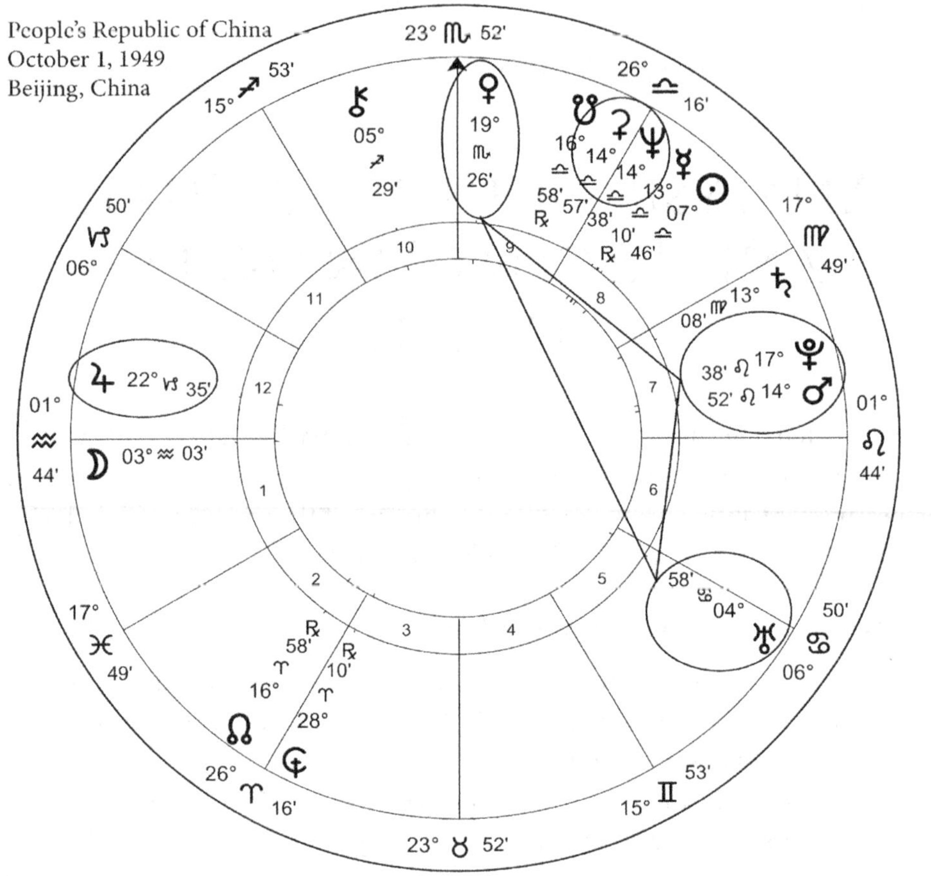

Furthermore, Uranus in Cancer is semi-square (45° angle) Pluto 17°38' Leo. The semi-square aspect is a harsh aspect, and as it is a separating aspect,[108] it has a second house influence. So, when triggered, this aspect in China's chart will impact the country's economy, financial system, and currency. This configuration will be triggered by transiting planets in late December 2018, when levels of corporate debt could affect the Chinese economy, and again in late December 2019, when the Chinese Communist Party's leadership may be affected by popular revolt.

108 All aspects (angles between planets within the zodiacal circle) have an "applying" or "separating" influence, based upon whether the faster moving planet is moving toward making the exact aspect with the slower moving planet, or moving away from the exact aspect. This technique gives houses (areas of life) through which the aspect will express itself.

Cancer is ruled by the Moon; therefore with China's Moon 3°03' Aquarius (in the sign co-ruled by Uranus), Uranus and the Moon are in mutual reception for China. The implications of the Uranus-Pluto semi-square have an enormous impact on the common people. Ruthless purges for the sake of enforcing an alternative financial system ideology have brought much suffering to the average person in China, which was definitely the case when transiting Uranus moved to conjunct transiting Pluto in 1966 at the time of Mao's Cultural Revolution. The conjunction at 16°06' Virgo conjoining China's natal Saturn 13°08' Virgo, near the cusp of the eighth house of transformation, indicated a major shift that would place severe restrictions on the population and have ugly consequences.

In the case of Latin America in the 1960's, the start of the new Uranus-Pluto cycle manifested for those countries as a shift in how they received funding, moving from loans from international development organizations to loans from private investment banks. But as noted above, in China the new cycle manifested as the Cultural Revolution, which was Mao's attempt to purge any remaining "capitalists" from society while reasserting and consolidating his own political power[109] (the heavy-handed force of Uranus-Pluto was applied to what was deemed a "backward" economic ideology). Transiting Uranus and Pluto first conjoining Saturn, and then moving into the eighth house, definitely indicated a major purge involving elements of the past that would ultimately damage the economy.

The natal Uranus-Pluto semi-square aspect forms a 45°–90°–135° triangle with Venus 19°28' Scorpio. This reinforces the interpretation of dramatic transformation that could involve the country's currency, as Venus is the natural ruler of finance and currencies. In addition, Venus is sesquiquadrate (135° angle) Uranus, an indication of volatile circumstances set in motion by impatience or irritation.

Venus squares Pluto, another indication of potential problems with China's economy and financial system, probably through issues with debt, foreign exchange rates, and/or foreign interest rates due to Pluto's connection with the eighth house.

China's second house of the economy, finance, and the currency is ruled by Pisces, so Jupiter and Neptune, the co-rulers of Pisces, will influence this area of the chart. Neptune 14°38' Libra is conjunct Ceres 14°57' Libra and Mercury

109 https://en.wikipedia.org/wiki/Cultural_Revolution

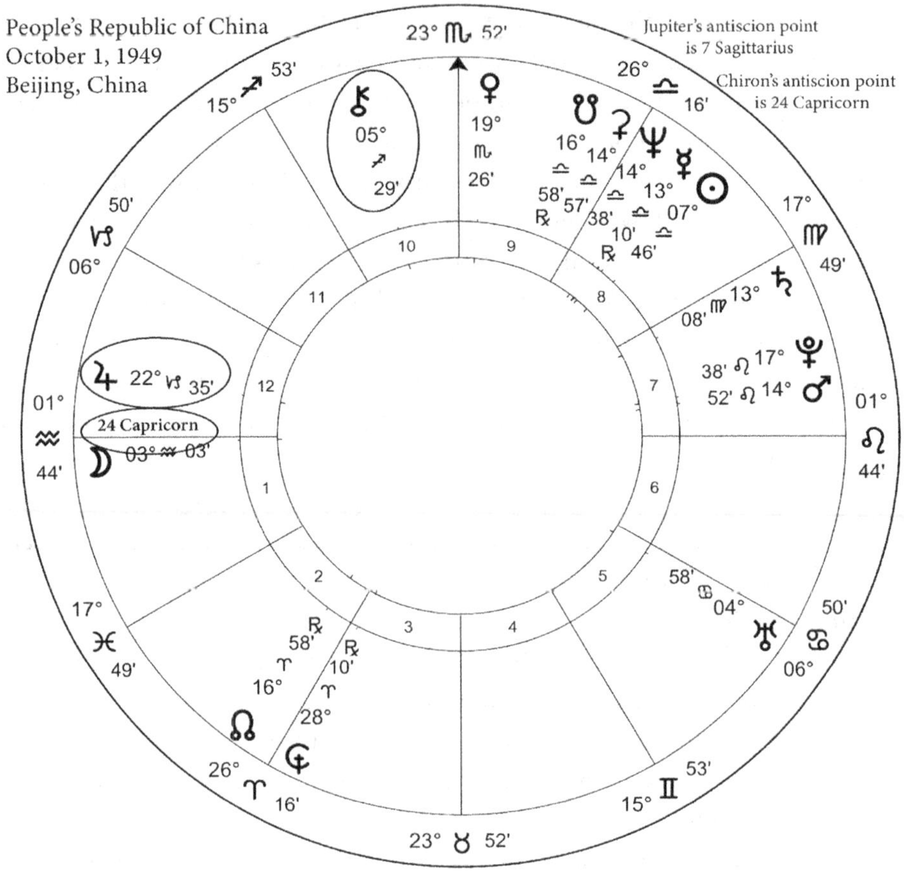

13°10' Libra in the eighth house, indicating that China's currency will be particularly sensitive to any developments affecting foreign exchange rates—and points to why China is often accused of manipulating their currency to their own economic advantage.

Jupiter 22°35' Capricorn is in the twelfth house, which is naturally ruled by Pisces/Neptune, accentuating the interpretation of Neptune given above. This is also confirmation that China does indeed manipulate their currency, although it backfires sometimes.

Jupiter is sextile (60° angle) Venus, indicating that China's economy and financial system has powerful support from foreign allies and competitors (due to Venus in the ninth house of international commerce), and Venus in Scorpio is ruled by Mars and Pluto, which reside in the seventh house of foreign allies and foes. China's economy is heavily interwoven with other countries' economies to the extent that China has to be respected as a major player, but it also indicates that China is very subject to what major competitors expect from her—with any tensions between China's actions and foreign expectations putting China at more risk than others.

China's natal Chiron 5°29' Sagittarius is semi-square Jupiter. Sagittarius/Jupiter rules the eleventh house of political parties in this chart, and because there is truly only one political party in China, Jupiter and the eleventh house represent the Chinese Communist Party (CCP).

With Jupiter in the twelfth house and ruling the eleventh house, the CCP is very sensitive to any dissent coming from the labor force. The twelfth house position is indicative of labor revolts because it is opposite the sixth house. In the older texts on astrology, the sixth house is said to rule servants and slaves,

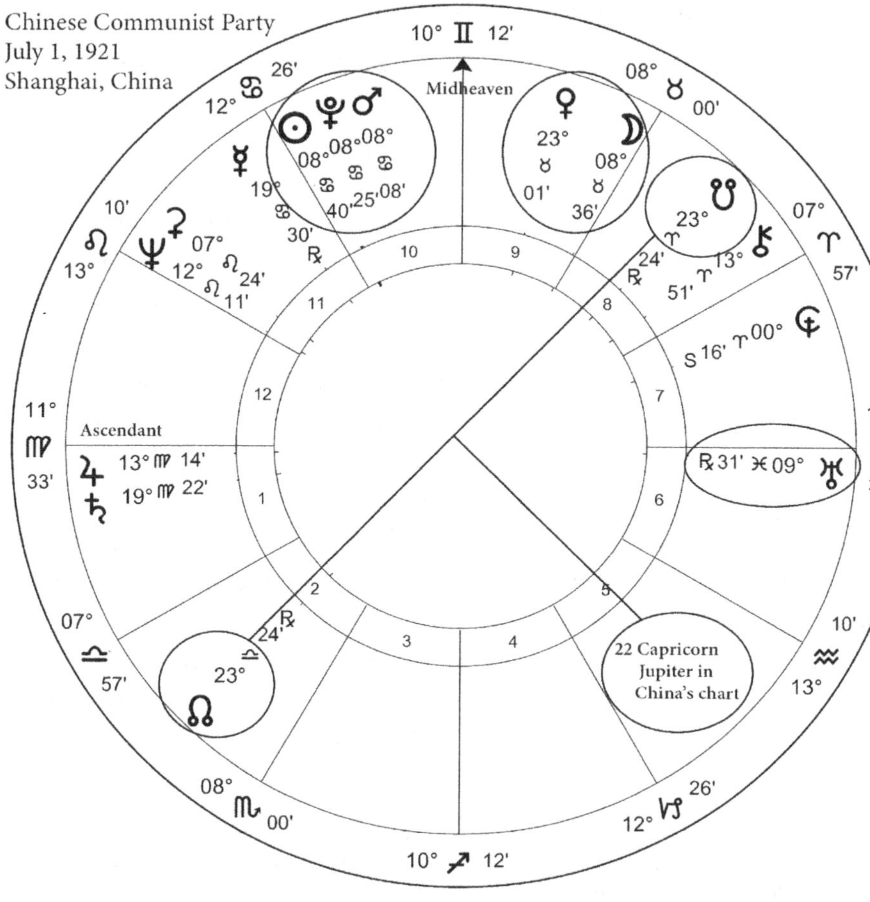

whereas the twelfth house rules "slave revolts." And because in the modern world the sixth house is associated with the labor force of a nation, in modern parlance the twelfth house has to do with strikes or revolts by the laborers, or the common people, who are still viewed pretty much as slaves by the ruling classes—especially in a dictatorship.

But this sensitivity to popular dissent and protest is made even stronger by the fact that the antiscion[110] of natal Chiron, at 24°31' Capricorn, is in close orb of natal Jupiter 22°35' Capricorn—and in the twelfth house, no less. With the Chinese Communist Party having a deeply ingrained fear of labor revolts, and Jupiter also ruling the economy in China's chart, maintaining a certain level of economic prosperity is considered essential by the CCP to control the masses.

Chinese Communist Party – Potential for Rigid Domination of Chinese Society

July 1, 1921 is the officially recognized founding date of the Chinese Communist Party.[111] This was the day of the opening session of the First National Congress of the Party in Shanghai, China. (See chart on page 133.)

The CCP chart has Sun, Mars, and Pluto conjunct at 9° Cancer, in the tenth house of status and government. The CCP is fiercely focused on their own security—which they equate with national security—and this triple conjunction also shows a sense of having the right to dominate, and even interfere, in people's most private lives. Aries/Mars rules the eighth house of foreign investment, foreign currency reserves, death, and transformation. With Mars conjoining the Sun and Pluto, the CCP sees no problem with using ruthless tactics to maintain their position of power. But this configuration also indicates that too tight of control of the financial system could backfire at times.

The Midheaven is 10°12' Gemini;[112] Mercury 19°30' Cancer sits on the antiscion point of the Midheaven. This reinforces the indications of the Party's tight control over Chinese society.

The Sun, Mars, and Pluto in Cancer are ruled by the Moon, which is in Taurus. This is a good setup for prosperity, especially as Venus 23°01' Taurus rules the sign Taurus. Also, the position of Venus in the CCP chart is trine (120°

110 See the Glossary.

111 *China Today,* The Communist Party of China, http://www.chinatoday.com/org/cpc/

112 This Midheaven degree is for the assumed time of 10:00 am; the actual time that the Party conference convened is unknown.

angle) the position of Jupiter 22°35' Capricorn in China's chart.

However, China's Jupiter 22°35' Capricorn forms a T-square with the CCP's Nodes 23°24' Libra/Aries. The ambitions of the Party can be detrimental to China's economy, especially through the currency (Jupiter rules the second house of the currency in China's chart). And with the CCP Venus 23°01' Taurus conjunct the cusp of China's fourth house, and inconjunct (150° angle) the CCP North Node in Libra, any imbalance in property rights and values could adversely affect China's economy.

Uranus 9°31' Pisces is trine (120° angle) the Sun-Mars-Pluto conjunction, and opposes (180° angle) Jupiter 13°14' Virgo. Uranus in Pisces indicates a conscious motive to redirect religious and spiritual devotion into Party allegiance; but with Uranus inconjunct (150° angle) Neptune 12°11' Leo, this effort eventually fails, due to coercive methods that alienate the people.

This trine of Uranus to Sun-Mars-Pluto also indicates the CCP's obsession with controlling the masses by providing economic conditions conducive to full employment, as Uranus is the co-ruler of the sixth house of the labor force.

The Jupiter-Saturn conjunction in Virgo shows that the CCP views the laboring classes as "opponents," as subjects to be controlled (Uranus opposing Jupiter), despite their outward claim that the Party was formed to favor the interests of the proletariat. Thus, Jupiter in both charts (China and CCP) indicates the Party's fear of protests by the labor force.

CHINA – Currency Devaluation in 2015

China's attempt to wean the yuan off its US dollar peg by a devaluation on August 11, 2015 caused global markets to swoon as China tried to stem excessive capital flight from the country. Attempts to rein in the overheated property market were then abandoned, as property speculation was allowed to rage again and interest rates were cut four times.[113]

China was depleting its foreign reserves in 2015 in order to maintain the yuan's peg to the US dollar. On December 12, 2015 China removed the peg to the dollar to relieve pressure on the economy as capital flight accelerated again due to expectations of the US Federal Reserve raising interest rates. The yuan is now pegged to a basket of currencies (which includes the US dollar).

113 Ambrose Evans-Pritchard, UK Telegraph, August 18, 2015 http://www.telegraph.co.uk/finance/comment/ambroseevans_pritchard/11810420/Chinas-August-scare-is-a-false-alarm-as-fiscal-crunch-fades.html

That a sudden and drastic currency devaluation by some nation was brewing in 2015 was indicated by transiting Pluto sesquiquadrate (135° angle) transiting Jupiter, an aspect that was shown to affect international currency exchange rates. This aspect was present in 1976, and was exact just prior to Mexico's devaluation of the peso in August 1976.

In June and July 1976, transiting Pluto and Jupiter formed a 135°–135°–90° triangle with Mexico's progressed Uranus 22° Aquarius, while transiting Ceres was opposing progressed Uranus (which rules the eighth house in Mexico's chart). Capital flight was excessive, draining Mexico's foreign reserves, forcing the devaluation. Thus, if this transiting aspect between Jupiter and Pluto forms a harsh configuration with the planet that rules a country's eighth house, that country could experience a severe devaluation.

In late July and August 2015, transiting Jupiter in Leo was sesquiquadrate Pluto in Capricorn. On August 5, 2015, transiting Jupiter and Venus were conjunct at 28°35' Leo, along with Mercury 25° Leo. All were square transiting Saturn 28°17' Scorpio. But they were also inconjunct (150° angle) China's progressed Venus 29°53' Capricorn (Venus is the natural ruler of the second house of the currency) and progressed Jupiter 1°01' Aquarius (Jupiter is the chart co-ruler of the second house) and the natal Ascendant 1°44' Aquarius.

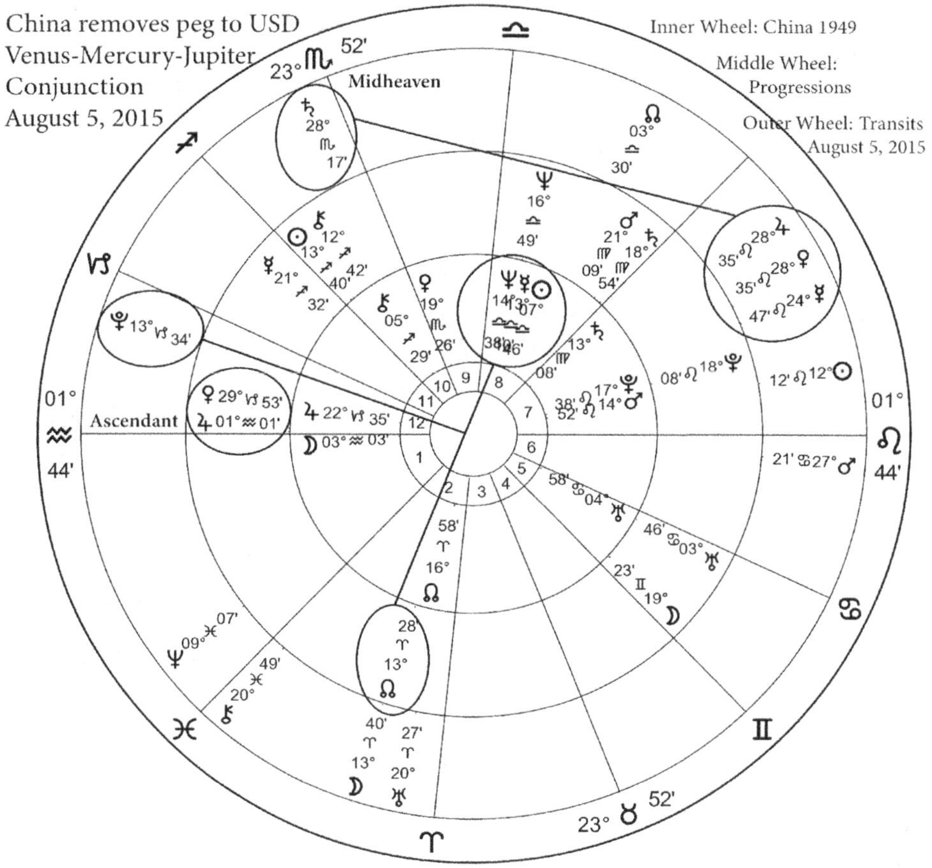

Mercury is the ruler of China's eighth house, and natal Mercury was involved in another configuration that linked to the Jupiter-Pluto aspect. The square between transiting Jupiter/Venus/Mercury and Saturn formed a 135°–135°–90° triangle with the progressed North Node 13°38' Aries—which was opposing natal Mercury 13°10' Libra in the eighth house.

In China's case, the triple conjunction involving Jupiter was a powerful trigger. In both cases (Mexico and China), Jupiter interacting with the ruler of the eighth house exaggerated the currency's move, but it's important to note that both countries were experiencing capital flight while also having an extreme buildup of debt at the time.

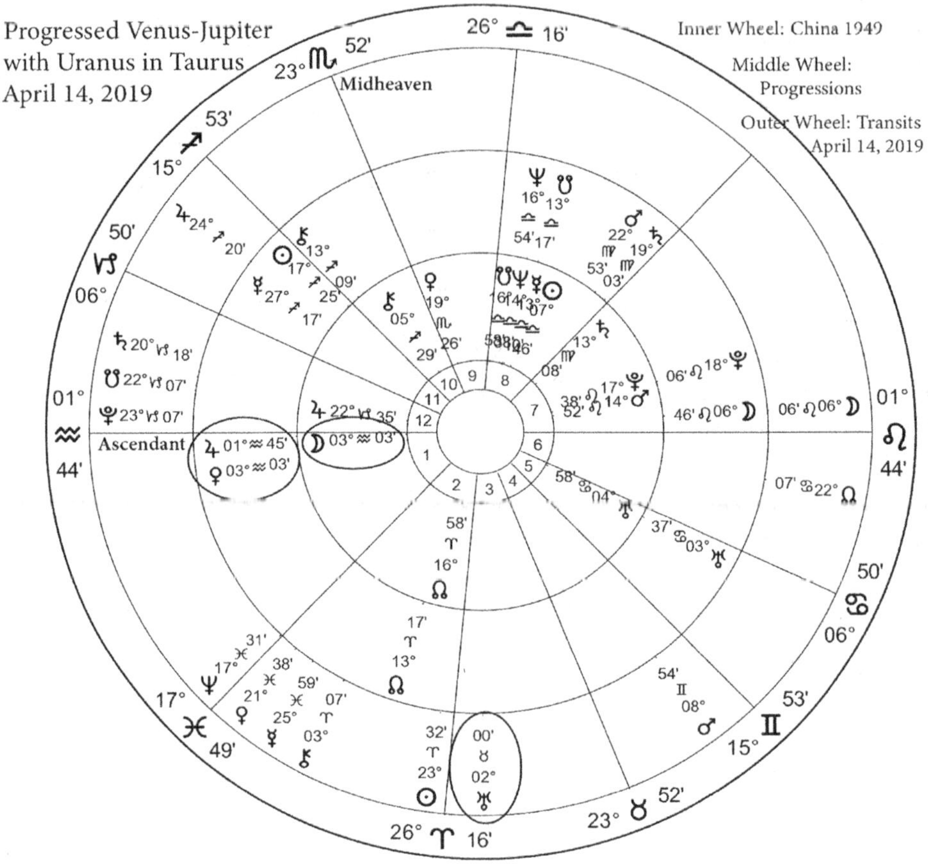

CHINA – Higher Trade Surplus and Increased Foreign Reserves, But Also More Corporate Debt in 2017

China's trade surplus with the US was its highest ever in 2017, at $275.81 billion.[114] After two and a half years of depleting its foreign reserves in order to prop up the yuan and staunch the effects of capital flight, China's reserves rose in 2017.[115]

China's outstanding debt has grown to fantastic levels since the financial crisis of 2008, as China has relied on bank loans usually extended by banks that are state-owned enterprises (SOE's) to maintain the country's growth rate. Corporate debt accounts for the largest share of China's total debt, at well over

114 https://www.cnbc.com/2018/01/11/chinas-trade-surplus-with-the-us-hit-a-record-high-in-2017.html

115 https://www.reuters.com/article/us-china-economy-forex-reserves/china-december-forex-reserves-rise-to-3-14-trillion-highest-since-september-2016-idUSKBN1EW061

100% of GDP for the last several years.[116]

Many SOE's in China are zombie companies, maintained by government subsidies and private sector loans. But workers are often put on furlough, or don't receive pay for months on end, which increases corporate debt in the domestic market.

A very similar situation existed in Indonesia in the 1990's, prior to the Asian currency crisis. Indonesia had a high level of foreign reserves and a trade surplus, which made the country look good on the surface, but there was a high level of corporate debt—just like China's situation now!

Indonesia's chart indicated this false prosperity by progressed Venus conjunct natal Jupiter, and progressed Jupiter conjunct natal Venus, both conjunctions falling in the sign of Aquarius.

China's chart has progressed Venus conjunct progressed Jupiter in Aquarius—it was exact in April 2017. This conjunction falls close to China's Ascendant and natal Moon in Aquarius. Things *look* good, or at least manageable, but China could lose control of the situation as multiple configurations involving outer planets impact China's chart in 2018 through 2021.

Although China raised its interest rates slightly in 2017 to keep pace with the Federal Reserve's rate hikes, this poses a problem for China as higher rates make it harder for China to maintain their currency's peg to a basket of currencies that includes the US dollar. Also, China's indebted companies need lower interest rates to service their debt, and China's leadership prefers low interest rates so as to stimulate the economy.

Perversely, China is getting squeezed by the resuscitation of the global economy. As global interest rates rise, China is forced to raise its domestic rates as well in order to maintain its currency's peg.

CHINA – Bubble in Property Values

In 2017, China again began to address a bubble in property values by raising interest rates and ending preferential lending rates for first-time home buyers.[117] Over recent years, China has alternately allowed a property bubble to form, as investment in infrastructure is what has been powering growth in the country

---

116 http://www.marketwatch.com/story/chinas-economic-problems-will-come-to-a-head-in-2017-2016-11-23?link=MW_latest_news

117 http://www.scmp.com/news/china/economy/article/2095438/chinas-interest-rates-poised-quick-rise-response-us-moves

in recent years, and then tightening conditions to deflate the bubble somewhat. Each time that Chinese policymakers apply stimulus to their economy in order to prop up their growth rate, property values rise and threaten destabilizing conditions.

That this property bubble is reaching its peak is another effect of the conjunction of progressed Venus and progressed Jupiter in the early degrees of Aquarius, as mentioned above. The conjunction was exact at 1°20' Aquarius in April 2017, conjoining China's Ascendant 1°44' Aquarius and emphasizing how this property bubble will probably acutely affect the economy, especially as Uranus moves into Taurus in 2018–2019 and squares these progressed planets.

CHAPTER 6

FORECAST FOR CHINA 2019 TO 2022

In 2019 through 2022, China's astrological chart is subject to very similar conditions as those that were identified for major financial crises and currency devaluations of the past. What is of concern in China's case is that several major conditions occur within a narrow timeframe, increasing the probability of a sudden and severe financial crisis.

Major Astrological Conditions that Apply to China's Chart in 2019 through 2022

- Stellium[118] in Capricorn that includes a Saturn-Pluto conjunction and makes a harsh aspect with the natal position of the chart ruler of the eighth or second house (Jupiter, in China's chart).
- Transiting Neptune opposing progressed Saturn.
- Transiting Saturn in harsh aspect with the progressed ruler of the eighth or second house.
- Transiting Jupiter in harsh aspect with the ruler of the eighth house (Mercury, in China's chart).
- Natal or progressed Venus conjunct natal or progressed Jupiter.
- Progressed Moon conjunct natal or progressed Mars—preferably in the second or eighth house.
- Transiting Mercury in harsh aspect with the progressed Moon/natal or progressed Mars configuration.
- Progressed Moon of an eclipse conjunct the natal Node of the eclipse chart.
- Eclipse point in harsh aspect with natal or progressed Saturn.

118 See the Glossary for the definition of a stellium.

Capricorn Stellium with Saturn-Pluto Conjunction 2020

The last occurrence of a stellium in Capricorn that included a Saturn-Pluto conjunction in the last ten degrees of Capricorn was in 1284.[119] The main impact of this stellium was a long-term shift in the relative values of gold and silver, due to control of the trading of these minerals by one player (Venice), which was profiting from the different currency standards of Europe and Asia. This shift, in combination with the buildup of debt by European monarchies, resulted in financial upheaval and the collapse of major banking companies. These events, in turn, stunted the development of emerging sovereign nations in Europe.[120]

In the 21st century, currency values are relative to the global reserve currency, the US dollar. The Federal Reserve can control the relativity of the dollar's value to a great extent by their policies. The Capricorn stellium and other transiting aspects in 2019 and 2020 impact the chart of the Federal Reserve, and its control of the modern form of currency standards will be enhanced at this time.

China's chart is heavily impacted by the 2020 Capricorn stellium, especially in areas associated with labor unrest, political groups or parties, the economy, financial system, and currency. The houses that represent these areas in China's chart are ruled by Jupiter, or natal Jupiter is in that house. The stellium, in particular the exact degree of the Saturn-Pluto conjunction, conjoins China's natal Jupiter at 22°35' Capricorn.

This stellium indicates a major upheaval in China, centered upon the Communist Party, and possibly triggered by a currency devaluation. The struggle for control will be brutal, and there will probably be ruthless suppression of any uprisings or protests by the people.

As co-ruler of the sign Pisces, Jupiter rules China's second house, the area of the chart representing the country's economy, financial system, and currency.

---

119 There was a Saturn-Pluto conjunction as part of a stellium in Capricorn in January 1518, but the conjunction occurred at 4°17' Capricorn. The 1284 stellium is examined in detail here because its Saturn-Pluto conjunction occurred at 26°21' Capricorn, nearly at the same degree at which the 2020 Saturn-Pluto conjunction occurs at 22°46' Capricorn. In addition, Pluto formed a harsh aspect (opposition) with Uranus in 1284, similar to the current cycle of Uranus-Pluto (square); in 1518, Pluto formed a soft aspect (trine) with Uranus.

120 The author is in no way inferring that Venice deliberately manipulated the collapse of other banking companies, or that Venice tried to suppress the developing power of European states. Nor is the author implying any such manipulation in the 21st century. Conspiracy theories will be left to others.

The constricting influence of the stellium will likely affect this area the most because the other co-ruler of Pisces—which is Neptune—is moving through Pisces, enters the second house, and then opposes progressed Saturn.

The first instance of the Capricorn stellium is in effect from November 16, 2019, when Ceres enters Capricorn and joins Saturn and Pluto in that sign,until March 31, 2020, when Mars leaves Capricorn. Other multiple configurations are present in the same time period, along with astrological triggers that make this the most intense period for a financial crisis centered upon events in China.

Saturn and Pluto are exactly conjunct at 22°46' Capricorn on January 12, 2020, conjoining China's natal Jupiter 22°35' Capricorn, ruler of the second house of the financial system and the currency. One day earlier, January 11, there is a lunar eclipse at 20°00' Cancer, interacting with Mercury, Saturn, and Pluto. There could be a major reversal in global financial markets around this date.

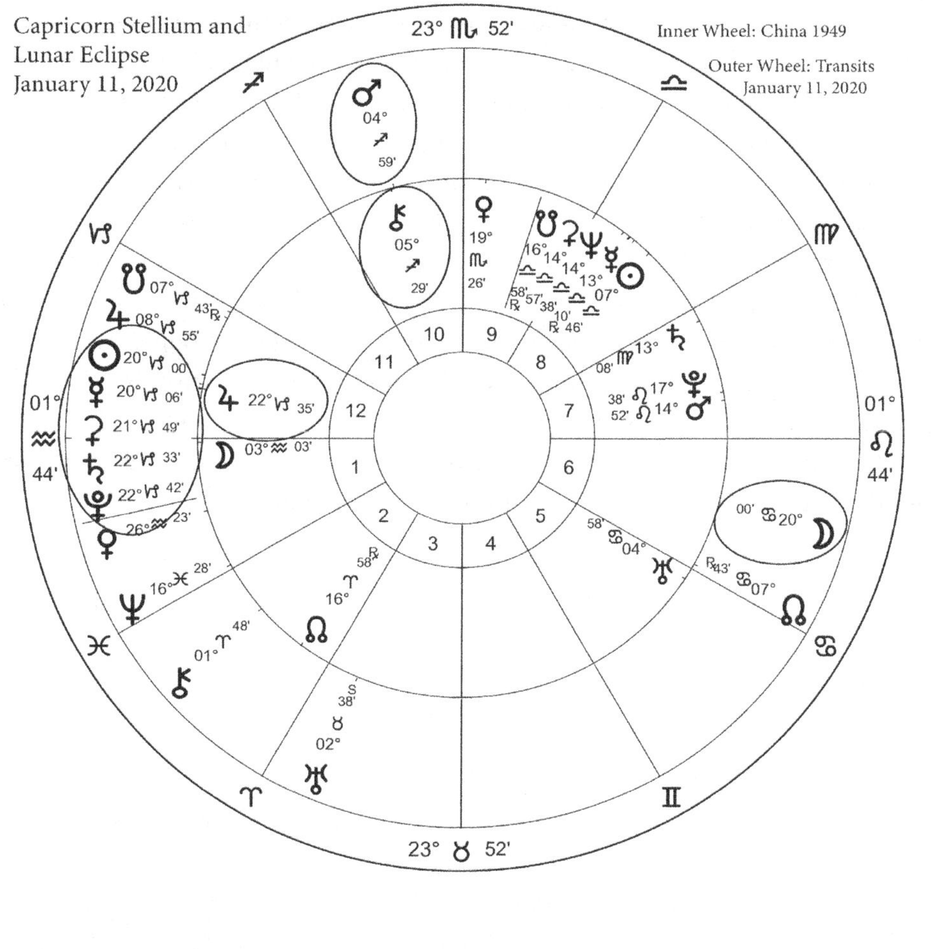

Also on January 11–12, transiting Mars 5° Sagittarius is conjunct China's natal Chiron, and thus triggering natal Jupiter through antiscion points, as discussed in Chapter 5. This configuration indicates an aggressive reaction triggered by fear of protests becoming widespread.

The stellium of Jupiter, Saturn, and Pluto occurs again from July 2 to December 17, 2020. From August 26 to October 2, 2020, transiting Neptune is once again in its closest opposition to progressed Saturn (due to retrograde motion). This time period could also impact the value of the yuan. On September 10, 2020, Mars goes retrograde at 28°08' Aries, conjoining China's natal Hades 28°10' Aries and forming a Grand Trine with progressed Mercury in Sagittarius and the progressed Moon 25°35' Leo (and the 2017 total solar eclipse point 28°52' Leo). Transiting Pluto is exactly conjunct natal Jupiter the same day, making this a prime time for events related to foreign interest rates to affect the yuan.

The value of the yuan could whipsaw in September through November 2020, due to the Mars retrograde period. From November 8 through November 13, 2020, Jupiter and Pluto are again conjunct China's natal Jupiter 22°35' Capricorn. They are exactly conjunct on November 13 at 22°52' Capricorn. Mars returns to direct motion the next day, November 14, at 15°14' Aries, opposing progressed Neptune and the natal South Node. Thus, China's policymakers could give confusing signals to investors on just what their priorities are for regulating the yuan's value and their financial system.

The 2020 Capricorn stellium affects the chart of the Chinese Communist Party, and therefore affects the leadership of China. It brings opposition of the Party to a head, with economic inequality and blatant corruption being the main grievances. But at the same time, it lends more power to the established leadership of China as it triggers ingrained fears about popular labor unrest, with China's leaders responding with sharp repression of any protests.

Transiting Neptune Opposition Progressed Saturn 2019–2021

From March 2019 to March 2021, transiting Neptune 16°–20° Pisces opposes China's progressed Saturn 19° Virgo. The Capricorn stellium occurs within this time band.

This long-term aspect is actually the most important for identifying which countries are most likely to experience a financial crisis, especially one related to debt and currency values, and in which time period such a crisis could occur. Transiting Neptune opposing natal or progressed Saturn was shown to be present at the times of the devaluations of the currencies of Thailand, Indonesia, Russia, Mexico, and the UK.

What is unfortunate for China about this aspect is two-fold: Neptune is co-ruler of China's second house of its financial system and currency; and the aspect becomes close to exact during the time when other harsh configurations form. Furthermore, progressed Saturn resides in China's eighth house, indicating that the consequences of past behavior with regard to debt buildup and depletion of foreign reserves can no longer be delayed—in other words, the can hits the brick wall at the end of the road.

The strongest effects of this aspect are most likely triggered in early 2020, first in the early January 2020 time period already discussed above, and again in late March 2020, due to a cluster of strong aspects:

- On March 20, 2020, transiting Mars conjoins transiting Jupiter and Pluto at 24° Capricorn, so it is translating the stellium that formed in January, and it is conjunct natal Jupiter.
- On March 22, Saturn enters Aquarius, the sign of China's Ascendant.
- On March 26, the progressed Moon in Leo exactly squares natal Venus.
- On March 27, transiting Neptune 19° Pisces exactly opposes progressed Saturn, which is in the eighth house.
- On March 28–29, the transiting North Node is exactly conjunct progressed Uranus in the fifth house of the stock market.

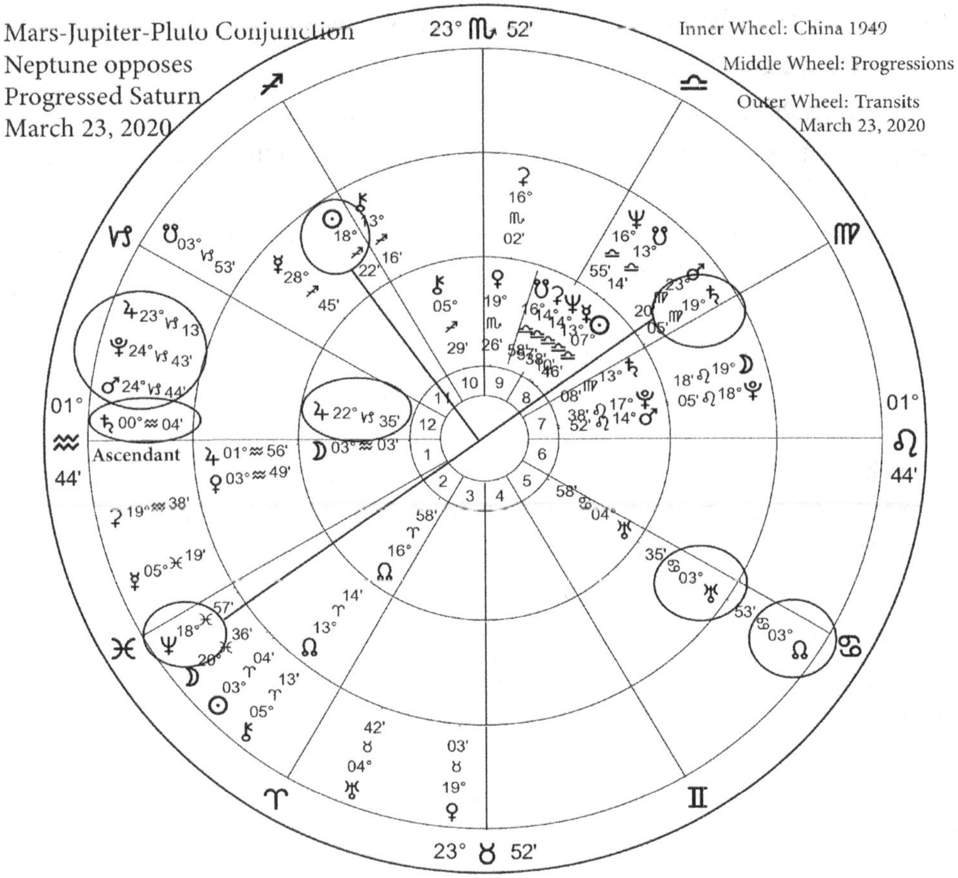

So, once again there is a time period in which the stellium is activated by a planet—in this case, Mars—and now Neptune exactly opposes progressed Saturn.

Transiting Saturn in Harsh Aspect with Progressed Ruler of the Second House 2020

The Saturn-Pluto conjunction, which is exact on January 12, 2020, is within 3° orb of natal Jupiter 22°35' Capricorn, co-ruler of China's second house, from December 16, 2019 to February 5, 2020.

Saturn is within 3° orb of progressed Jupiter and China's natal Ascendant from March 7 to July 18, 2020,[121] and again from December 5, 2020 to January 30, 2021.[122] In the case of Brazil, this configuration indicated Brazil's decision to increase their level of debt, despite obvious problems. China may have to resort to using debt to fund stimulus to their economy, but this could backfire in a big way, as the planet of influence here, which is transiting Saturn, is within range of squaring transiting Uranus, the planet of the unexpected, during these two time periods.

With transiting Uranus in Taurus, it could be that property values complicate the scenario, for Uranus will square China's progressed Venus and progressed Jupiter. As explained below, the conjunction of progressed Venus and progressed Jupiter also refers to China's trade surplus and level of foreign reserves. The combination of Uranus in Taurus and Pluto in Capricorn could reveal that China's financial situation is much more dire than previously thought.

Transiting Jupiter in Harsh Aspect with Progressed Ruler of the Eighth House November 2019

For China, Mercury is ruler of the eighth house. Transiting Jupiter, along with Ceres, Venus, and the Sun pass over China's progressed Mercury in November 2019.

Extremely volatile conditions in China's financial system and property market erupt in November and December 2019, especially November 3 through December 25. This will likely affect the yuan's exchange rate and, by extension, global financial markets.

On November 24, 2019, transiting Jupiter is exactly conjunct transiting Venus 28°11' Sagittarius, and both are conjunct progressed Mercury 28°14' Sagittarius in the eleventh house.

121 From 28°44' Capricorn, back to 28°44' Capricorn, due to retrograde motion.

122 When Saturn enters Aquarius again.

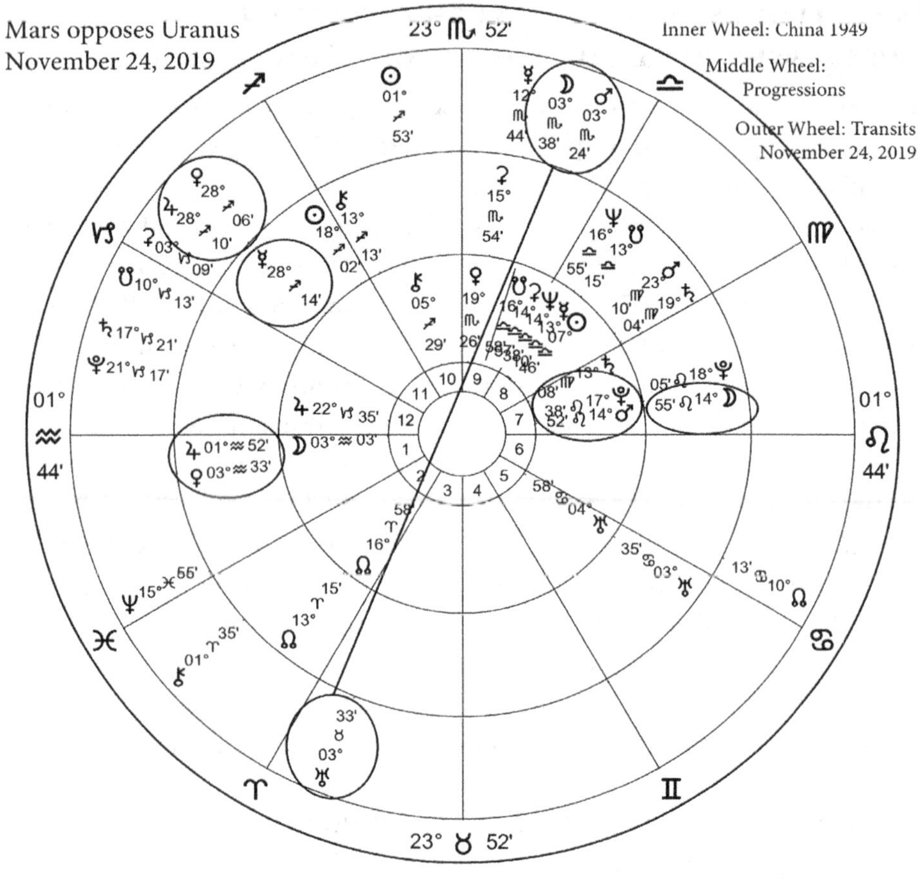

On the same day, transiting Mars and the Moon in Scorpio are exactly opposing transiting Uranus 3°32' Taurus, forming an exact T-square with progressed Venus 3°33' Aquarius, indicating the exposure of the depth of China's debt problems.

With the progressed Moon exactly conjunct natal Mars 14°52' Leo also on this date, this would seem to be when global markets decide that the amount of China's corporate debt and its property valuations are excessive, and investors run for the hills. With the aspects to Uranus mentioned above, a decline in China's stock market and the yuan could lead a rout in global markets.

Progressed Venus Conjunct Progressed Jupiter 2012–2022

Progressed Venus is within 3° orb of conjunction with progressed Jupiter from November 23, 2012[123] to January 25, 2022.[124] They were exactly conjunct at 1°20'–21' Aquarius from April 1–14, 2017.

The overall effect of this long-lasting configuration is complacency on the part of investors over the state of China's economic and financial health. Specifically, it denotes a peak in property values, a trade surplus, and a high level of foreign reserves—all of which are deceiving.

Essentially the same configuration was present for Indonesia in the 1990's, prior to the Asian currency crisis, when Indonesia's chart had progressed Venus conjunct natal Jupiter *and* progressed Jupiter conjunct natal Venus, both falling in Aquarius. Indonesia had a high level of foreign reserves and a trade surplus, which made the country look good on the surface, but there was a high level of corporate debt, just like China's situation is now.

When this configuration first moved into range of 3° of exactness, it was in the twelfth house of hidden issues, indicating that the amounts of debt in both the property market and the shadow banking system of China were (and still are) more than anyone suspects.

In 2018, transiting Uranus moving into Taurus—the sign that rules China's fourth house of real estate, land, and mines—begins a volatile transition in the property market, and by extension, in China's overall economy and financial system.

An economic slowdown, based upon declining property values and high levels of corporate debt, begins in earnest in 2019. Lack of information about levels of corporate debt, especially in the shadow banking system, contributes to investors' negative perspective on China's prospects and financial solvency. Property values in China begin to cool down in early 2019 as a powerful shift occurs that is interwoven with the value of the yuan.

Perversely, China is getting squeezed by the resuscitation of the global economy. As global interest rates rise, China is also forced to raise its domestic rates in order to maintain its currency's peg. But this puts pressure on domestic companies that have borrowed heavily in order to stay afloat, including state-

123 Venus 27°29' Capricorn, Jupiter 0°29' Aquarius

124 Venus 5°18' Aquarius, Jupiter 2°18' Aquarius

owned enterprises, for most of these loans have short-term durations. Uranus will put the unexpected into the mix.

The Chinese Communist Party will have a very hard time containing the fallout of these configurations. They may have to resort to heavy-handed efforts in order to survive.

The events of 2019 through 2021 will have long term effects, and will reverberate through the time period of May 2022 to May 2023 as transiting Uranus passes through 13°–19° Taurus forming a T-square by squaring China's natal Mars and Pluto in Leo and opposing China's natal Venus in Scorpio. When Uranus is conjunct the transiting North Node in July through August 2022, that T-square configuration forms a Grand Cross with transiting Ceres in Leo and Saturn in Aquarius.

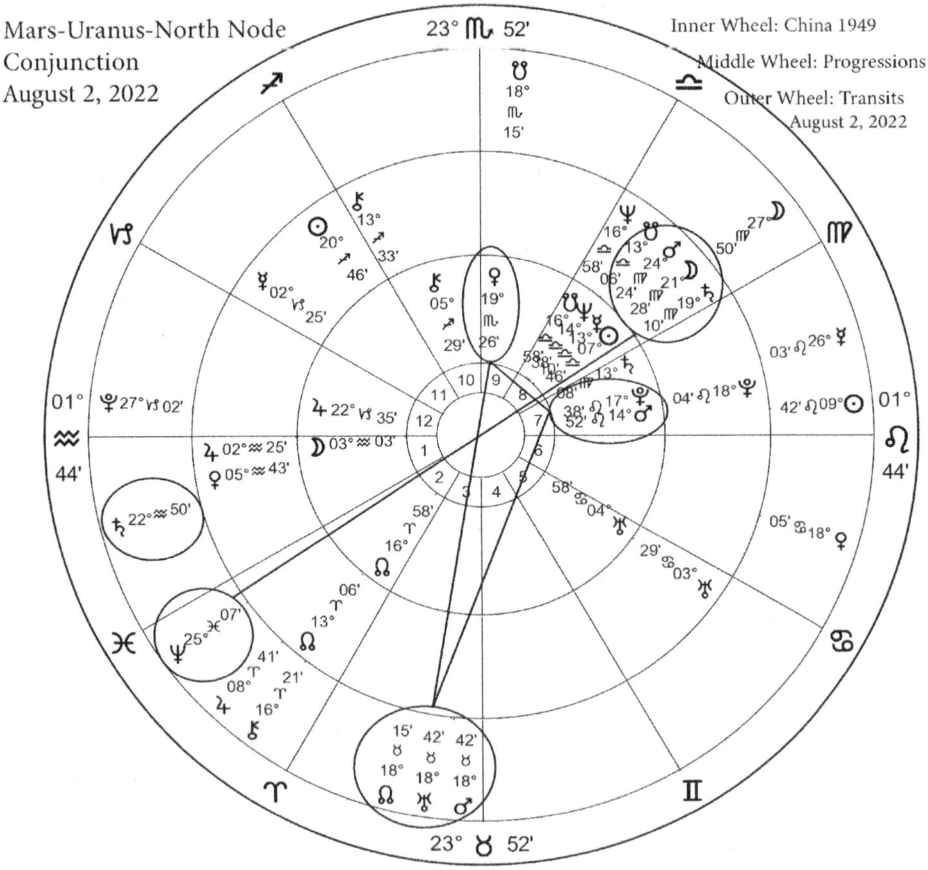

Drastic events intertwining changes to China's leadership with the stability of its economy and currency could occur in this July through August 2022 time period. Foreign interest rates and capital flight may again weaken China's economy, as transiting Neptune opposes progressed Mars in the eighth house at the same time. An important change in leadership is brewing, with corruption and power plays within the CCP inciting upheaval.

Progressed Moon Conjunct Natal Mars November 2019

From October 30 to November 27, 2019, China's progressed Moon conjoins natal Mars 14°52' Leo (see the chart for November 24, 2019 on page 148). This is a trigger aspect, and as this conjunction is exact on November 24, on the same day that other astrological triggers occur, this would seem to be when global markets decide that the amount of China's corporate debt and its property valuations are excessive, and global markets experience a sell-off.

Transiting Mercury in Harsh Aspect with Progressed Moon and Natal Mars

This is another trigger aspect; in Thailand's case, transiting Mercury was conjunct the Moon/Mars pair (as discussed above), and it timed Thailand's devaluation of the baht to the day. For China, on November 27, 2019, transiting Mercury 14°–15° Scorpio squares the progressed Moon and natal Mars.

Progressed Moon of an Eclipse Conjunct Natal Node of the Eclipse Chart

There is a total solar eclipse on July 3, 2019 at 10°37' Cancer. The progressed Moon of this eclipse chart reaches the natal North Node 18° Cancer *of the eclipse chart* on January 2, 2020 while the Capricorn stellium is in effect, and within the time band of the Saturn-Neptune aspect.

Configurations involving the position of an eclipse can act as triggers to other configurations occurring together within a narrow time band (usually of about two to three weeks), and have often been found to time an event to the day. As this eclipse condition is met within the timeframe of the Capricorn stellium and other important configurations, January 2 is a critical date.

Progressed Moon conjunct
Eclipse Node
January 2, 2020

Inner Wheel:
July 3, 2019 Solar Eclipse
Outer Wheel:
Progressed Moon
January 2, 2020

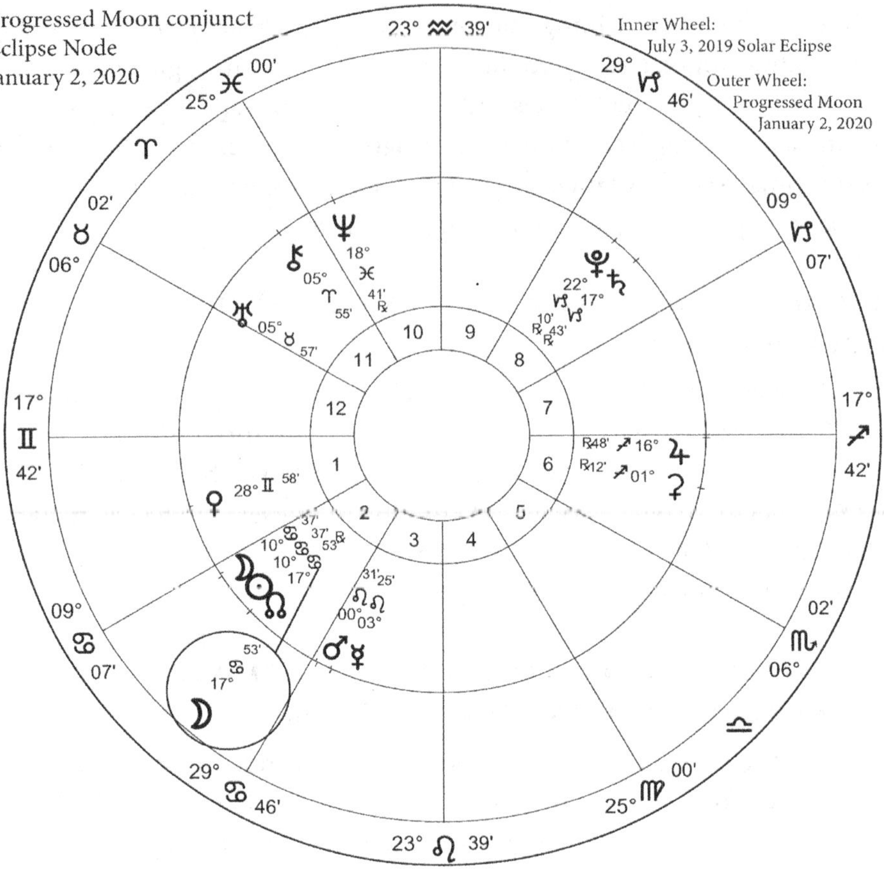

The chart for the time of this solar eclipse for the location of Beijing has the eclipse point falling in the second house.[125] This emphasizes what the eclipse's effect will be on China, that it will mainly affect China's financial system and currency.

Additionally, there is a solar eclipse on December 26, 2019 at 4°6' of Capricorn. This solar eclipse opposes China's natal Uranus. The progressed Moon of the chart for this eclipse will be conjunct the eclipse chart's South Node from April 12 to May 9, 2020. It is exact on April 26, 2020. This time period will likely see more fallout from the events of November 2019 through January 2020.

125 Using the Placidus house system.

Eclipse Point in Harsh Aspect with Natal or Progressed Saturn

The total solar eclipse on December 15, 2020 at 23°08' Sagittarius squares China's progressed Mars 23°40' Virgo. On the day of this eclipse, the progressed Sun, also in Sagittarius, exactly squares progressed Saturn, and progressed Saturn is sesquiquadrate (135°) progressed Venus 4°25' Aquarius. This eclipse occurs during the second time band of the Capricorn stellium, as discussed above.

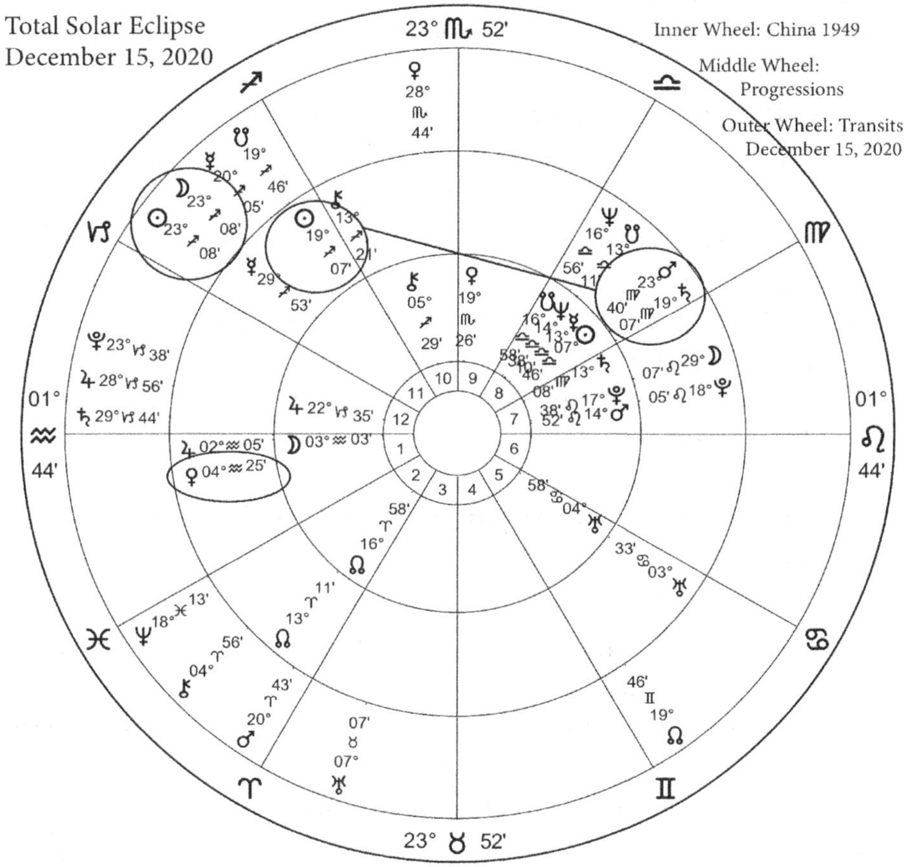

Due to Venus's rulership of China's fourth (real estate, national security) and ninth (international commerce, shipping, maritime issues) houses, this eclipse could motivate China to assert its position in disputed territory, especially with regard to the seas off China's coast. China sees itself as the rightful dominant player in this region, and makes it clear that it will not tolerate any encroachment—whether physical or by international law—that limits its activity in the region. China feels that such limitations are a threat to its security.

The solar eclipse on June 10, 2021 at 19°47' Gemini opposes China's progressed Sun, forming a T-square with progressed Saturn 19°08' Virgo. This eclipse could aggravate the issue that arose in mid-December 2020, as discussed above.

Transiting Mars Conjunct Eclipse Point

On March 20, 2020, transiting Mars conjoins transiting Jupiter and Pluto at 24° Capricorn (see the chart for March 23, 2020 on page 146). These three planets are conjoining the position of the July 16, 2019 lunar eclipse. They are also passing over the degrees of the stellium that formed in January, and so are conjunct natal Jupiter. The last ten days of March 2020 could see more financial fallout from the events of November 2019 through January 2020. China's leadership may be trying to compensate, or "clean up" from those events at this time, but they could cause even greater turmoil in the process.

The Saturn-Pluto and Chiron-Pluto Cycles 2007 and 2013

The Saturn-Pluto and Chiron-Pluto cycles do *not* coincide in the 2019–2020 time period, as they did in 1284, 1299, 1340, 1966, 1973, and 1992. They coincided by soft angles in 2013 when Saturn in Scorpio was trine Chiron in Pisces, and both were sextile Pluto in Capricorn. They were within 1° orb of these aspects in March 2013. Xi Jinping became President of China on March 14, 2013 under this configuration, thus Xi's continuing accumulation of power in the CCP and the Chinese government plays a major role in upcoming changes to the global financial system.

However, these cycles coincided by harsh angles in 2007, from late February through June, with Saturn in Leo opposing Chiron in Aquarius, and Chiron semi-square (45° angle) Pluto in late Sagittarius. Saturn was passing over China's natal Mars and Pluto at 15°–18° Leo, indicating that China's status in the world

(Mars and Pluto rule Scorpio, the sign of the tenth house of government and public status) would change, with China becoming more crucial to the global economy but also that her financial system would become strained due to increased domestic debt.

Maintaining the appearance of a healthy growth rate was funded by domestic debt, especially in the property market. China's economic growth probably truly peaked in 2007, for throughout that year progressed Venus 22°–23° Capricorn was conjunct natal Jupiter 22°35' Capricorn (they were exactly conjunct from August 21–26). As progressed Venus moved away from progressed Jupiter 1°20' Aquarius in 2017, and she passed over China's Ascendant in late August 2017, investors' concern over China's debt problem increased and China has made some (insufficient) attempts to tame it. China's trade surplus increased, and her foreign reserves rebounded some in 2017, as discussed in the Introduction, but as the planetary picture shifts, with the Saturn-Pluto conjunction occurring in 2020 and then Saturn and eventually Pluto passing over China's Ascendant, the pressure of mounting debt will impact China's financial system.

Thus, the Saturn-Pluto and Chiron-Pluto cycles coinciding in 2007 did signal a big shift for China's financial system, just as these cycles coinciding in the 1960's indicated an upcoming serious change for Latin American economies.

CONCLUSIONS

As these astrological conditions cluster together, there are three critical time periods for China's financial system:

- November 2019 through January 2020.
- Mid-March through April 2020.
- Late August through mid-November 2020.

An economic slowdown in China begins in earnest in 2019. China is getting squeezed by the resuscitation of the global economy as global interest rates rise. Investors' concerns about levels of corporate debt, especially in the shadow banking system of China, contribute to their negative perspective on China's prospects and financial solvency.

By November 2019, the consequences of corporate debt buildup and depletion of foreign reserves can no longer be delayed. In late 2019 and early 2020, China must decide if it wants to maintain the yuan's peg to a basket of currencies—in which case it must raise domestic rates—or if it should devalue the yuan and break the peg, thus keeping afloat domestic companies which have accumulated much debt. Either course will bring a crisis.

Opposition to China's leadership and the Chinese Communist Party will intensify at the same time. An economic crisis would add fuel to the fire of the opposition's cause.

But China's financial system will likely receive an unavoidable shock at this time. The spring of 2020 could see another financial crisis, probably in response to events of January 2020. China's policymakers may be trying to make adjustments in an attempt to "correct" what happened in January.

The Chinese Communist Party will have a very hard time containing the fallout of these events. Having delayed reforms in favor of maintaining the appearance of strong economic growth, their only recourse at this point is to be reactive. It is the inherent nature of CCP leadership to resort to force when facing a challenge to their survival.

Turmoil continues throughout 2020 and well into 2022, with scattered intense events that make it difficult for the Chinese Communist Party to rectify their mishandling of both financial system problems and domestic political opposition. Their knee-jerk reaction is to apply force, purge their ranks of "corrupt" members, and further restrict the personal freedoms of the Chinese people.

Longer Term Effects of the Capricorn Stellium

The dates used here for the calculation of astrological charts to signify the "inception" of influence of the 1284 and 2020 Capricorn stelliums are based on the occurrence of solar eclipses when the stellium planets were within range in Capricorn. The 13th century stellium chart is calculated for the moment of the December 8, 1284 solar eclipse; the 21st century stellium chart is calculated for the moment of the December 26, 2019 solar eclipse.

By progressing the positions of the 1284 stellium chart, progressed Saturn and progressed Pluto were exactly conjunct in the summer of 1296. This was a critical time period in which a severe drain of capital (papal reserves) occurred in the European financial system; war intensified between France and England; and the influence of the Catholic Church began its long decline due to Philip IV's feud with the Pope and his insistence on taxing the clergy. Thus the period of progressed Saturn closely conjunct progressed Pluto is one of serious disputes revolving around taxation and territorial claims, and an upset to the amount of capital in the international finance system.

Applying the same calculation to the 2019 solar eclipse/stellium chart, progressed Saturn and progressed Pluto will be exactly conjunct between May 24 and July 14, 2037.

In the summer of 2037, transiting Saturn in Leo opposes transiting Pluto in Aquarius, aggravating China's relations with foreign allies and competitors. The beginning of this period— May 24, 2037—has the transiting South Node exactly conjunct China's Ascendant. Progressed Mars 0°40' Libra is on the cusp of that sign, and forms a T-square with the progressed Sun 6° Capricorn opposing natal Uranus 5° Cancer. Thus, the co-rulers of China's Ascendant (Saturn and Uranus) are making significant configurations at this time. China's leadership could be antagonistic and push back on what they consider undue pressure from other countries. If the events of 1294 through 1296 are any precedent, military conflict over territorial issues could emerge. And this interpretation would certainly fit the astrological configurations in China's chart at the time.

CHAPTER 7

Timeline for China 2019 to 2022

Broad Overview

2019 through 2022

2019 through 2022 could see a massive overhaul of China's financial system. The Chinese property market figures prominently in how this overhaul is generated and conducted.

China may become defensive against foreign investment in their country, especially their property market, perhaps even to the point of reverting to total control of all property use rights by the state. Thus, the holding of property use rights by foreign investors could be declared null and void, with all control reverting to the Chinese state.

China may initiate harsh changes to control the level of debt in the property market, with the purpose being twofold: To rid the financial system of the burden of bad loans; and to keep the Chinese state and Chinese Communist Party firmly in control of how China develops its financial system according to Party ideology.

Conflicts could develop between China and foreign nations. There could also be a domestic revolt over economic conditions and enforced changes on society.

There are several time periods that indicate financial crises resulting in large fluctuations in China's currency and/or several devaluations. The level of debt, capital flight, and China's change in attitude toward foreign investment contribute to investors' anxiety over China's financial solvency.

March 2019 through March 2021

This is the time band in which there is the greatest probability of a major default on debt (probably domestic debt) within China. It is also a time of increased capital flight, increased currency fluctuations, and possible devaluations of the yuan.

The CCP may see foreign investment in China's markets, especially the property market, as an existential threat at this time. The Chinese government may opt to take draconian measures to control debt and foreign investment sometime during this two-year period.

The events of this time period may lead to a major overhaul of China's financial system, with the country's leadership preferring to revert to a more socialist/communist system.

February 2019 through May 2020

Issues concerning wealth distribution, the solvency of shadow banks and wealth management products, and property rights could all contribute to problems within China's financial system and reverberate in foreign exchange markets.

An economic slowdown, based upon declining property values and high levels of corporate debt, begins in earnest in 2019. Lack of information about levels of corporate debt and the shadow banking system of China contributes to investors' negative perspective on China's prospects and financial solvency. Property values in China begin to cool down in early 2019 as a powerful shift occurs that is interwoven with the value of the yuan.

Perversely, China is getting squeezed by the resuscitation of the global economy. As global interest rates rise, China is also forced to raise its domestic rates in order to maintain its currency's peg. But this puts pressure on domestic companies that have borrowed heavily in order to stay afloat, including state-owned enterprises, for most of these loans have short-term durations.

Xi Jinping may face obstacles which are pernicious and difficult to root out, and which undermine his position as Supreme Leader, for they erode

China's financial standing in the world. A challenge to the CCP emerges, one that is difficult to counter, as the opposition is "hidden." In November–December 2019, this challenge could morph into a popular revolt over economic conditions and demands for democracy and rule of law. This revolt will most likely be crushed aggressively and decisively by the Chinese government.

Xi is getting pushback by those who want to limit his authority, and he will need to institute new rules in order to expand his grip on power. Xi seems able to do just that—although this fosters growing opposition to him.

March 2020 through April 2021

This period could see a slow wearing away of legal rights with regard to property use rights, and also an erosion of property values. It heralds a return to a more socialist policy regarding property ownership, with a return to more state-owned enterprises.

Monthly and Daily Timeline

February 2019

2019 begins with the easing of property value mania, and reality setting in. China is faced with the necessity of an overhaul of not only their property market, but also their financial system, as both are intertwined. Foreign investors in China's property market may find that their rights are suddenly blurry, with the state using them as an excuse for the fallout in the financial system.

A peak in Chinese property values could form February 5, 2019, the day of the New Moon.

Developments in the foreign exchange market on February 7 could mark a sudden, drastic turn in market sentiment toward Chinese property values.

February 5 to June 10, 2019

Capital flight from China could accelerate, in expectation of higher foreign interest rates, and in late November there are indications of that expectation becoming a reality.

March 2 to May 19, 2019

Wealth distribution, the solvency of shadow banks and wealth management products, and property rights become important issues. Discontent is centered on real estate, but also on the rule of law. In general, China's banks, financial system, and currency come under stress. These issues surface again from November 12, 2019 to March 8, 2020 and become more pronounced in November and December 2019.

March 25 to March 29, 2019 China may make changes to property rights as they apply to foreign investors that are vague and could possibly be interpreted as giving the state the power to rescind such rights.

April 9 to April 24, 2019 is a time period in which China's currency could be most adversely affected by these issues.

Foreign investors in anything in China may want to reexamine those holdings before the start of 2019, and definitely before May 2019.

June 14 to August 2, 2019

Changes to China's regulation of its property market (and property use rights) are in the air from June 14 to July 7, 2019. Constraints on foreign ownership of property are possibly put into legal form. A sudden decline in real estate values could occur around July 8. The air is now escaping from the property bubble in a steady stream.

A sudden reversal in China's stock market could also occur, which has repercussions in the currency market.

Agitation for reform of labor market regulations and conditions could manifest in mid-June as protests.

Alternately, these issues could surface around July 31 to August 2, 2019.

September 2019

In mid-September 2019, popular grievances that have been growing for some time burst forth in protests. A serious, well-organized opposition challenges China's existing leadership whose image has been damaged, possibly by a corruption scandal. The opposition gains favor with the general population.

However, Xi Jinping seems able to use these events to his advantage and cements his dominance of the CCP.

A major currency devaluation is looming, due to excessive debt. Capital flight could accelerate in mid-September.

October 2019

The possibility of a major default by a Chinese state-owned enterprise, or failure of a Chinese bank, is more pronounced in early October, especially on October 2, 2019.

The general populace could be roused into active protest, due to events in the financial system. These protests could become violent, especially between October 9 and December 9, 2019. On October 22, 2019, there could be an escalation of the conflict.

November 12, 2019 to March 8, 2020

Issues from the March to May 2019 time period (wealth distribution, the solvency of shadow banks and wealth management products, and property rights) surface again. China's banks, financial system, and currency come under extreme stress.

October 30 to November 27, 2019

There is increased pressure to devalue the yuan, due to concerns over levels of debt and possibly over a military conflict. If a conflict with a foreign power or domestic opposition has been brewing, it boils over now.

November 19, 2019 to March 30, 2020

During this time band, investors' concerns intensify over the buildup of debt in China. One or multiple devaluations of the yuan are indicated on the horizon.

Extremely volatile conditions with respect to China's property market and its currency could develop in November–December 2019. The Chinese government and CCP will have a very hard time containing the fallout of these events. They may have to resort to heavy-handed efforts in order to survive.

November 19 to December 2, 2019

Attempts by the Chinese government to quell popular protests are frustrated by escalating violence.

Investors are very anxious over debt levels in the Chinese property market and the shadow banking system.

November 22 to November 27, 2019

November 24, 2019 may be the day when global markets decide that the amount of China's corporate debt and property valuations are excessive, and investors run for the hills, prompting a global sell-off. This could be due to an unexpected rise in foreign interest rates which puts enormous pressure on the yuan. China's leaders are faced with the choice of raising domestic interest rates to maintain their currency's peg to the US dollar—and thus increase the debt burden of companies already squeezed to the asphyxiation point—or letting the peg break and inducing massive capital flight. Either option will introduce chaos into their financial system. The overall level of risk of investing in China is perceived as too high.

November 23 and 24, 2019 indicate a dramatic event, probably a major confrontation between the ruling leadership and the opposition. The established government has more power in this conflict, and a heavy-handed response by China's leadership could lead to violence and death. Although global markets are primarily concerned with China's financial status, this confrontation adds impetus to dump any investment in the country. The global financial system may be taking a hit; global speculative markets most definitely will be.

November 24 to 26, 2019 could be the start of a wild ride in the foreign exchange market.

December 3 to December 11, 2019

It's probable that the established order will crush the opposition in January 2020, but the configurations of November 23 and 24, 2019 show a fierce fight to do so.

But once Jupiter enters Capricorn on December 3, 2019, the government has the upper hand. By December 11, order will begin to be re-established, although probably at great cost. China may pay the price of maintaining political stability of the CCP by seeing itself shut out of some aspect of the global financial system. This could even be voluntary on China's part, in order to keep control of their society on the CCP's terms. In other words, China may abandon certain aspects of capitalism and revert to a more socialist/communist economic model.

December 11, 2019 to January 5, 2020

Several astrological configurations come together in this time period that were shown to have indicated financial upheaval in the past. Trouble accelerates on December 26, 2019, the day of a solar eclipse that impacts China's natal chart.

Due to severe pressure on China's financial system, the yuan could be forcibly devalued at least once in this time band, especially close to January 2, 2020.

January 11, 2020

There could be heavy suppression of protests and upheaval in China due to labor unrest. There is a lunar eclipse at 20°00' Cancer on January 11, 2020, the same day that Saturn and Pluto, as part of the Capricorn stellium, conjoin China's natal Jupiter, triggering a configuration within China's natal chart that indicates a fear of labor unrest that is inherent in the reactions of the CCP.

Protesters could use more violent tactics than in the past, but the government may show far less patience this time, perhaps choosing to crack down aggressively much sooner in the course of the protests than they did in 1989.

Overwhelming astrological evidence points to the government crushing any dissent, especially around January 7–11, 2020. China's established leaders exert more control than ever.

January 12, 2020

Correction to an overvalued currency becomes inevitable. There could be a reversal in global stock markets.

March 20 to March 29, 2020

This is a critical time period for a financial crisis centered on China. This period could see (another) devaluation of the yuan, perhaps more than expected, and a reversal in China's stock market.

This marks a further shift in the legal status of foreign capital and/or property investment. Property use rights and regulations surrounding them that were introduced in the past could be voided.

May through June 2020

The crackdown on dissent now impacts the Chinese Communist Party, with the arrest of scapegoats being used as a way to justify purges within the Party.

May 12, 2020 could be the start of a slow but important shift in China's financial system and value of the yuan.

July through September 2020

The stellium of Jupiter, Saturn, and Pluto in Capricorn occurs again from July 2 to December 17, 2020. More crisis events could occur in this time band, especially in August and September.

There may be radical reforms to China's financial and banking system around August 2, 2020 which enhance the power of the CCP.

August 26 to October 2, 2020 indicates events related to foreign interest rates and/or China's debt levels that impact the yuan. September 10 could see a sharp reversal in the value of the yuan.

August 24, 2020 to January 14, 2021

The Mars retrograde period in Aries in the last quarter of 2020 indicates a serious conflict with another country. A neighbor could become belligerent, and not necessarily toward China, but its actions have serious ramifications for China. A belligerent neighboring state is putting obstacles in the way of China's efforts to project leadership and power in the Pacific region.

This conflict affects China's currency and economy. The level of debt in China's property market becomes a critical issue again in September 2020.

Major changes to China's financial system may be discussed as solutions at this time. The ownership of some assets may revert to the state.

If China was caught off guard by the events at the beginning of the retrograde period, the tables are turned when Mars goes direct in mid-November 2020, with China becoming more aggressive and gaining the upper hand into early January 2021. However, China may need to resort to extreme tactics to maintain control of the situation after January 6, 2021.

December 15 to December 27, 2020

China's leadership asserts itself as the dominant power of the Pacific region, disregarding the concerns of foreign powers. The actions of foreign powers are perceived by China as blocking its rightful place in the region.

January 2021

January 7, 2021 starts a shift in China's leadership, though this may not be outwardly apparent at the time. Opposition to the established leadership is gaining ground again.

January 21, 2021 indicates conditions that bring the Chinese state to act harshly and decisively. There may be sudden changes in China's financial system regarding foreign investment and/or capital controls. Some property use rights that were enacted in the past could be dissolved. The changes will strongly favor the Chinese state in the assignment of property rights.

There could be a serious rupture of China's financial system with the global financial system. It could be that China is shut off from certain portions of the global financial system, due to their "confiscation" of foreign investment capital that was paid for property rights that have been rescinded.

February 13 to February 15, 2021

Pressure that has been building on China's financial system and the yuan could reach the breaking point.

July through August 2021

This time period could see another aggressive move by China against foreign investors (possibly confiscating assets for the state) or in some way involving foreign capital. China makes some sort of unilateral move at this time, in relation to global financial markets, possibly currency-related. It could also be the trigger of a big shift involving the yuan in the foreign exchange market.

December 2021

Serious levels of debt could threaten the credibility of China's leadership; perhaps they are not seen as having addressed the issues of the past two years. Capital flight accelerates. There doesn't seem to be an available means to address the problems with China's financial system, and this adversely affects the currency.

July through October 2022

Drastic events intertwining China's leadership with its economy and currency could occur from July through August 2022. Foreign interest rates and capital flight may again weaken China's economy.

Speculators may sense deteriorating conditions for China's currency in July 2022. There could be a big move in the yuan's value, associated with an extreme drain of foreign capital, from October 4 to October 25, 2022.

CHAPTER 8

POPULAR REVOLT IN CHINA 2019–2020

Astrological configurations forming in 2020 to the natal charts of China and the Chinese Communist Party have similar patterns to what occurred astrologically in 1989, the time period of the Tiananmen Square protests and suppression of dissent.

ANALYSIS OF THE 1989 TIANANMEN SQUARE PROTEST FOR CHINA'S CHART

Just as in 1307, Saturn, Uranus, and Neptune were traveling closely together from December 1988 through December 1989. Although there was never an exact conjunction involving all three planets in the 20th century, each pair made exact conjunctions (three passes due to retrograde motion).

During the Tiananmen Square incident, Saturn, Uranus, and Neptune were traveling through 0° to 13° Capricorn. It was in 1989 that Saturn was exactly conjunct Neptune, at 11°–12° Capricorn. This position was sextile (60° angle) the position of the Uranus-Saturn-Neptune conjunction in 1307, of 11° Scorpio. The 1307 conjunction in Scorpio heralded the decay of institutions and destruction of crops due to floods, and massive depopulation due to disease. The 1989 Saturn-Neptune conjunctions in Capricorn, along with the 1988 Saturn-Uranus conjunctions in late Sagittarius (conjoining the Galactic Center at 26°–27° Sagittarius[126]) and the 1993 Uranus-Neptune conjunctions at 19°–20° Capricorn, brought the collapse of the Soviet Union, independence to former Soviet republics, and the reunification of Germany. These conjunctions also brought the hardening of authoritarianism in China and the consolidation of power into a few positions within the Chinese Communist Party.

126 The Galactic Center is a supermassive black hole which is the rotational center of the Milky Way.

Although economic and political reforms had begun in China in the 1980's, they were shelved due to the Tiananmen Square protests. In 1993, the year of the Uranus-Neptune conjunction, China began implementing economic reforms again,[127] but suppression of political debate and dissent is still heavy-handed to

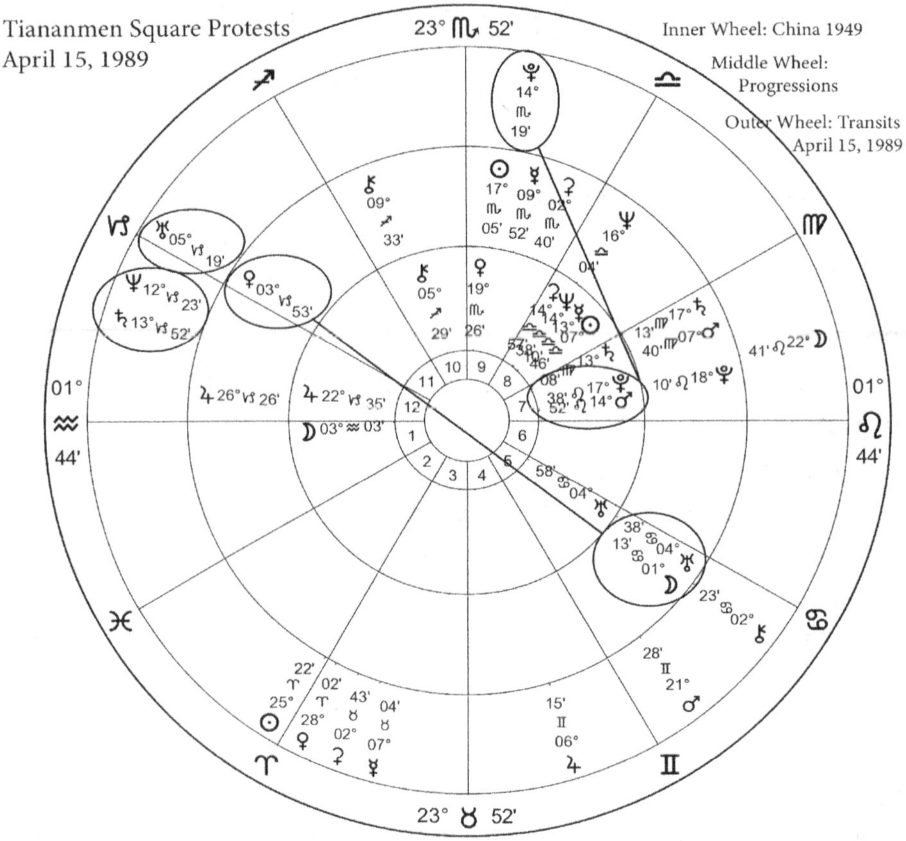

this day. In fact, it's increasing. And economic reform has been implemented in such a way as to encourage corruption and accrue the most benefit to the CCP. So, although the common people in China have benefited by being lifted out of poverty, they are still the ones paying the high price of social disorganization, a lack of basic freedoms, and environmental ravage that has characterized China's selective acceptance of certain aspects of capitalism, while rejecting other aspects.

China's Chart in Spring 1989

The Tiananmen Square protests began on April 15, 1989. Configurations

127 https://en.wikipedia.org/wiki/Tiananmen_Square_protests_of_1989

affecting China's chart at this time put transiting Saturn 14° Capricorn and Neptune 13° Capricorn in the twelfth house. They were both trine (120° angle) to natal Saturn 13°08' Virgo in the seventh house, indicating that the flow of events would favor the established ruling party.

The twelfth house position is indicative of popular revolts because it is opposite the sixth house. In older astrology texts the sixth house is said to rule servants and slaves, whereas the twelfth house rules "slave revolts." But in the modern world, the sixth house is associated with the labor force of a nation. Thus, in modern parlance, the twelfth house has to do with strikes or revolts by laborers—the common people (who are still viewed pretty much as slaves by the ruling classes, especially in a dictatorship). Although the Tiananmen Square revolt began as a student protest, the students were quickly and massively joined by the work force of China. In the crackdown and arrests that followed the protests, laborers were given much harsher sentences than the students, whose parents were members of the elite classes.[128]

So, why did revolt break out in April–June 1989 in spite of the fact that dissent was growing amongst students and workers as early as 1986, when Professor Fang Lizhi began lecturing at Chinese universities about human rights, democracy, and especially, the separation of powers within government?[129]

It was in April 1989 that not only were these three transiting planets together in Capricorn, but within two weeks each of them turned retrograde.

On April 14, Neptune turned retrograde, and the protests began on April 15 with the death of Hu Yaobang,[130] the former General Secretary of the CCP who had been forced to resign due to his empathy with the ideas of the intellectual elite and the students. Uranus turned retrograde on April 9, and Saturn went retrograde on April 23.

This huge shift in the undercurrents of society coincided with China's progressed Moon 1°13' Cancer moving to conjoin natal Uranus 4°55' Cancer, opposing transiting Uranus 5°19' Capricorn and progressed Venus 3°53' Capricorn. Over the three-month time period of April–June 1989, the progressed Moon made exact aspects to these natal, progressed, and transiting planets—especially the opposition between transiting Uranus and natal Uranus. This was the first occurrence of transiting Uranus opposing natal Uranus for China's chart,

128 https://en.wikipedia.org/wiki/Tiananmen_Square_protests_of_1989

129 Ibid.

130 Ibid.

and the progressed Moon just happened to be there to trigger it. As Cancer/Moon rules China's sixth house of the labor force, it was the mobilization of the labor force that accelerated the revolt.

Chinese Communist Party's Chart in Spring 1989

In the natal chart for the Chinese Communist Party, Saturn, Uranus and Neptune at 5°–14° Capricorn, in the fourth and fifth houses, opposed the natal Sun, Mars, and Pluto, all at 9° Cancer in the tenth house of the ruling authority

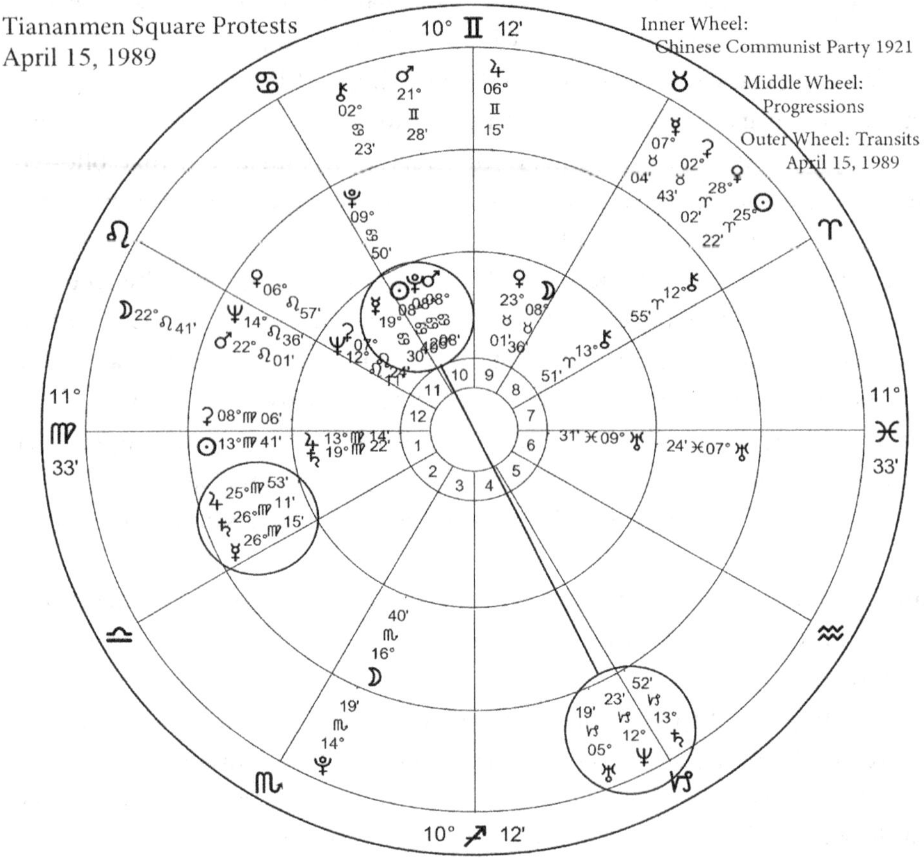

or leadership. It was the Saturn-Neptune conjunction at 11°–12° Capricorn that most directly opposed these natal planets. As explained in the analysis of China's chart above, and also as stated by astrologer Andre Barbault,[131] the Saturn-Neptune cycle is associated with "popular insurrections that are usually

131 Andre Barbault, *Planetary Cycles – Mundane Astrology*, (The Astrological Association, 2016), p. 85

fired by ideological beliefs." The fourth house of a mundane chart is associated with opposition to the ruling party. A cycle associated with popular revolts was situated in the area of the chart denoting opposition.

These three planets turned retrograde in the CCP chart's fourth house. As the fourth house denotes the past, Saturn, Uranus, and Neptune all backtracking within this house perfectly described the result of the protests: The CCP rescinded the reforms that had begun in the early 1980's, and reverted to a mostly traditional Leninist form of government.

That the CCP would prevail is also confirmed by this chart, for progressed Saturn 26°11' Virgo was conjunct progressed Mercury 26°16' Virgo. Both are conjunct progressed Jupiter 25°53' Virgo. Mercury rules the sign of the tenth house, Gemini, and the sign of the Ascendant, Virgo. The established authority was favored by this configuration.[132]

Astrological Configurations in 1989 Favored the Chinese Government's Suppression of Revolt

From first glance, however, the astrological configurations of spring 1989 for China's chart might have caused an astrologer to forecast that a popular revolt would go in favor of the protesters. But the position of transiting Pluto 14°19' Scorpio indicates that this could not be the case. Pluto is in the sign it rules, and Scorpio is associated with transformation. With Pluto in the ninth house of expansion of ideals, it would seem that the time was ripe to favor increased reform, not the cancelling of previously implemented reforms.

But transiting Pluto in Scorpio squares China's natal Mars 14°52' Leo and natal Pluto 17°38' Leo. This is a potent configuration. Mars and Pluto are the co-rulers of Scorpio, and Scorpio is the sign on the cusp of China's Midheaven, the tenth house of the ruling government. Pluto's influence is heavily on the side of the CCP—the Chinese Communist Party *is* the government of China—and the square to these natal planets indicates their heavy-handed response.

Furthermore, transiting Mars moved into Cancer as the protests wore on, and thus made exact aspects to natal Uranus, the progressed Moon, and transiting Uranus. Mars shows violence inflicted upon the masses (the Moon always represents the general population, and even more so in China's case, as the natal Moon is conjunct the Ascendant, another point that indicates a

132 These house rulerships are dependent upon the time used for the chart. The exact time is unknown, but it is probably safe to assume that the conference that initiated the CCP began midmorning (10 am).

country's populace). This violence has its source in the government—Scorpio, ruled by Mars, on the cusp of the tenth house.

As transiting Mars moved through Cancer in May and June 1989, it conjoined the CCP natal Sun, Mars, and Pluto at 9° Cancer. Transiting Mars was triggering China's progressed Moon, but triggering the CCP's natal Sun, Mars, and Pluto. This Sun-Mars-Pluto conjunction in the tenth house of the CCP chart indicates that the CCP is fiercely focused on their own security, which they equate with national security, and the protesters felt the full force of the government's power to enforce their position.

The Sun indicates a nation's leadership in a mundane chart. China's progressed Sun 17°05' Scorpio also indicates a harsh reaction by leadership, and not just because it is in Scorpio. The contra-antiscion[133] of 17°05' Scorpio

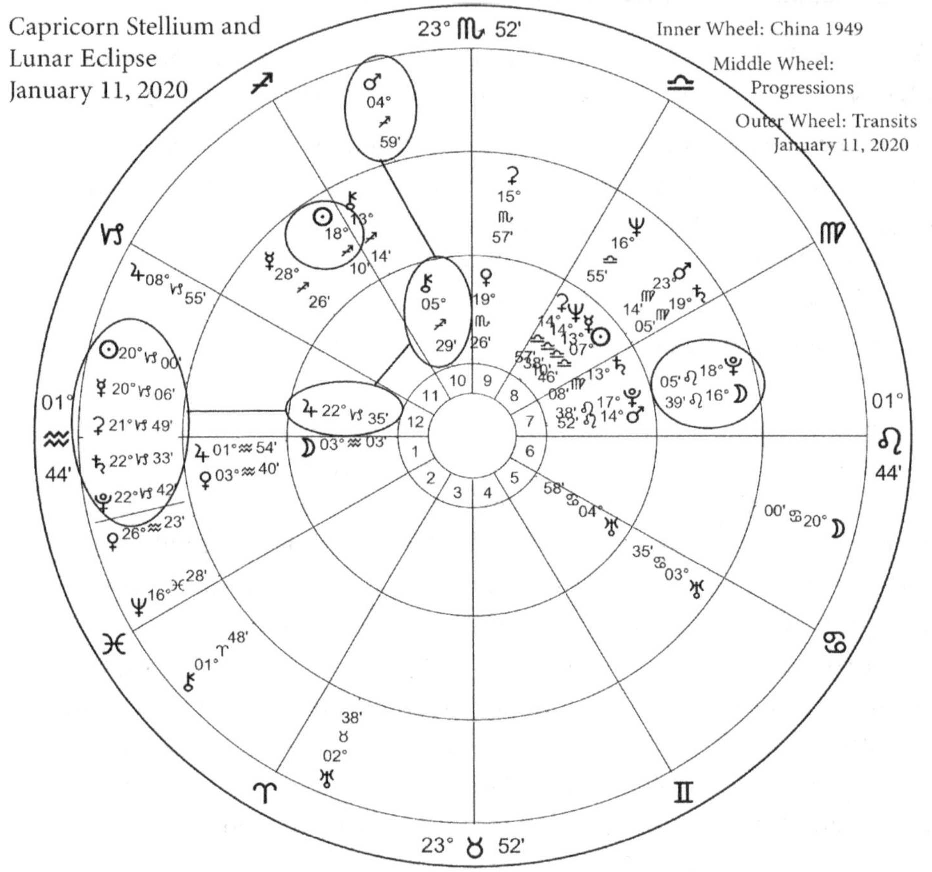

133 See the Glossary.

is 12°55' Leo, very near the position of natal Mars 14°52' Leo. This setup acts as if the progressed Sun and natal Mars are in a harsh aspect—another indication of heavy-handed use of power.

But perhaps the real key to proper interpretation of how these configurations would play out is transiting Jupiter 6°15' Gemini opposing China's natal Chiron 5°29' Sagittarius. Sagittarius/Jupiter rules the eleventh house of political parties, and because there is truly only one political party in China, Jupiter and the eleventh house represent the CCP.

The CCP is very sensitive to any dissent coming from the labor force. This is shown by the antiscion[134] of natal Chiron, at 24°31' Capricorn, being in close orb of natal Jupiter 22°35' Capricorn—and in the twelfth house, no less. The CCP has a deeply ingrained fear of labor revolts, which was triggered in the April 1989 time period as transiting Jupiter opposed natal Chiron and formed a T-square with progressed Mars 7°40' Virgo. It is the square to Mars that increased the government's fear and resulted in a violent response.

CHINA – Astrological Conditions of Suppression of Popular Revolt in 1989

What astrological conditions can be defined from this situation in 1989 as indicative of a massive popular revolt *in China* that is suppressed? (Some of these conditions apply to certain nations, but not all.)

- Outer planets in the twelfth house, particularly Saturn.
- Transiting or progressed planet in harsh aspect to either natal Jupiter or natal Chiron.
- Transiting or progressed planet in harsh aspect to natal Mars and Pluto.
- Involvement of Sun, Mars, Pluto, and/or the sign Scorpio.
- Natal or progressed Moon in harsh aspect to natal, progressed, or transiting Uranus.

134 See the Glossary.

CHINA – Astrological Conditions of Suppression of Popular Revolt Repeat in 2019–2020

The Capricorn stellium of 2020 falls in China's twelfth house. On January 11, 2020 Saturn and Pluto are conjunct at 22°46' Capricorn—and they are conjunct the Sun's position in a lunar eclipse.

Saturn and Pluto conjoin natal Jupiter 22°35' Capricorn, and thus they trigger the Jupiter-Chiron link by antiscion as explained above. Saturn and Pluto are planets whose transits can induce fear, and at this time they are triggering a configuration within China's natal chart that indicates a fear of labor unrest that is inherent in the reactions of the CCP. (See chart on page 174.)

China's natal Jupiter-Chiron link is also triggered by transiting Mars 5° Sagittarius, which conjoins natal Chiron. Mars sparks action, especially when in a Fire sign such as Sagittarius.

The progressed Moon 16°39' Leo conjoins natal Mars and Pluto, putting emphasis on what these planets represent (aggression, action, deeply felt emotions, destructive tendencies) and the things ruled by the seventh house (interactions with others, war, peace, legal issues) where the conjunction occurs. This conjunction ties to another aspect at the time: The progressed Sun 18°10' Sagittarius has moved to (almost) exactly trine progressed Pluto 18°05' Leo. This aspect indicates that the power dynamics of the situation once again favor the established government and leadership, as Scorpio/Pluto rules the tenth house.

The progressed Moon is also semi-square (45° angle) to progressed Uranus 3°35' Cancer. Emphasizing this aspect between progressed planets is transiting Uranus 2°33' Taurus, turning direct on the same day as this lunar eclipse, being in square aspect to the natal Moon 3°03' Aquarius.

Thus, all five conditions that were present in 1989 are also present in 2020.

But no event repeats exactly. In 1989, the protesters were taken by surprise (progressed Moon conjunct progressed Uranus) by the government resorting to shooting its own people. Although there were riots in April 1989, the government vacillated in its response. But in June, it came out with tanks and guns.

In 2020, things could unfold differently, with more violent tactics being used by the protesters (progressed Moon conjunct natal Mars and Pluto), but also by the authorities (progressed Moon semi-square progressed Uranus). The government may show far less patience this time, perhaps choosing to crack down aggressively much sooner in the course of the protests than they did in

1989 due to the overt friction and mistrust shown by the semi-square aspect between the progressed Moon and Uranus.

CHINA – Political Forecast for September 2019 through January 2020

In mid-September 2019, popular grievances that have been growing for some time burst forth in protests. On September 16, 2019 while transiting Saturn makes its station, about to return to direct motion, Saturn and the South Node are conjunct at 13°53' Capricorn. This pair interacts with points in China's chart and the CCP's chart, triggering these outbursts.

In the CCP chart, Saturn and the South Node are trine natal Jupiter 13°14' Virgo, progressed Venus 13°30' Virgo, and progressed Mars 11°10' Virgo. But they form a T-square with the progressed Sun 13°28' Libra opposing natal Chiron 11°51' Aries, in the second and eighth houses respectively. A serious, well-organized opposition challenges the existing leadership, whose image has been damaged (possibly by a corruption scandal). The opposition gains favor with the general population.

From September 14 to October 8, 2019, the progressed Sun in China's chart is similarly impacted: Transiting Mars 17°–19° Virgo is conjunct progressed Saturn in the eighth house and opposes transiting Neptune 17° Pisces. Transiting Jupiter is passing over the progressed Sun 18° Sagittarius and they form a T-square to this opposition. This configuration, with a transiting Jupiter-Neptune square, in harsh aspect to progressed Saturn, definitely indicates a scandal coming to light that involves CCP leadership. The opposition between transiting Neptune and progressed Saturn is also a condition of a major currency devaluation that is looming, due to excessive debt.

In this same time period, Pluto returns to direct motion on October 3, opposing natal Mercury in the CCP chart—another indication of an opposition movement (both within the CCP and in the general populace) against the existing leadership of both the CCP and the country. On the same date, the progressed Moon 13°01' Leo in China's chart is exactly sesquiquadrate (135° angle) progressed Mercury 28°01' Sagittarius. The general populace (the labor force of China) is roused into active protest. As the progressed Moon is moving to conjunct natal Mars and Pluto, it is likely that the protests will escalate into violence. From November 19 to December 2, transiting Jupiter in late Sagittarius is in orb of a sesquiquadrate aspect (135° angle) to natal Mars and the progressed Moon in China's chart. Attempts to quell popular protests are frustrated by escalating violence.

In late November 2019, the transiting North Node 10° Cancer exactly conjoins the CCP progressed Pluto, and is moving to conjoin natal Sun/Mars/Pluto (the Nodes move backward through the zodiac). So although these transits to China's natal chart indicate some sort of confrontation by political opposition, the CCP chart confirms that the government will prevail.

Configurations for both China's chart and the CCP's chart on November 23–24, 2019 indicate a dramatic event, probably a major confrontation between the ruling leadership and the opposition. Transiting Venus and Jupiter are conjunct at 28°12' Sagittarius—in China's chart, they are conjunct progressed Mercury; in the CCP's chart, they are conjunct the progressed Moon. This degree in Sagittarius is trine to the point of the August 21, 2017 total solar eclipse at

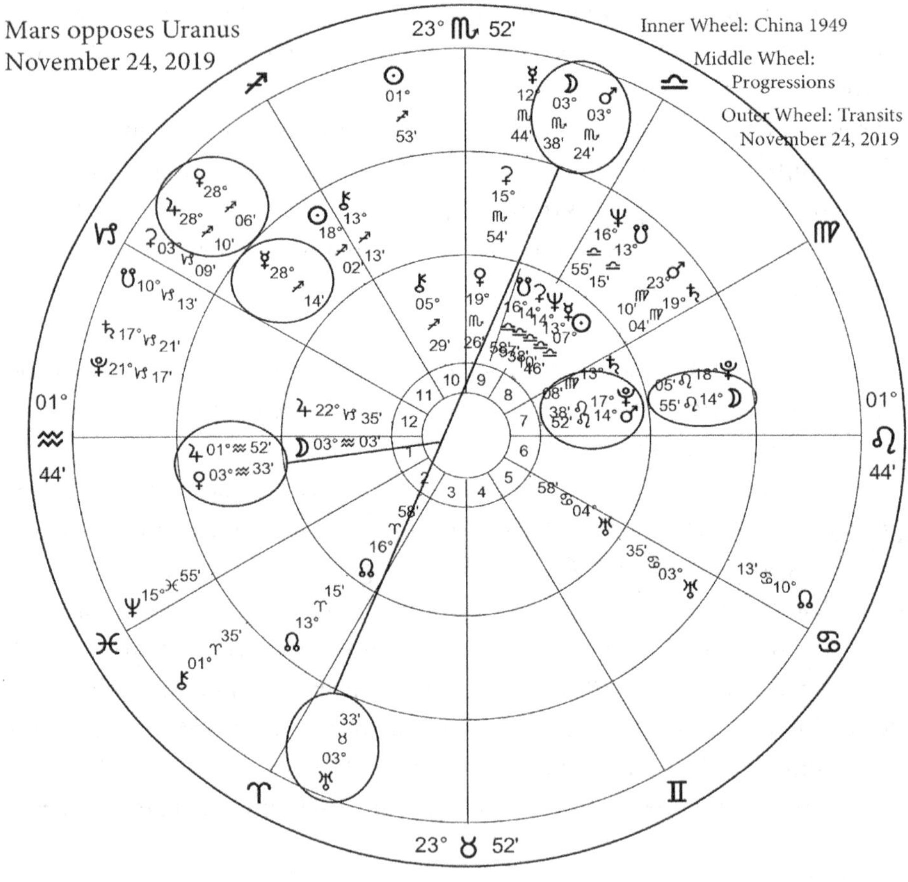

28°52' Leo. The trine aspect, and the position of Jupiter in Sagittarius, lend more power to the established government. They also indicate a very negative reaction from the rest of the world.

Violent conflict is indicated by transiting Mars and the Moon in Scorpio exactly opposing transiting Uranus 3°33' Taurus. This opposition forms an exact T-square with progressed Venus 3°33' Aquarius in China's chart. And transiting Uranus is exactly sextile China's progressed Uranus 3°35' Cancer.

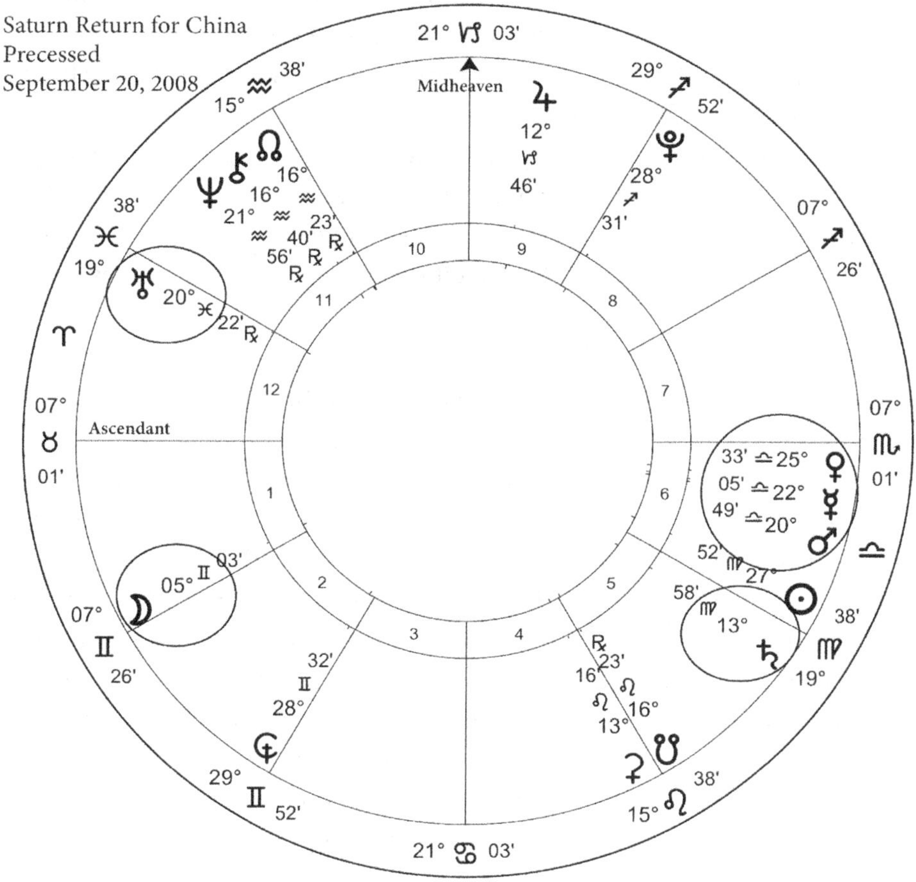

It's just too easy for both sides to be ideologically inflamed and righteous under this configuration.

Due to the indications from the configurations in January 2020, it's probable that the established order will crush the opposition—with the configurations of November 23–24, 2019 showing a fierce fight to do so.

Once Jupiter enters Capricorn on December 3, 2019, the government has the upper hand. By December 11, order will begin to be re-established, but probably at great cost. The transiting Sun square progressed Saturn in Virgo, and transiting Uranus 3° Taurus squaring the natal Moon in Aquarius, show the situation being brought under control, although not without violence due to transiting Mars in Scorpio squaring natal Mars and the progressed Moon in Leo. By December 24, the government and CCP may use more violence to exert control, as Mars moves over China's Midheaven 23°52' Scorpio. The solar eclipse of December 26 at 4°06' Capricorn conjoins transiting Jupiter and opposes China's natal Uranus, another indication of a massive response by the government to maintain control.

In January 2020 when the Capricorn stellium occurs, transiting Hades 8° Cancer[135] conjoins the CCP natal Sun/Mars/Pluto, and transiting Jupiter and the South Node 8°–9° Capricorn oppose them. This appears to be another period of consolidation of power for the CCP, but it is achieved in a ruthless way.

2008 Saturn Return for China

China's current Saturn return[136] confirms this October 2019 through January 2020 time period as one of protest and crackdown.

The potential for serious opposition to the established rule is shown in the precessed Saturn return itself: Saturn is in Virgo, ruled by Mercury 22°05' Libra conjoining Mars 20°49' Libra and Venus 25°33' Libra in the sixth house of the labor force—and also of the military. This Mars-Mercury-Venus conjunction in Libra is trine Neptune 21°56' Aquarius in the eleventh house of groups, and inconjunct (150° angle) Uranus 20°22' Pisces in the twelfth house of corruption and labor unrest. This indicates a destabilizing influence for the country that involves underground elements, as well as the work force. This opposition movement is very idealistic, but it lacks cohesion (Uranus and Neptune in mutual reception) as it is composed of various groups which are not bound by one, strong, unifying purpose.

---

135 See the Glossary for an explanation of Hades.

136 A comparison of the precessed and non-precessed Saturn return charts in effect for China at the time of the 1989 Tiananmen Square protests shows that both have close aspects with transits to progressions, but perhaps the precessed return works slightly better. And there was only one Saturn return in 2008; transiting Saturn did *not* pass over its natal position three times due to retrograde motion.

All of this has an effect on the functioning of Saturn in the twenty-nine-year period of this return. Capricorn/Saturn rules the return's Midheaven, the cusp of the tenth house of the ruling government, so Saturn functions mainly through the established government. Saturn is in the fifth house of new forms and projects—but any new form, or reform, to government will be difficult to

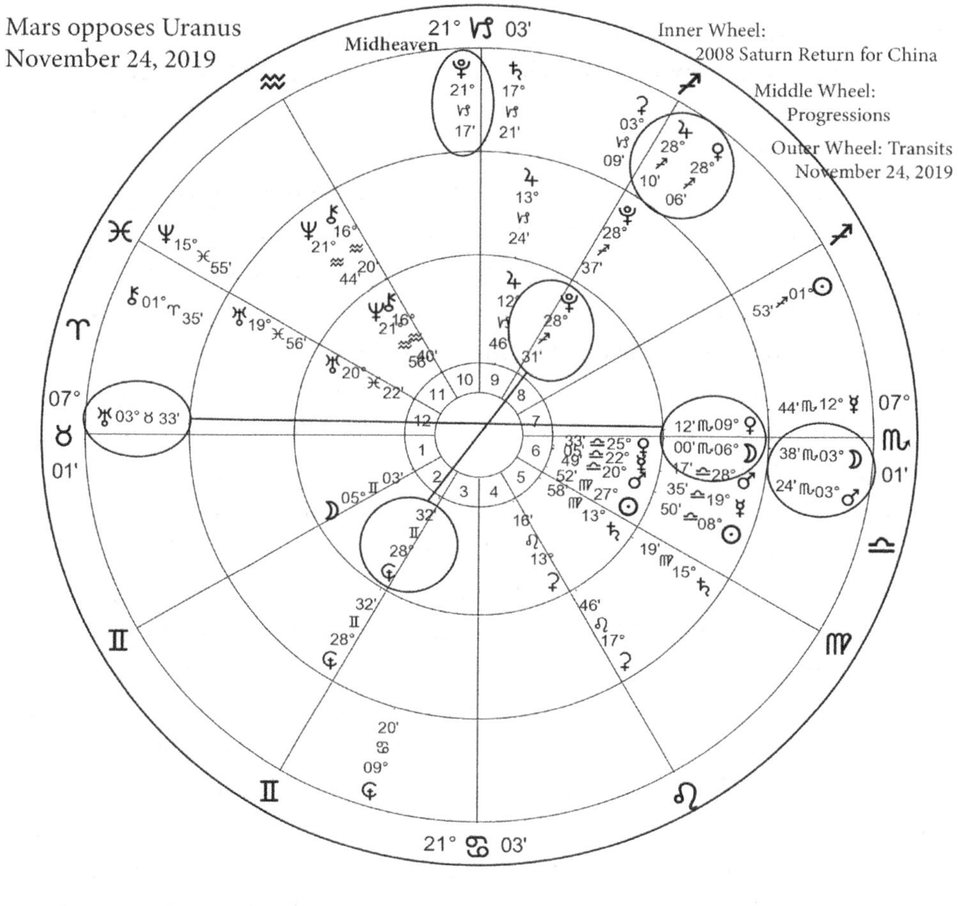

implement, if not outright rejected, due to the South Node also in the fifth house, which makes old habits hard to break. In this case, a break with the past is felt as keenly painful, due to Chiron conjunct the North Node in the eleventh house.

A violent attempt at reform that is suppressed by leadership is indicated by Pluto 28°31' Sagittarius (on the Galactic Center) in the eighth house opposing Hades 28°22' Gemini, forming a T-square with the Sun 27°52' Virgo. Pluto rules the Descendant 7° Scorpio, which represents foreign allies and enemies. When this configuration is triggered by progressions and transits, it has the potential to result in suppression and elimination of foreign influences in the country.

But by far the most important element indicating that a popular revolt will challenge China's leadership is the position of the Moon in the Saturn return, at 5°03' Gemini. This indicates widespread opposition by the work force, triggering the CCP and government leadership's dread of such threats to stability. The trigger is that the return's Moon opposes natal Chiron in China's chart, triggering the Jupiter-Chiron link by antiscion points. That the opposition movement could become violent is shown by Mercury conjunct Mars in the sixth house of laborers (Gemini, sign of the return's Moon, is ruled by Mercury).

Two dates stand out when checking the progressions and transits to the Saturn return for late 2019 and early 2020. Configurations on October 22, 2019 show suppression of student protests, with the work force also coming out in larger numbers to protest. Transiting Uranus in Taurus (in the twelfth house of labor revolt) exactly opposes the progressed Moon 4°52' Scorpio, while transiting Saturn and progressed Jupiter in Capricorn (in the ninth house of higher learning—university professors and students) are trine the return's Saturn in Virgo. This trine gives support to the established leadership's position.

November 24, 2019 is another date that stands out (just as it did for both China's natal chart and the CCP's natal chart). Violence and death are shown, due to a heavy-handed response by China's leadership. The transiting Venus-Jupiter conjunction at 28° Sagittarius on that day conjoins natal Pluto in China's Saturn return, in the eighth house of death, debt, and foreign currencies. This triggers the Pluto-Hades-Sun T-square of the Saturn return. House rulerships indicating much violence and death are shown, for Sagittarius/Jupiter rules the eighth house of death, Taurus/Venus rules the first house of the general populace, and Libra/Venus falls in the sixth house of the work force.[137] Transiting Pluto is conjunct the return's Midheaven, eliciting an excessive response from leadership. With transiting Mars about to conjoin the progressed Moon at 6° Scorpio while opposing Uranus (at the same time that the transiting Moon conjoins progressed Mars 28°17' Libra), emotions are running wild, resulting in extreme actions.

137 This configuration also has heavy implications for China's economy and the value of the yuan. See Chapter 6.

The lunar eclipse of January 11, 2020 falls on the Midheaven axis of the precessed Saturn return. With the transiting Sun, Saturn, and Pluto at 20°–23° Capricorn conjunct the Midheaven (MC), China's established leaders exert even more control than ever.

APPENDIX A

LIST OF NATAL CHARTS WITH DATA

BRAZIL

Event: Proclamation of independence from Portugal
Date: September 7, 1822 4:47 pm Local Mean Time (LMT)
Location: Ipiranga, Brazil
Source: Nicolas Campion, *The Book of World Horoscopes*, Wessex Astrologer, 2004, pg. 63

CHINA

Event: Proclamation of formation of government of People's Republic of China at a rally in Peking (Beijing)
Date: October 1, 1949 3:01 pm LMT
Location: Beijing, China
Source: Nicolas Campion, *The Book of World Horoscopes*, Wessex Astrologer, 2004, pg. 81

CHINESE COMMUNIST PARTY

Event: Formation at opening session of the First National Congress of the Party
Date: July 1, 1921 10:00 am LMT (assumed time)
Location: Shanghai, China
Source: *China Today,* The Communist Party of China, http://www.chinatoday.com/org/cpc/

CLERICIS LAICOS

Event: Issuance by Pope Boniface VIII
Date: February 5, 1296 1:48 am LMT (moment of the New Moon)
Location: Rome, Italy
Source: Wikipedia, Clericis Laicos, https://en.wikipedia.org/wiki/Clericis_laicos

European Exchange Rate Mechanism

Event: Initiation
Date: March 13, 1979 0:00 am Greenwich Mean Time (GMT)
Location: Brussels, Belgium
Source: Wikipedia, European Exchange Rate Mechanism
https://en.wikipedia.org/wiki/European_Exchange_Rate_Mechanism

Indonesia

Event: Independence granted by the Netherlands
Date: December 27, 1949 9:22 am GMT
Location: Jakarta, Indonesia
Source: Nicolas Campion, *The Book of World Horoscopes*
Wessex Astrologer, 2004, pg. 160

Mexico

Event: Signing of constitution at Constitutional Assembly
Date: January 31, 1917 4:00 pm LMT
Location: Queretaro, Mexico
Source: Nicolas Campion, *The Book of World Horoscopes*
Wessex Astrologer, 2004, pg. 212

Reign of Philip IV of France

Event: Philip's reign began with the death of his father, Philip III
Date: October 5, 1285 12:35 pm LMT (time rectified by the author)
Location: Paris, France
Source: Wikipedia, Philip IV of France
https://en.wikipedia.org/wiki/Philip_IV_of_France

Russia

Event: Raising of the Russian flag over the Kremlin after Soviet Union disbanded
Date: December 25, 1991 7:45 pm LMT
Location: Moscow, Russia
Source: Nicolas Campion, *The Book of World Horoscopes*
Wessex Astrologer, 2004, pg. 274

South Korea

Event: Independence granted by the United States
Date: August 15, 1948 12:00 pm LMT
Location: Seoul, South Korea
Source: Nicolas Campion, *The Book of World Horoscopes*
Wessex Astrologer, 2004, pg. 180

Thailand

Event: Military coup that instituted constitutional rule
Date: June 24, 1932 5:00 am LMT
Location: Bangkok, Thailand
Source: Nicolas Campion, *The Book of World Horoscopes*
Wessex Astrologer, 2004, pg. 314

United Kingdom Chart #1

Event: Union of Great Britain with Ireland
Date: January 1, 1801 0:00 am LMT
Location: Westminster, United Kingdom
Source: Nicolas Campion, *The Book of World Horoscopes*
Wessex Astrologer, 2004, pg. 344

United Kingdom Chart #2

Event: United Kingdom Reorganization
Date: December 7, 1922, 3:28 pm GMT
Location: Westminster, United Kingdom
Source: Nicolas Campion, *The Book of World Horoscopes*
Wessex Astrologer, 2004, pg. 345

Venice, Italy

Event: Venetian tradition
Date: March 25, 421 12:00 pm LMT
Location: Venice, Italy
Source: John Julius Norwich, *A History of Venice*, Vintage, 1989, p. 5

All charts use the Placidus house system.

Glossary of Astrological Terms

A

Antiscion – The reflex position of a planet's degree in the zodiac, as measured from the 0° Cancer–0° Capricorn axis. For example, if a planet is located at 13° Taurus, it is 47° away from 0° Cancer. The antiscion of that planet's position is then 47° on the other side of 0° Cancer, at 17° Leo. When a transiting or progressed planet conjoins a natal planet's antiscion point, that natal planet can be triggered. The antiscion point is also called the solstice point. See also Contra-antiscion.

Applying – A condition of any aspect in which the faster moving planet is approaching the exact aspect with the slower moving planet. Each aspect has a specific house (and its areas of life) associated with its applying condition. See also Separating.

Ascendant – The point in the zodiac that was on the eastern horizon for the location and time for which the chart was cast; along with the Midheaven, considered a very sensitive point in a chart. The cusp of the first house of the chart. Denotes the character of the entity represented by the chart. In political astrology, where charts are cast for countries, the Ascendant denotes the general population, the overall condition of the country, and the characteristics of its citizens.

Aspect – The relationship between two planets, as measured by longitude or declination. An aspect by longitude is the central angle between two positions in the zodiac, as viewed from the Earth as the center of the zodiacal circle. Divisions of the circle (360°) by two and three are the commonly used aspects, such as the conjunction (0°), semi-square (45°), sextile (60°), square (90°), trine (120°), sesquiquadrate (135°), inconjunct (150°) and opposition (180°). An aspect by declination is measured by the distance of the planet from the projection of the equator onto the heavens; these are the parallel (both planets are the same number of degrees either north or south of the projection) and the contraparallel (one planet is north of the projection and the other is the same number of degrees south of the projection). Aspects indicate how the two planets will work together, either in harmony or discord.

C

Ceres – An asteroid that is part of the asteroid belt orbiting the Sun between Mars and Jupiter. Named after the Roman goddess of vegetation, especially corn. Ceres was associated with law and justice as defining the norms of society. Ceres appears to influence national borders and currency exchange rates.

Chiron – A minor planet orbiting the Sun between Saturn and Uranus; also classified as a comet. Named after the Roman centaur. Chiron was a gifted healer, but was unable to heal himself when he was struck by a poisoned arrow. Chiron is referred to as the "Wounded Healer" in astrology and represents a blind spot, weakness, sensitivity, or wound from the past which the chart entity finds it difficult to move past.

Conjoin – When two planets occupy the same degree of the zodiac, or are within a tight range (3° to 10°) of being at the same point in the zodiac; same as the conjunction.

Conjunction – When two planets occupy the same degree of the zodiac, or are within a tight range (3° to 10°) of being at the same point in the zodiac. The conjunction is the end of one cycle of the pair of planets involved, and the beginning of a new cycle. The conjunction aspect can be favorable, denoting agreement or success, or unfavorable, denoting a clash of wills, depending upon the planets involved.

Contra-antiscion – The point exactly 180° opposite the antiscion of a planet or point in the chart. See also Antiscion.

Contraparallel – An aspect by declination in which one planet is north of the projection of the equator upon the heavens, and the other is the same number of degrees south of that projection. See also Parallel; Declination.

Cusp – The boundary line (at a specific degree in the zodiac) between two houses in a chart.

Cycle – For a single planet, its cycle is a complete revolution of the zodiac (any degree of the zodiac can be taken as the starting point of the cycle). For a pair of planets, their cycle (referred to as their synodic cycle) begins with their conjunction, progresses as the faster moving planet moves away from the slower moving planet, and ends when they are conjunct again, usually at a different point in the zodiac from the conjunction which started their cycle. A cycle of a planetary pair has a waxing phase and waning phase, and culminates when they reach opposition, 180° apart in the zodiac. See Waxing; Waning.

D

Debilitated – An astrological condition in which the Sun, Moon, or a planet is in a sign or a house, or is part of an aspect that blocks or distorts its expression of its nature. In the system of essential dignities, the Sun, Moon, and five planets of traditional astrology (Mercury, Venus, Mars, Jupiter, and Saturn) each have sign placements in which they are designated as in their fall or their detriment; these are debilitated placements.

Declination – The distance between a planet and the projection of the equator on the heavens. A planet can be north or south of the equator. Declination is the basis of the parallel and contraparallel aspects.

Descendant – The point exactly 180° opposite the Ascendant. It is the cusp of the seventh house. Denotes other people with whom the chart entity has significant relationships, such as spouse, business partners, etc. In political astrology, denotes allies and open enemies, foreign countries.

Dignity, Dignified – An astrological condition in which the Sun, Moon, or a planet is in a sign, or a house, or part of an aspect that strengthens or freely allows its expression of its nature. In the system of essential dignities, the Sun, Moon, and five planets of traditional astrology (Mercury, Venus, Mars, Jupiter, and Saturn) each have sign placements in which they are designated as in their rulership or their exaltation; these are dignified placements.

Domicile – The sign or signs ruled by a planet; the sign in which that planet most strongly expresses its intrinsic nature.

E

Eclipse – The phenomenon that occurs when the Sun, Moon, and Earth are aligned so as to block the view of the Sun (solar eclipse) or the Moon (lunar eclipse) as seen on Earth. When the Moon aligns between the Sun and the Earth, a solar eclipse occurs and the Sun is blocked from view. This can happen only during a New Moon (though not at every New Moon). When the Earth aligns between the Sun and the Moon, a lunar eclipse occurs and the Moon is blocked from view. This can happen only during a Full Moon (though not at every Full Moon). The traditional view is that eclipses are malefic in nature, but that is not always the case. However, eclipses are one of the most powerful configurations in astrology.

Ecliptic – The great circle on the celestial sphere that is the apparent path of the Sun as it moves around the Earth, from the perspective of an observer on Earth. The constellations that align with the ecliptic are those that define the signs of the zodiac.

Element – A fourfold division of the zodiac signs into designations of Fire, Earth, Air, or Water, which describe the basic nature of the sign, and which condition how planets in those signs will function.

Essential Dignities – A categorization of certain positions in the zodiac in which the Sun, Moon, and five traditional planets (Mercury, Venus, Mars, Jupiter, and Saturn) have either strength or weakness.

Exalted – An astrological condition that is one of the essential dignities. The Sun, Moon, and five planets of traditional astrology (Mercury, Venus, Mars, Jupiter, and Saturn) each have one sign in which they are said to be exalted; i.e., they express their fundamental nature freely. Exaltation is considered to be very beneficial, but not quite as powerful as rulership.

G

Grand Cross – A configuration that forms among four planets when two of them are in opposition, and the other two are also in opposition, and the second pair are square (at a 90° angle) the first pair.

Grand Trine – A configuration that forms among three planets in which each is 120° apart from the other two, forming an equilateral triangle in the heavens.

H

Hades – The Transneptunian point in Uranian astrology that represents decay, loss, criminal activity, sinister influences, the occult, buried issues, and filthy conditions. Named after the god of the underworld. Hades is not an actual planetary body in the heavens, it is a calculated point that has been found to have an effect astrologically as it moves very slowly through the zodiac.

House – A division of an astrological chart that represents an area of life. There are twelve divisions, based upon the Ascendant as the beginning of the first house. There are many different methods of determining the houses. These methods can be classified according to the basis of their calculation: Those based upon the ecliptic; those based upon the volume of the celestial sphere; and those based upon time—the rotation of the Earth. The Whole Sign method of house division uses the 0° point of the sign in which the Ascendant falls as the cusp of the first house, and then each house is comprised of the 30° of a single sign, so that each sign of the zodiac is assigned to a house. Each astrologer has their preferred method of house division. The charts in this work use the Placidus method.

I

Inconjunct – An aspect by longitude in which two planets are 150° apart in the zodiac. The inconjunct aspect indicates an unbalanced situation.

M

Midheaven – The point in the zodiac which was the zenith for the location and time for which the chart was cast; along with the Ascendant, considered a very sensitive point in a chart. The cusp of the tenth house of the chart. Represents the career and outward status for an individual's chart; represents the government and leadership in power for a country's chart.

Mode – A classification of the signs that determines the basic manner in which planets in those signs function. The three modes are cardinal, fixed, and mutable. Each mode is assigned to four signs which are at 90° angles to each other in the zodiac. Aries, Cancer, Libra, and Capricorn are cardinal signs. Taurus, Leo, Scorpio, and Aquarius are fixed signs. Mutable signs are Gemini, Virgo, Sagittarius, and Pisces. Planets in cardinal signs act directly and forcefully, and want quick results. Planets in fixed signs act with determination and focus, and tend to preserve the status quo. Planets in mutable signs are adaptable, changeable, and are more easily influenced. The modes are also called quadruplicities.

Mutual Reception – A planetary condition that occurs between two planets when one planet is in a sign ruled by the other planet, and that other planet is in a sign ruled by the first planet; e.g., when Saturn is in Taurus (ruled by Venus) and Venus is in Capricorn (ruled by Saturn), Venus and Saturn are in mutual reception. Planets in mutual reception will work together, somewhat like a conjunction.

N

Natal – A chart calculated for the moment that an entity is considered to have begun its existence. For an individual, the natal chart is based upon the moment and location of their birth. For a country or an organization, many different events can be considered the "inception" of existence. For example, a country's natal chart could be calculated for the moment and location of a declaration of independence, or the ratifying of a constitution, or other events.

Node – The Moon's Nodes (North and South) are the points at which the Moon's orbit intersects the ecliptic. The Nodes are always 180° apart in the zodiac. The North Node indicates the destiny of an entity, the best that it could strive for. The South Node indicates influences from the past, or a regression to old habits or methods.

O

Opposition – An aspect by longitude in which two planets are 180° apart in the zodiac. The opposition aspect indicates conflict, open hostility, or a situation that has reached a climax.

Orb –The range (in degrees) in which an aspect is considered active. Each aspect is defined as a certain number of degrees, but the aspect is active before the aspect becomes exact, and also after it is exact, as long as the two planets involved fall within a certain degree range of each other. For example, Venus and Mars could be close to an exact trine of 120° apart, but they are only 115° apart; still, the aspect is active. Usually an orb of 8° is used for the major aspects (conjunction, square, trine, and opposition) between planets, but an orb of 10° or more is allowed for most aspects between the luminaries (Sun and Moon) and the planets. A smaller orb of 3° is often used for the other aspects (semi-square, sextile, sesquiquadrate, and inconjunct).

P

Parallel – An aspect by declination in which both planets are the same number of degrees either north or south of the projection of the equator upon the celestial sphere. See also Contraparallel; Declination.

Placidus House System – A time-based method of dividing the astrological chart into twelve sections that represent areas of life.

Precessed Return – Calculation of solar or planetary return charts that takes into consideration the precession of the equinoxes that has occurred since the date of the natal chart; thus the position of the Sun (or planet) moves slightly forward in the zodiac as the chart entity increases in age.

Progressed – The position which the Sun, Moon, or a planet occupies at a certain time after the birth or inception time, as calculated by the formula of "a day for a year." This technique is termed secondary progressions. The progressed positions of the Sun, Moon, and planets for the nth year of life correspond to their positions for the nth day after the birth date; e.g., the progressed positions for the tenth year of life are those of the Sun, Moon, and planets for the tenth day after birth. These progressed positions show the changes in the entity's situation as their life unfolds.

R

Retrograde – The phenomenon of a planet appearing to move backward through the zodiac. This optical illusion occurs because of the geometrical relationship that exists between the planet and a viewer on Earth as both the Earth and the planet revolve around the Sun. All planets have retrograde periods. When a planet is moving retrograde, the areas of life with which that planet is associated will experience delays and obstacles, or unresolved issues reappear. Mercury goes retrograde three or four times a year for about three weeks each time. Venus moves retrograde once every 18 months for about six weeks. Mars goes retrograde every two years for about two months. The outer planets go retrograde every year.

Ruler – The planet which has its strongest, fullest expression in a specific sign of the zodiac. In traditional astrology, each sign has a ruler: Mars rules Aries; Venus rules Taurus; Mercury rules Gemini; Moon rules Cancer; Sun rules Leo; Mercury rules Virgo; Venus rules Libra, Mars rules Scorpio; Jupiter rules Sagittarius; Saturn rules Capricorn; Saturn rules Aquarius; Jupiter rules Pisces. When the outer planets Uranus, Neptune and Pluto were discovered, these planets were assigned as co-rulers of the signs Aquarius, Pisces and Scorpio, respectively.

S

Saturn return – A predictive technique in which a chart is calculated for the moment that transiting Saturn returns to its position at birth. As Saturn takes about 29 years to revolve around the zodiac (from the Earth's perspective), an individual will have their first Saturn return at about 30 years of age, the second return at 59, and possibly a third return at 88. The Saturn return is considered to give indications of major life trends in career and maturity. For a country's chart, the Saturn return is especially applicable to trends in government and leadership.

Semi-square - An aspect by longitude in which two planets are 45° apart in the zodiac. The semi-square is a harsh aspect that indicates disagreement and irritation.

Separating – A condition of any aspect in which the faster moving planet has already formed the exact aspect with the slower moving planet and is now moving away from that aspect. Each aspect has a specific house (and its areas of life) associated with its separating condition. See also Applying.

Sesquiquadrate - An aspect by longitude in which two planets are 135° apart in the zodiac. The sesquiquadrate is a harsh aspect that indicates agitation and irritation.

Sextile - An aspect by longitude in which two planets are 60° apart in the zodiac. The sextile is a favorable aspect that indicates opportunity and harmony.

Square – An aspect by longitude in which two planets are 90° apart in the zodiac. The square is a harsh aspect that denotes obstacles to be overcome.

Stellium – A cluster of four or more planets in one sign. However, because Mercury and Venus are always close to the Sun from the Earth's perspective (and thus are often in the same sign as the Sun), the Sun, Mercury, and Venus being in one sign count as only one "planet" in a stellium. A stellium places strong emphasis on the energy of the sign which it occupies, and also on the ruler of that sign.

Synodic Cycle – The cycle between a pair of planets that begins with their conjunction, progresses as the faster moving planet moves away from the slower moving planet, and ends when they are conjunct again, usually at a different point in the zodiac from the conjunction which started their cycle. A cycle of a planetary pair has a waxing phase and waning phase, and culminates when they reach opposition, 180° apart in the zodiac. See also Waxing; Waning.

T

T-square – A planetary configuration in which two planets oppose (180° angle) one another, while also squaring (90° angle) a third planet, forming a 180°–90°–90° triangle. The T-square presents a stark conflict that can be an either/or situation.

Transit – The movement of planets as they are in the heavens at the current time (versus being a planet in the natal chart, or a progressed planet).

Translating – A condition that occurs when a transiting planet moves to a degree of the zodiac such that it forms an aspect with another planetary aspect that was exact in the recent past, or that is moving to be exact in the near future.

Trine – An aspect by longitude in which two planets are 120° apart in the zodiac. The trine is considered the most favorable aspect, as it indicates ease of expression and harmony between the two planets, but a trine can also indicate a low point in the entity's life.

W

Waning – The last half of a planetary pair's synodic cycle, as the faster moving planet moves from opposing (180° angle) the slower moving planet, to being conjunct the slower planet once again.

Waxing – The first half of a planetary pair's synodic cycle, as the faster moving planet moves away from conjunction (0° angle) with the slower moving planet and moves to opposing the slower planet.

Y

Yod – A planetary configuration consisting of three planets that form a 150°–150°–60° triangle with each other. As the inconjunct aspect (150° angle) indicates imbalance and the need to reorganize, the yod shows a situation that demands a readjustment.

About the Author

MARIE SCHOEPPEL has been practicing astrology for over 25 years, with an emphasis on financial and political astrology. She studied financial astrology with Michael S. Jenkins, author and publisher of *Stock Cycles Forecast*. She has a Bachelor of Science degree in Mathematics from UCLA. Read more of her astrological analyses at:

www.globaltrendscycles.com

Made in the USA
Monee, IL
06 December 2025

37637706R00125